The Presidential Road Show

The Presidential Road Show

Public Leadership in an Era of Party Polarization and Media Fragmentation

Diane J. Heith

Paradigm Publishers
Boulder | London

Published in the United States by Paradigm Publishers, 5589 Arapahoe Avenue, Boulder, Colorado 80303 USA.

Paradigm Publishers is the trade name of Birkenkamp & Company, LLC, Dean Birkenkamp, President and Publisher.

Library of Congress Cataloging-in-Publication Data

Heith, Diane J., author.
The presidential roadshow : public leadership in an era of party polarization and media fragmentation / Diane J. Heith.
pages cm. — (Media and power series)
Includes bibliographical references and index.
ISBN 978-1-59451-851-5 (pbk. : alk. paper)
1. Presidents—United States—History—21st century. 2. Presidents—United States—History—20th century. 3. Political leadership—United States—History—21st century. 4. Political leadership—United States—History—20th century. 5. United States—Politics and government—1989- I. Title.
JK511.H45 2013
352.23'60973—dc23

2012039108

Printed and bound in the United States of America on acid-free paper that meets the standards of the American National Standard for Permanence of Paper for Printed Library Materials.

17 16 15 14 13 5 4 3 2 1

For Owen

Contents

Tables and Figures

Tables

Figures

Preface

In the past twenty-five years, the political environment in which presidents function has changed significantly. It is more partisan, more fragmented, and more uncertain. Presidents face a party system characterized by purity, where moderate presidential and congressional candidates cannot easily survive primaries when challenged by their party ideologues. In addition, presidents face a public sphere replete with voices. No longer do the big three television networks and a handful of newspapers and radio stations dominate the dissemination of the president's message. Cable channels parse presidential politics 24/7. Television pundits flourish by offering opinions presented as facts. Online, the Internet magnifies citizen voices, and the pundocracy has expanded to include bloggers with and without traditional credentials.

These changes in the political environment have changed the context under which the president governs. More significantly, these changes put constraints on presidential leadership. In *The Presidential Road Show*, I contend that the electoral and media environments are what provide the president a perch from which to govern nationally. Specifically, the election, which gives the president his office, also provides the president with his constituency, be it large or small. The election determines how national, and thus how supportive, the presidential audience is. Presidents who sail into office with large Electoral College victories can claim to represent the nation at large. Conversely, presidents with narrow victories have trouble claiming a national audience let alone national support.

The media environment in which presidents try to reach their audience also influences the type of leadership presidents can exercise. As scholars and presidents have noted, since 1992, a different tone has pervaded media coverage of the presidency, replete with negativity, cynicism, and the perceived bias of the national press corps. Moreover, the myriad of media outlets makes it difficult for any president to count on reaching the majority of the nation in a given speech or press conference.

In *The Presidential Road Show* I argue that the way in which the electoral and media environments intersect constrains opportunities for public leadership. Presidents with a national constituency and a national media environment can take the traditional route to reach their audience, delivering national addresses and occasionally traveling around the country in support of the presidential agenda. In contrast, a president with a narrow electoral victory and thus little national support cannot rely on national addresses alone, so he travels the country exercising rhetorical leadership targeted toward specific sectors of his constituency. A president who won a narrow victory in a contentious media environment also travels, seeking friendlier media coverage and the opportunity to influence members of Congress directly.

I use the presidential rhetoric of Bill Clinton, George W. Bush, and Barack Obama to determine how the mythology of national representation competed with the partisan warfare in which they governed (unless otherwise noted, all excerpts of presidential speech in this book come from the American Presidency Project, http://www.presidency.ucsb.edu). I find that presidents speak with one voice, to one nation, only in areas that are truly national: disasters, wars, crises, and foreign policy. However, across the president's domestic agenda, the ideal of national representation collapses under the political realities of partisanship and communication requirements. Partisanship and the new media environment combine to shape a different leadership context, one that makes national leadership strategies, even at the local level, less appealing to the president and his staff.

Acknowledgments

For multiple reasons, this book took what felt like an eternity to complete. At every stage there were supportive people without whom this project might have collapsed under its own weight. At St. John's University, I was granted a timely research leave, which moved the project from a solid idea to something more coherent, substantial, and supported by data. Dozens of graduate assistants and student workers toiled over the tedious data-gathering the book required. Special thanks go to Patricia Bittner for supervising the crew and to Kathleen McTigue, Michael Perez, Jamie Beran, Brian Meehan, and Ryan Covino for working as quickly as possible to input the seemingly endless stream of data. I would also like to thank David Paletz, Jennifer Knerr, and the anonymous reviewers for their assistance and encouragement.

Many friends and colleagues influenced the quality of data and argument presented here. Roderick Hart and his text analysis software, DICTION, offered me a means to measure what at times seemed immeasurable. I owe an enormous debt of gratitude to John Woolley and Gerhard Peters and their American Presidency Project for providing the text of all presidential speech in a searchable format. This book would not have been possible without their incredibly comprehensive website and their assistance with the data. I am also grateful to the scholars who provide me with support, scholarly assistance, and friendship: Kristin Le Veness, Lori Cox Han, Tim Groeling, and Victoria Farrar-Myers. Two friends and scholars, one a political scientist and one a linguist, went above and beyond the call of duty and provided thoughtful and skillful assistance at a critical moment. Endless thanks to you both, Mary Ann Borrelli and Angela Reyes!

My friends and family always provide generous love and support; I am lucky to have all of you. Rosalyn and Elliott Heith, I treasure the extra effort you put forth, which made it possible for me to devote extra time to finishing the book. Most importantly, Stephen and Owen Kline, I could not have done this without my two best editors. Three is absolutely a magic number!

Chapter I

Redefining Presidential Leadership

The American people may have voted for divided Government, but they didn't vote for a dysfunctional Government. So I'm asking you all to make your voice heard. If you want a balanced approach to reducing the deficit, let your Member of Congress know. If you believe we can solve this problem through compromise, send that message.

—Barack Obama, Address to the Nation on the Federal Budget, July 25, 2011

But we've got to give them a little help to do the right thing. So I'm asking all of you to lift up your voices, not just here in Richmond—anybody watching, listening, following online—I want you to call, I want you to e-mail, I want you to tweet—[Laughter]—I want you to fax, I want you to visit, I want you to Facebook, send a carrier pigeon. [Laughter] I want you to tell your Congressperson, the time for gridlock and games is over. The time for action is now. The time to create jobs is now.

—Barack Obama, Richmond, Virginia, September 9, 2011

Ever since Franklin D. Roosevelt magnificently employed rhetoric to persuade a nation to put money in the bank, to believe in leadership, and to fundamentally change the way in which the federal government functioned in the economy, presidents have relied on rhetoric as a cornerstone of their leadership efforts. President Barack Obama's July 25, 2011, address to the nation is the epitome of this kind of presidential speech, urging the public to support his goals and pressure Congress to approve his agenda. However, President Obama, like his predecessors Bill Clinton and George W. Bush, exercised public leadership much more frequently in local settings, such as his stop at the University of Richmond on September 9, 2011. In fact, in the summer of 2011, 57 percent of President Obama's rhetoric occurred outside of Washington, while only 2 percent had the pageantry and spectacle of national addresses.

Most presidents experience the isolation of the White House and Washington very soon after taking office, a stark contrast to the crowds on the campaign trail. As President Obama noted just two months into office, "It's always nice to get out of Washington—at least for a little bit—and to come to places like this. The climate is nicer. So is the conversation sometimes. *[Laughter]*"[1] As the nation's capital, Washington, DC, is a highly partisan and politicized arena that exudes tension. Travel can be an enjoyable and even uplifting change for the president, particularly when he is met with an adoring throng of supporters.

The use of presidential travel in support of the presidential agenda continues a trend that began in the early 1990s. Since 1992, local venues outside of Washington have increasingly provided the arena where presidents exercise their public leadership in support of their domestic agenda. The use of travel as a leadership tool emerged because of changes in the environment in which the president functions. The 1990s ushered in a period of intense partisanship, where ideological battle lines were starkly drawn and "compromise" became a dirty word. At the same time, the media marketplace changed dramatically: The traditional media outlets for political information underwent massive horizontal and vertical consolidation, while nontraditional media outlets grew in number. Specifically, the Internet moved from an unheralded information exchange system to the dominant means of communicating all manner of information. Consequently, the primary means by which the president delivered information to a national audience multiplied and fragmented. These changes to the electoral arena and media environment profoundly influenced how presidents exercise public leadership.

All presidents since FDR have attempted, with varying degrees of effectiveness, to use rhetoric to translate the unique lever that a national election yields (a national audience and a national constituency) into agenda success. However, the non–State of the Union, non-inaugural policy address to the nation is almost extinct; recent presidents have reserved the pageantry of the national address for foreign policy and crisis response, only occasionally venturing into national exercises of public persuasion. The abandonment of this uniquely presidential tool is a result of the constraining effects of the electoral and communications environments. A president cannot wield a tool he no longer has in his toolbox.

Presidential rhetorical leadership exists within a continuum created by the electoral victory, which propels a president into office, and by the media environment, which he confronts. A national leadership strategy stems from electoral victories that yield a broad national presidential coalition and a broadcast media capable of reaching a national audience. A local strategy results from a narrow and small presidential coalition in a fragmented media environment. Consequently, presidential behavior ranges from the national tactics of national addresses for national audiences with infrequent local travel to infrequent national addresses and an exponential increase in the exercise of local rhetorical leadership before targeted audiences. The persistence of increasingly dispersive forces in the political environment, as found in post-2000 politics, has encouraged a shift toward the local, partisan end of the rhetorical leadership continuum. The effects of partisanship and media fragmentation have continued to shape presidential leadership, the seemingly unifying election of 2008 notwithstanding. The divisiveness of the 2012 election demonstrates that this pressure on presidential leadership shows no sign of abating.[2]

The Effect of Environment

Presidents are strategic actors. Consequently, they are responsive to changes in their environment. The political pressures stemming from partisanship, fragmentation, and uncertainty present significant challenges to efforts to exercise presidential leadership. Presidents now face increasingly demanding party ideologues who seek strict adherence to core party principles. The diversification of the media environment magnifies the political echo chamber. It is much harder for the president to dominate the agenda of all the participants in the political sphere: the mainstream press, cable news, bloggers, radio personalities, and ordinary citizens. Consequently, these changes have altered and constrained the choices presidents make.

The Rise of Partisanship

Prior to 1992, conventional wisdom, particularly scholarly wisdom, articulated a long-standing view of American politics: Parties and partisanship were on the wane. The decline of party identification, brought about by the rise of independents, explained just about everything in the 1970s and 1980s, particularly the decline in political participation. However, as Bartels notes, authors like Niemi and Weisberg, who focused on the rise of independents in the late 1960s and early 1970s, "were writing precisely at the nadir of party identification in the American public."[3] By the 1990s party identification was on the upswing, especially among those who actually voted. Thus, partisanship was once again a significant determinant for voters at the voting booth and for politicians in office. The rise of partisanship, and a particularly virulent form of partisanship, changed the environment for the president by limiting the national nature of the office.

Partisanship is felt most intensely in campaign combat. The most intense battle for office is the one between Democrats and Republicans during the campaign for the presidency. Scholars heralded the decline of partisanship in part because of the large disparities in electoral victory at the presidential level. Voters were clearly abandoning party voting in favor of candidate-centered decision making.[4] Table 1.1 demonstrates two distinct patterns of voting behavior and electoral outcomes. In Period 1, 1972–1988, presidents won their office with, on average, 83 percent of the Electoral College votes, a very healthy margin

Table 1.1 Vote Totals, 1972–2008

	Year	*Popular vote (%)*	*Electoral College total*	*Electoral College won (%)*	*Victor*
Period 1	1972	60–37	520–17	96–3	Nixon
	1976	50–48	297–240	55–44	Carter
	1980	51–41	489–49	90–9	Reagan
	1984	59–41	525–13	97–3	Reagan
	1988	53–46	426–111	79–21	Bush 1
Period 2	1992	43–37	370–168	68–31	Clinton
	1996	49–41	379–159	70–30	Clinton
	2000	48–48	271–266	50–49	Bush 2
	2004	50–48	286–251	53–46	Bush 2
	2008	53–46	365–173	68–32	Obama

	Average popular vote margin (%)	*Average Electoral College won (%)*
Period 1 (1972–1988)	5.25	83
Period 2 (1992–2008)	4.60	59

for victory. Moreover, those same elections produced an average popular vote margin of 5.25 percentage points. In Period 2 (1992–2008), however, a new voting and electoral pattern emerged: Table 1.1 shows a significantly narrower margin of popular vote victory (4.60 percent) and a narrowed average Electoral College majority (59 percent). The winnowing of the Electoral College margin in Period 2 is perhaps more notable, since the Electoral College system typically exaggerates victory.

Table 1.2 demonstrates that it was not an increase or decrease in turnout that caused the change in outcomes; newer partisan voters did not enter the arena. In fact, turnout among registered voters dipped slightly from Period 1 to Period 2, and the turnout among the voting age population did not change at all. Thus, a comparison of turnout alongside a comparison of outcomes in these eras reveals that the percentage of Americans participating changed negligibly but the way in which they participated changed significantly.

The trends revealed in Tables 1.1 and 1.2 naturally resulted in changes in the behavior of presidential candidates and their campaigns. Candidates employ vastly different campaign strategies according to how close the race is. In Period 2, presidential campaigns shifted their strategies from competing widely and nationally to competing narrowly and only in battleground states.

Table 1.2 Voter Turnout, 1972–2008

	Year	*Registered voters (%)*	*Voting age population (%)*	*Victor*
Period 1	1972	80	55	Nixon
	1976	78	54	Carter
	1980	76	53	Reagan
	1984	75	53	Reagan
	1988	73	50	Bush 1
Period 2	1992	78	55	Clinton
	1996	66	49	Clinton
	2000	67	50	Bush 2
	2004	73	56	Bush 2
	2008	89	57	Obama

	Average turnout (%)	*Average voting age*
Period 1 (1972–1988)	76.4	53
Period 2 (1992–2008)	74.6	53

Despite this evolution in candidate strategy, voting behavior in presidential elections has not changed since the publication of V. O. Key's *The Responsible Electorate* in 1966. As Brams and Davis put it, "Most people make up their minds about whom they will vote for in a presidential election well before the onset of the campaign . . . [but] for the typically 20–40 percent of the electorate who are normally undecided about their choice of candidate . . . the campaign will not only be decisive for [them but also for changing] the outcome of almost all elections."[5] Thus, candidates, pollsters, and campaigns have long been aware that there are decided voters and undecided voters and that the battle for victory lies in turning out one's supporters and reaching those who are uncommitted.

In terms of allocation of resources, in Period 1, population defined strategy. In 1974, Brams and Davis argued that the Electoral College forced "candidates—and after the election incumbent presidents—with an eye on the next election to pay much greater attention in terms of their allocation of time, money, and other resources to the largest states."[6] Brams and Davis dramatically suggest that California was 8.13 times more "attractive per electoral vote" than Alaska.[7] Larry Bartels agreed with Brams and Davis that instrumental resources (money and time) were allocated disproportionately toward populous states but contended that ornamental resources (state funds and personnel) were more universally allocated.[8] Colantoni, Levesque, and Ordeshook argued that the competitiveness of the state as well as population influenced allocation.[9] Population was a reasonable, even rational, guide for the allocation of a scare resource considering the voting patterns of the time. In this era, bigger, competitive states had more undecided voters to sway.

However, between 1992 and 2008, population ceased to drive campaign decisions regarding resources. Competitiveness remained an important factor, but only in terms of whether or not the state was a swing state. Consistency in voting patterns could render even the largest states, such as California and New York, irrelevant in instrumental resource allocation. Rather than compete across the nation, campaigns focused on states where the outcome was in doubt. The net result was a narrowing of campaign behavior. This intensely targeted campaign behavior resulted in different electoral outcomes. As noted above, net voter participation remained relatively unchanged, yet the distribution of those voters changed considerably.

The increased focus on battleground states versus blackout states significantly influences the composition and turnout of the voting electorate. Turnout and mobilization increase in battleground states as campaign and candidate activity increase.[10] Direct contact with the parties and the candidates increases voter participation.[11] Moreover, the disparity in influence over participation is not only geographical in nature but also socioeconomic.[12] Turnout increases among the committed and uncommitted in battleground states. In predictable states, turnout remains stable or actually declines, since only the continually active partisans participate while uncommitted or inactive citizens remain unmotivated or inattentive.

A presidential campaign's strategic choices depend largely on its classification of the country. Hill and McKee found that the campaigns tended to agree on which states were in play, although they disagreed as to whether a state was marginally in play or competitive.[13] In the 2000 presidential campaign, only twelve states met the criteria of being on both the Gore and Bush campaigns' competitive states lists.[14] Thus, twelve states received intense attention from the campaigns irrespective of population while thirty-eight received less robust campaigning and some received no attention at all. The net result is a wholly different campaign environment than the one that existed in Period 1.

Between 1972 and 1988, candidates focused on large, populous states, attempting to win each state as a whole. This approach allowed for the nationalization of the campaign from a candidate-centered perspective as campaigns focused on the differences between the candidates rather than the parties. Thus, the strategy suppressed partisan differences and focused instead on what connected a candidate to his constituency. It was possible for candidates to attract voters who traditionally voted for the opposing party by stressing different appeals. This was also a period where candidates and presidents learned to exploit public opinion polling and the ability to categorize voters.[15] Candidates could view individuals in terms of what categories they fell into, from the traditional variables (e.g., citizens, voters, primary voters, gender, ethnicity, race, income level, homeownership) to the shorthand currently in vogue (e.g., soccer moms, NASCAR dads), and connect those groupings to likelihood of voting.

Increasing partisanship produces conflicting needs but simplified strategies. In a highly partisan era, candidates need to turn out their base because the likelihood of conversion is nearly nonexistent. Candidates facing increased partisanship focus on candidate-centered strategies geared toward uncommitted voters as well as party strategies to turn out the base, but they do so in a narrowed arena—only in the battleground states. In 2012, there were only nine states that could be considered toss-ups.[16] Therefore, victorious presidential candidates since 1992 have faced an almost impossible dilemma upon entering office, one not faced by their predecessors: the need to move from divisive battleground electoral politics to governing.

The Changed Media Marketplace

In the "golden age" of news broadcasting, from the 1960s to the 1980s, the institution of the presidency could count on the institution of the media to provide essentially homogenous news in terms of content and a predictable audience.[17] The relationship between the media and the president was conflictual, as they had competing goals and interests, but their interdependence (the press needed stories and the president needed a vehicle for outreach) moderated their behavior.[18] Although every president at some point complained about his press coverage, a norm of shared dependency between the president and the press corps existed in terms of coverage and tone.[19]

The content, audience size, tone, and reliability of the media changed rather dramatically in the 1990s and 2000s. This period represents an epoch of change for the media and its relationship to the president. Jeffrey E. Cohen argues that five specific changes in the media significantly affected presidential leadership during this time frame: "(1) the increase in competition across news organizations, (2) the decline in hard news, (3) the rise of negativity in presidential news, (4) the decline in the size of the news audience, and (5) the erosion of trust in the news media."[20] Cumulatively, these changes diminished opportunities for presidential leadership.

The changes that Cohen highlights reflect the growth in consumers' choice of media outlets, which went from a prix fixe menu to a buffet. Upon taking office in 2009, President Obama faced a multilayered media approach in which citizens self-select where and how they receive their news. In the 1990s and early 2000s, during the transition from the golden age to what Cohen terms the "new media age," the media sowed the seeds for presidential leadership disjunction. Increased competition among media outlets in turn resulted in a decrease in the convergence of news stories and tone, which resulted in both a decrease in credibility for the media and a decreased ability to influence opinion as the multiplicative effect was lost. When reporting on the presidential message differed across news outlets, the president lost the opportunity to reinforce his message. A decrease in credibility and trust in the media potentially weakens the presidential message as well.

The larger threat to presidential efforts to lead the public and lead via the public stemmed from the changed content of presidential news. As Cohen notes, the decline in hard news changed the content and tone of information about the president, which changed the public's receptiveness to leadership efforts.[21] As hard news declined, soft news rose in its place. Hard news, according to Patterson "refers to coverage of breaking events involving top leaders, major issues, or significant disruptions in the routines of daily life, such as an earthquake or airline disaster."[22] By contrast, soft news is "typically more sensational, more personality-centered, less time-bound, more practical, and more incident-based than other news."[23] Any medium can provide hard or soft news.[24] Scholarly attempts to define the differences center on the lines between the politics and policy of hard news versus "celebrity gossip, crime dramas, disasters or other dramatic human interest stories" on the softer side.[25] Furthermore, Patterson finds that a different style of language (i.e., first-person references rather than group and collective terminology) characterizes soft news.[26] However, Baum notes also that the "difference between soft and hard news is one of *degree* rather than *kind*."[27]

Soft news appealed to audiences. During Period 2, citizens began fleeing traditional hard news outlets for alternate forms of media and information. Local TV news stations and newspapers boosted their ratings and circulation by adopting an increasingly softer focus.[28] Moreover, soft news appeared to be as popular as hard news.[29]

Scholars fretted over the flight of citizens to soft news. For example, Patterson argued, "Soft news and critical journalism are weakening the foundation of democracy by diminishing the public's information about public affairs and its interest in politics."[30] The problem, according to John Zaller, is that when "news becomes too soft, or . . . its political information quotient is too low," the news fails to provide the requisite information for citizen participation.[31] W. Lance Bennett argues that the shift to soft news and sensationalism resulted in the "turning off" and "tuning out" of citizens.[32]

The scholarship that bemoans the decline of hard news exists because of the inherent rejection of the quality of information presented in "talk shows, documentaries, magazines and breakfast television."[33] If "the news discourse constitutes a masculine narrative form," then altering this discourse is to both diminish and/or feminize hard news.[34] Carter, Branston, and Allan contend that the move away from the masculine style of probing, process-driven questions, indeed hard news, was driven by female consumers' demand for less argumentative coverage.[35] In addition, Nichols and McChesney argue that investigative reporting is a phenomenon of the past, as the media is now too corporate to "stray beyond the comfort zones of the nation's economic elites" and ask the tough questions women dislike.[36] However, van Zoonen contends that the softening or "soap opera" approach to political discourse actually benefits citizens, as softer approaches move, engage, and mobilize citizens.[37]

The strategic president must adapt to a media environment that no longer routinely broadcasts for a mass public. The viewership of national nightly news programs continues to decline, while newspapers remain troubled. Cable news appears to be flourishing, but its ratings do not suggest anywhere near the domination of information exchange that the "big three" networks enjoyed in the broadcast golden age. The quality of news has changed as well: Hard news contains increasingly negative and cynical coverage that dilutes the president's opportunities to lead, while soft news potentially provides less depth and substance with which to engender a response to leadership.[38] The net result for the president is an inability to exercise and control presidential outreach on a mass scale.

A Continuum of Public Leadership

As the past five presidential races demonstrated, environmental change in the electoral arena produced electoral uncertainty and instability. In the governing arena, these changes encouraged the development of a new pathway for public leadership. The changes in the environment in which presidents function naturally yielded changes in presidential strategic behavior. National, Washington-based public leadership was once the standard model, but as Obama's summer of 2011 illustrated, presidents now have an array of public leadership strategies from which to choose.

Figure 1.1 illustrates the effect of context on presidential behavior. It demonstrates how the Electoral College victory and the media marketplace influence the range of public leadership activities that presidents can pursue. The two components of environmental effect influence two areas of strategic presidential behavior. The electoral side influences constituency strategy while the media marketplace influences communication strategy. In Figure 1.1, the extent of the president's Electoral College victory yields a range of constituency strategies from national to narrow and partisan. The range of media outlets from narrow and few to fragmented and many similarly yields a range of activity.

In this model, a large Electoral College victory results from an electoral coalition of multiple states, both large and small. A narrow victory rises from a narrower coalition, often of similarly sized and located states. Incoming presidents with large Electoral College vote totals can behave as if they represent one nation. These presidents can target a single audience through speeches from the Oval Office, from Congress, or on location in Peoria. Presidents with narrow Electoral College victories cannot appeal to a universal audience as easily, since they were unable to garner a large majority in the election. Narrow victories lead presidents to target the multiple narrow constituencies that create their smaller

Figure 1.1 Systemic Influences on Presidential Leadership

Electoral College victory	***Media environment*** — *Narrow*	*Fragmented*
Large (>65% of total Electoral College vote)	Target a single audience Employ national rhetoric Less likely to travel	Target a single audience Employ national rhetoric Likely to travel
Narrow (<65% of total Electoral College vote)	Target multiple audiences Employ coalition base rhetoric Less likely to travel	Target multiple audiences Employ coalition base rhetoric Likely to travel

governing coalition. The cornerstone of this coalition is, of course, their party's political core.

The content of the president's speeches, the rhetoric itself, is also affected by the president's coalition. The relative friendliness of the audience shapes rhetoric designed to be persuasive. An audience of supporters requires different language than an audience divided between supporters, nonsupporters, and neutral parties. Presidents with large victories can universally employ what I term the "national voice" since their constituency remains the same wherever they travel. In contrast, presidents with narrow victories lack a majority coalition, and thus nonsupporters are as prevalent as supporters in the national audience. In local travel, where the event is scripted, the audience is designed to be relatively friendly. A president with a narrow electoral victory will give a different speech to a national audience than to a supportive local audience.

The large number of media outlets distinguishes the current media environment. A narrow media environment contains a few powerful national outlets. A fragmented media environment contains multiple media outlets and media formats. A president governing in a narrow media environment has the luxury of not having to travel as much to disseminate his message. A president facing media fragmentation cannot be certain which media platform or outlet will reach his coalition, nor can he control his message when it is disseminated by so many voices. In a fragmented media environment, the president must travel more frequently and employ diverse communication strategies to disseminate his message.

Therefore, when it comes to agenda leadership, the degree to which a president engages in wholly national outreach, wholly base rhetorical outreach, or a combination thereof rests on his access to a nationalized coalition. The national coalition is comprised of partisans, moderates, independents, and even members of the other party afforded the president by the size and strength of his incoming electoral coalition and limited by the degree of fragmentation and confrontation present in the media environment.

Applying this analysis to the presidents of the past 40 years reveals interesting patterns. As Figure 1.2 demonstrates, up until 1992 all presidents governed in a narrow media environment consisting of the big three television networks and a few national newspapers. After 1996, Presidents Clinton, George W. Bush, and Obama all faced a fragmented media environment that necessitated travel as a mechanism to get the presidential message out. However, these three presidents entered office with different opportunities for rhetorical leadership based on their Electoral College victory margins. Figure 1.2 suggests that Obama and Clinton could employ national appeals in their first terms while Bush could not. However, it also suggests that Bush and Obama would be challenged to disseminate their message during their first terms, while Clinton would not.

This book tests the argument that a president's public leadership strategies are highly dependent on the environment in which he functions. I argue that presidents with narrow Electoral College victories and low popular vote totals functioning in a confrontational, multiplatform media environment, such as George W. Bush, exercise leadership dependent on motivating the base via direct interaction and alternatives to the Washington press corps. Presidents with large Electoral College victories functioning in a confrontational, multiplatform media environment, such as President Obama, do not distinguish between national

Figure 1.2 Systemic Influences on Specific Presidents

Electoral College victory	***Media environment***	
	Narrow	*Fragmented*
Large (>65% of total Electoral College vote)	FDR (1932) Nixon (1972) Reagan (1980, 1984) Bush I (1988) Clinton (1992)	Clinton (1996) Obama (2008)
Narrow (<65% of total Electoral College vote)	(Ford) Carter (1976)	Bush 2 (2000, 2004)

and base leadership strategies but do seek direct interaction and alternatives to the Washington press corps. President Clinton seems to represent the last of the national presidents. However, as he governed during the cusp of change, President Clinton faced some of the same dilemmas his successors did, particularly with the Washington press corps. Correspondingly, Clinton's strategies changed over time in response to the changing media environment. In contrast, both Bush and Obama remained tied to their incoming strategies—despite national polls that improved dramatically for Bush and worsened dramatically for Obama. My findings suggest that these systemic features are more enduring predictors and descriptors for presidential public leadership strategy than short-term indicators like approval ratings. Interestingly, both Clinton and Bush won larger Electoral College victories in their second presidential contests despite their local, participant-driven strategies, which emphasized different voices to different groups. The slightly narrower Obama victory in 2012 offers compelling support for adopting the Bush and Clinton approaches, despite Obama's large initial Electoral College victory.

In the following chapters I explore my argument in more detail, using the cases of Presidents Bill Clinton, George W. Bush, and Barack Obama. I begin in Chapter 2 by investigating the concept of national leadership. If the presidency has a national audience, then all presidents face the same audience. Thus, while different presidents have different goals and ideologies, a leadership style based on appealing to the same audience using rhetoric would have some similarity across presidents. By exploring the tone of rhetoric in national and international speeches using the text analysis program DICTION, I find that there is a similarity in rhetoric across these three presidents, which I deem the "presidential voice."

Chapter 2's investigation of presidential speech focuses on what most consider presidential speech: rhetoric delivered to a national audience in prime time from the Oval Office, the House of Representatives, or a special location. However, those national speeches represent only a fragment of the president's rhetoric. Chapters 3–5 explore the different types of presidential leadership that stem from the bulk of presidential rhetoric, which occurs at the local level. Chapter 3 explores the type of leadership described in the top left box of Figure 1.1, which I call the national leadership style. By virtue of his Electoral College victory and time of tenure, President Clinton falls into this category. I demonstrate how Clinton's large Electoral College victory and narrowed media environment enabled a national leadership style. Clinton's behavior did not fit perfectly within the model, underscoring the environmental changes occurring at the time. The differences will be explored further in Chapter 7.

Chapter 4 turns to the bottom right box of Figure 1.1 and the president facing the most constraints from his environment. George W. Bush's Supreme Court–adjudicated Electoral College victory combined with a fragmented media environment led to a particular style of leadership. A president constrained by a narrow victory and a fragmented media cannot target a national audience he does not have and cannot reach. Consequently, President Bush traveled frequently, spoke before audiences that did not reflect the nation, and used different rhetoric to reach these specific groups.

In Chapter 5 I delineate the behavior of a president with a national audience working within a fragmented media environment (see the top right box in Figure 1.1). President Obama's leadership style reflects the conflict inherent in a presidency shaped by this environment. President Obama had a national audience by virtue of his large Electoral College victory, but he had to use the tactics of a constrained president to reach that audience due to the limitations imposed by the media environment.

Chapter 6 considers whether these distinct leadership styles yielded different results for the presidential agenda. Did the local efforts compensate for the environmental changes (e.g., media fragmentation and a diminished electoral coalition) that precipitated the decline in national rhetoric? Using the four primary agenda items of each president, I find that presidents engaging in local rhetoric do get better media coverage locally. However, they actually depress state approval ratings on legislative efforts. Most importantly, there is evidence of local public leadership exerting some influence on congressional voting.

Chapter 7 explores the effectiveness of my model of presidential behavior. Specifically, I consider alternatives to the contextual constraints used to define the model. I find that using the popular vote outcome does not provide the same explanatory power in distinguishing presidential behavior. Using the tone of media coverage rather than the proliferation of media outlets provides an interesting perspective on the change in President Clinton's behavior, but it does not better predict his strategy.

Chapter 8 concludes the book by considering the consequences of the new approach to public leadership. *The Presidential Road Show* demonstrates that presidents can provide outside pressure in a manner that is more strategic and meaningful for members of Congress. Moreover, the focus on local behavior emphasizes bipartisanship on a small scale with individual members rather than party leaders. Potentially, the abandonment of the national voice in favor of this local voice will result in a loss of skill in exercising national leadership.

Chapter 2

The Depth and Breadth of National Leadership

My fellow citizens, today we celebrate the mystery of American renewal. This ceremony is held in the depth of winter, but by the words we speak and the faces we show the world, we force the spring.

—William J. Clinton, January 20, 1993

President Clinton, distinguished guests and my fellow citizens: The peaceful transfer of authority is rare in history, yet common in our country. With a simple oath, we affirm old traditions and make new beginnings.

—George W. Bush, January 20, 2001

My fellow citizens, I stand here today humbled by the task before us, grateful for the trust you have bestowed, mindful of the sacrifices borne by our ancestors.

—Barack Obama, January 20, 2009

As the introductions from these three inaugurals demonstrate, when presidents speak, they underscore national representation. The emphasis is on shared identity between leader and citizens. However, almost eighty days earlier, these presidential candidates had been emphasizing "us" versus "them" and the creation of a winning candidate-centered coalition. That coalition, formed around winning the election, creates the foundation for the president's leadership base.

The campaign and election define the president's starting point with the public. Historically, presidents usually entered office with a majority of the popular vote and a majority of the Electoral College vote, but not always. A victory based on the majority of voters provides a president with a mandate for action, or at least a mandated level of support, which can be termed a national presidential coalition. Presidents with narrow victories lack a comfortable majority coalition, which means they enter office with almost as many citizens having voting against them as voted for them.

Most views of presidential leadership from scholars, the press, and the public start anew with the inauguration. The president, once a partisan fighter for victory, magically morphs into a figure who not only makes national appeals but also receives national support and acknowledgment of this national representation. The nationalization of the office in a sense institutionalizes the notion of the presidential audience. The president's audience in this view is not the candidate's audience. From this perspective, all presidents represent the same constitutionally defined audience, which in turn suggests that all presidents appeal to the same national public when pursuing their agenda. Viewing the president's audience this way also simplifies measuring the president's effectiveness in leading his audience as public opinion polls, specifically approval ratings, emerge as the measurement proxy for the nation.

I argue in this book that the type of rhetorical leadership available to the president stems from the political context and media environment in which he functions. Thus, when the context changes, there should be an observable effect on presidential strategy, tactics, and behavior. If context does not influence leadership strategy and the president's national audience is a feature of the presidency, then there should also be some observable effect of that institutionalization on presidential rhetoric. In this study, I use rhetorical tone as the representation of leadership style. If the presidency were truly a national office with a national constituency, then across all presidents and all speeches there would be similarities. All presidents would make different substantive appeals with different rhetorical skill sets but in a similar tone. A universal tone would be present whether the president was elected with a wide majority or a narrow margin, or whether he was speaking from the Oval Office or a day care center. Colloquially, there would be a "presidential voice."

However, if context influences presidential strategy, then either there would be no common tone or the tone would shift as the environment changed. In this chapter, I evaluate the tone of presidential speech in the rhetoric where universality is most likely to be found, speech that is specifically designed for broad audiences:

national and international addresses. Using the text analysis program DICTION, I find that there is a national presidential voice, regardless of electoral context, in speeches given to the nation and the international community.

Delineating the Presidential–Public Relationship

Historically, the public was intentionally distanced from the presidency, a result of the struggle over the nature of the public's role during the constitutional debate. Over time, however, suffrage and participation expanded exponentially, and the role of the mass public expanded concurrently. Yet, the public remained limited to its electoral role via party politics. Not until FDR decoupled the relationship between the public, the party, and the presidency did the public offer the president a leadership tool. In the sixty years following FDR's approach, presidents have deployed the public as an agenda tool, with varying degrees of success and skill.

First Conceptions of the Role of the Public

The role of the public and whether it was to be directly or indirectly involved in policy debates was one of the core disputes of the founding period. The Republicans and the Federalists had substantial differences of opinion concerning the public. According to Colleen Sheehan, James Madison and Alexander Hamilton represented opposing sides of the debate during the 1790s: "For Madison, republicanism meant the recognition of the sovereignty of public opinion and the commitment to participatory politics. Hamilton advocated a more submissive role for the citizenry . . . [where] public opinion [w]as 'confidence' in government."[1] By the time of the election of Thomas Jefferson, Hamilton recognized he had lost the battle over the role of the people: "Reluctantly, Hamilton reconciled himself to the fact that he and his fellow Federalists would also have to give much more attention to cultivating public opinion."[2] However "unworthy of a republican statesman" the new politics appeared to Hamilton, the "'disciples of the new creed' had won the battle to make public opinion queen of the world."[3] It was the Madisonian view—that the public should not be restricted to participation only at election time—that triumphed. However, for much of the nineteenth and twentieth centuries, the president did not actively recruit the public for political purposes beyond electoral activity.

Traditional interpretations of the nineteenth century presidency assert that political norms, born out of the constitutional debate discussed above, rejected direct presidential appeals to the people on policy matters.[4] This nineteenth century president was involved in public affairs but kept out of the public spotlight, allowing Congress the primary connection with citizens.[5] Mel Laracey challenges the notion of a silent nineteenth century presidency, arguing that there are four models of presidential public behavior and that nineteenth century presidents were as likely as twentieth century presidents to be the mobilizer (who goes public), the deliberator (who works only with Congress), the celebrator (who rallies the nation), or the reserved (who remains silent). Laracey challenges the concept of the traditional presidency by focusing on an expansive definition of policy support and by redefining the partisan newspapers of the nineteenth century as presidential newspapers. Laracey argues that communications through the presidential newspaper have been dismissed by most scholars because speechmaking is their sole definition of going public. Laracey asserts that a focus on the modern mechanisms of relating to citizens has prevented scholars from giving written rhetoric its due in terms of presidential going-public efforts.[6] Categorizing the partisan newspapers as a tool of the president dramatically recasts the notion of presidential public relations exercises. Using these criteria, Laracey finds that eleven nineteenth century presidents went public and eleven did not: not exactly a ringing endorsement for going public. Moreover, all the presidents who went public did so within a limited time frame, between 1829 and 1860.

Laracey's findings, however, highlight an important miscasting of the presidential–public relationship: Focusing on connecting public leadership to the nineteenth century president obscures the tie between the party and the presidency. Laracey contends that scholars cast going public as a twentieth century tool because they "treat presidential newspapers more as quasi-independent partisan echoes of the president rather than the primary presidential communication tools they were."[7] However, partisan newspapers cannot be considered echoes or primary tools of the president because the president cannot be considered an independent entity. The newspapers were party tools and partisan organs, as was the president of the nineteenth century.[8] With the exception of a few strong individuals who dramatically altered the institution of the presidency, most nineteenth century presidents were instruments of the party rather than the other way around, as scholars perceive the modern-day relationship. Laracey's own findings underscore the connection: The nineteenth-century presidents who appealed to the public for policy support did so as part of the national, partisan dialogue that led up to the Civil War.

The Second Coming of the Public

As Tulis and even Laracey find, the nineteenth century president was neither verbally active in the policy arena nor nationally oriented.[9] The presidential audience in the nineteenth century was a partisan audience. The notion of a national audience and a national mandate is a modern one, emerging out of evaluations of the FDR presidency. Neustadt's classic conception of the presidency, *Presidential Power*, rests on the success of FDR and the failures of subsequent presidents to duplicate his skill and success.[10] Part of the skill set of FDR was clearly rhetorical, building on the efforts of Woodrow Wilson and Theodore Roosevelt. The mass public was the not-so-secret extra-constitutional weapon that FDR used to prod a nation of citizens, not just partisans, to engage in politics to end an economic crisis and support a war. FDR's triumph was not merely reaching out against traditional norms *but reaching out to the nation in its entirety*, not just to members of his own party.

By 1960, the ability to motivate and mobilize the mass public in its entirety was being portrayed as what set the president apart and as potentially making up for his lack of specific constitutional tools within the domestic policy sphere. As FDR demonstrated, the ability to focus and rally public attention could focus government. Neustadt's early formulations of the indirect power of the public for the presidency employed the vague "public prestige" as a symbol for public support, while Cornwell's conception employed presidential approval ratings to indicate support or lack thereof.[11] Scholars and pundits followed Cornwell's route, and the national approval rating became the de facto symbol for the president's mass, nonpartisan constituency. Beginning in the 1940s, Gallup and other polling organizations queried citizens as to whether they approved of the job the president was doing, both in general and specifically by issue area.

Ronald Reagan's administration epitomized a presidency successfully utilizing a national audience in the service of the president's agenda. In 1986, Samuel Kernell articulated the new view of the presidential–public relationship, terming it "going public."[12] Sidney Blumenthal, watching the Reagan White House, nicknamed their approach "a permanent campaign."[13] The permanent campaign and going-public styles of leadership are characterized by addresses to the nation, travel around the nation, and reliance on public opinion polls, and their success lies in the representative nature of Congress and the presidency. Going public utilizes the intense media spotlight on presidential rhetoric to produce changes in public opinion, which in turn affect responsiveness in Congress. Congress is responsive to shifts in public attitudes produced by presidential rhetoric because of their electoral imperative, which compels attention to citizen desires. The permanent campaign links citizen support to campaign techniques, such as speeches and public opinion polls.

The post-FDR, post-Reagan model of rhetorical leadership rests on conceptions of national representation. In particular, the practice of using the public to pressure Congress to act requires that the president have a different constituency than members of Congress. The president's power stems from the notion that the national constituency trumps local, partisan needs and wants. However, the ability to mobilize a national presidential constituency requires either that the office imbues the presidency with a national constituency or that the president entered office having won with one.

Measuring the Relationship

As noted in Chapter 1, around 1992, politics in the United States started to become more partisan, and the partisanship was of a particularly uncompromising type. In addition, the media coverage changed as soft news became increasingly prevalent while media outlets proliferated. During this period, scholars and others noted a change in the effectiveness of presidential leadership. Presidents appeared less able to motivate their national audience and less able to use that audience as political leverage.

After Samuel Kernell argued in *Going Public* that presidents were forgoing bargaining with Congress because public pressure provided enough of a threat, presidential spoken rhetoric became the mechanism by which presidential leadership was evaluated.[14] Kernell's formulation adds specificity to the theory put forth by Neustadt and Cornwell: Presidents speak to the nation to achieve their goals individually, apart from the party. However, the rhetoric itself became less important than the result of the rhetoric: influencing public opinion.

The ability to measure and track the president's approval rating dominated the understanding of the relationship between the president and the public and became the mechanism for evaluating presidential effectiveness and success. The focus on popularity made the approval rating the barometer by which to judge whether presidential messages were successfully transmitted and whether the mass public supported the president. For pundits, the political world, and scholars, the approval rating became the key measurement of presidential leadership.

Myriad studies correlating presidential rhetoric with approval and also correlating approval with congressional success yielded mixed results. In particular, a score of arguments challenged both the concept of going public (that the pressure of approval ratings influenced members of Congress) and the notion that presidential rhetoric is for mass consumption. George Edwards argued in *On Deaf Ears* that the president may be speaking to the nation, but the nation is not listening to the president and is certainly not acting on any presidential requests.[15] Yet presidents continue to go public, and they do so frequently. For example, Han finds that Clinton spoke to the public 1.5 times a day—more than six hundred times a year.[16]

If the mass public is not listening, then who is? And if the mass public is not listening, then why speak so often? Edwards postulates that perhaps others, not the mass public, are the targets of presidential rhetoric.[17] Building on Edwards's theory, Eshbaugh-Soha argues that the president speaks to influence Congress and the bureaucracy directly through policy cues, which he terms "presidential signaling."[18] In this way, Eshbaugh-Soha bypasses the awkward assumption inherent in Kernell's work that presidential approval ratings influence Congress regardless of whether citizens directly respond to presidential appeals by voting or contacting their congressperson. Eshbaugh-Soha contends that the increase in presidents going public emerges from either a desire to maintain what they have or a desire to influence, move, and motivate policy elites—not a desire to move or motivate the public. Canes-Wrone returns to the indirect scenario, arguing that presidents are not leading, following, or pandering through their rhetoric; rather, they are choosing to maximize their success with Congress by resting their public appeals on policies already consistent with mass opinion.[19] Rottinghaus comes full circle and argues that going public can work, but it does not necessarily work all the time or because presidents utilize the bully pulpit.[20]

The concept of the public in all of these scholarly arguments remains intact as a monolithic, nonpartisan force. Moreover, the inherent concept that Neustadt and Kernell articulated and Edwards tested also remains intact: The national public is a tool for presidential use. When the president uses this tool skillfully, these arguments assert that he can count on national support. Even arguments that challenge the notion of the public as a preeminent tool conceive of the public as a distinctive monolith, an undifferentiated mass for presidential use.

Talking to the Nation

The epitome of the nationalized presidency is the speech to the nation from the Oval Office or from the well of the House of Representatives. Presidential addresses to the nation garner a lot of attention from the press, pundits, and scholars. Reams of scholarship exist that dissect the content of State of the Union addresses, their effect on public opinion, and their influence on congressional voting from a myriad of methodological perspectives.[21] However, presidents do not give many national addresses. There is a yearly address: the inaugural in the first year and the State of the Union in the years following. Other national addresses are typically crisis driven (responses to national disasters, national tragedies, or foreign incidents, like war) but are occasionally driven by the president's legislative agenda. Second only to the inauguration as moments of national representation, presidential trips abroad showcase the president as not only the head of the government but also head of state. Addresses in foreign countries serve a similar purpose, allowing the president to identify American goals, ideals, and policies for a singular audience: the world.

Analyzing National Rhetoric

To evaluate whether presidents employ a national leadership strategy regardless of political circumstances, I focus on the rhetoric of three presidents who confronted partisan and media change: Presidents Clinton, George W. Bush, and Obama. I investigate first terms only in order to exclude lame duck and legacy rhetoric. In addition, in order to capture strictly domestic governing constituency appeals, I exclude fourth years, since the reelection campaign substantively influences that year's rhetoric. Furthermore, I exclude remarks that merely thank or welcome individuals at a particular event. I also exclude question-and-answer sessions. The focus here is on planned rhetoric. Moreover, I consider presidential speeches given in prime time (after 8 p.m. EST) and across news networks as national addresses intended for a national audience. Foreign speeches are speeches given outside the United States or its territories, not including question-and-answer sessions with the leader of the host country.

To determine whether presidents are employing a nationalized leadership approach, I developed a mechanism to compare presidential rhetoric internally and externally; in essence, I aimed to compare presidents to themselves and to each other. Presidents have different agendas and thus make different appeals, but do they make those appeals using similar language? In short, to determine if there is a singular national audience for the president, I needed a mechanism that explored what was intrinsic to speechmaking and rhetoric. Consequently, my methodology utilizes the text analysis software DICTION.

DICTION is a software program that evaluates the tone of verbal messages. It analyzes text by processing all the words in a given speech to "determine the global variables Certainty, Activity, Optimism, Realism and Commonality by evaluating 31 minor variables."[22] According to Roderick Hart, the creator of DICTION, verbal tone is based on these five global variables. The Activity variable contains "language featuring movement, change, implementation of ideas and the avoidance of inertia."[23] Optimism in verbal tone employs "language endorsing some person, group, concept, event or highlighting their positive entailments."[24] The Certainty variable captures "language indicating resoluteness, inflexibility and completeness, a tendency to speak as the authority." Realism aggregates "language describing tangible, immediate, recognizable matters that affect everyday lives."[25] Commonality in verbal tone utilizes "language highlighting agreed upon values of a group and rejecting idiosyncratic modes of engagement."[26]

The DICTION variables provide an effective means by which to identify a presidential voice in rhetoric without comparing content. Instead, this analysis examines the way in which presidents address their audiences. If different presidents in different settings discussing different context employ the same rhetorical style and tone, then it is likely that a universality exists in audience perception of speeches from the White House. Simply put, different presidents would not use the same language style, nor would the same president use the same language style all the time, *unless their perception of the audience remained constant.* Thus, if nationalized leadership exists, then I expect when comparing national speeches that:

H_1: Presidential rhetorical tone in national speeches, evidenced by DICTION's five global variables, will be statistically similar across presidents.

Moreover, if the role of head of state reflects an institutionalism of the national voice, then I expect when comparing foreign speeches that:

H_2: Presidential rhetorical tone in foreign speeches, evidenced by DICTION's five global variables, will be statistically similar across presidents.

Electorally Challenged Presidents

The speech to the nation is the quintessential act of the modern presidency. Scholars contend that the State of the Union is both a substantive[27] and a symbolic[28] mechanism for advancing presidential leadership. In terms of substance, Cohen argues that the more attention a president pays to issues in the State of the Union address, the more concerned the public becomes about those issues.[29] If presidential leadership requires motivating the public via oratory, then speechmaking becomes an integral component of governing.[30] The importance of motivating the citizenry (enough so that they contact their congressperson or, at a minimum, register approval or disapproval in an opinion poll) imbues all presidential oratory with an obligation of effectiveness. As discussed earlier, presidential oratory is rarely successful in changing public opinion.[31] Echoing Neustadt's 1960 work, Edwards contended in 2008 that "public support gives a president, at best, leverage, but not control."[32] Presidents are rarely able to motivate a majority of the mass public to support them let alone act in support of their policies.

Relying entirely on the movement of national public opinion polls, Rottinghaus is a bit more sanguine about national leadership efforts. Rottinghaus contends that the ability to move national public opinion polls is provisional but possible. Specifically, "the communication strategies that most directly connect to the public find the most success in leading the public opinion."[33] However, it was easier to move national opinion prior to the increase of the countervailing forces of a fractured media and a partisan public environment.

Edwards takes the argument a step further, contending that presidential mass public efforts—the permanent campaign—are actually "antithetical to governing" because they frustrate coalition building, prevent compromise, and seek to "mobilize an intense minority of supporters as [much as they seek] to persuade the other side."[34] The failures that Edwards cites as evidence of the lack of public leadership are a lack of public attention, an inability to control the frame of an issue, and the diminishment of the available audience for the message. On these counts, national speechmaking fails as a presidential tool. Thus, it is logical that presidents are not increasing the number of speeches they give to the entire nation.

During their first three years in office, Presidents Clinton and George W. Bush each gave fewer than twenty speeches to the nation, about the same number as their predecessors.[35] Both presidents gave one inaugural and two State of the Union addresses. Including these constitutionally required addresses, Clinton averaged 4.6 speeches a year. Moreover, his national speeches actually declined over time. George W. Bush gave, on average, 5.6 speeches a year (see Table 2.1).

Clinton and Bush covered a range of international and domestic subjects in their national addresses. Clinton's speeches focused on his campaign agenda as well as issues forced onto his presidential agenda by current events, such as the

Table 2.1 Presidential Speeches to a National Audience

Clinton		*Bush*	
Speech	*Date*	*Speech*	*Date*
Year 1		**Year 1**	
Inaugural	1/20/93	Inaugural	1/20/01
Economic program	2/15/93	Administration goals	2/27/01
Administration goals	2/17/93	Stem cell research	8/9/01
Iraq	6/26/93	9/11	9/11/01
Economic program 2	8/3/93	Response to 9/11	9/20/01
Health care	9/22/93	Al Qaeda strikes	10/7/01
		Homeland Security	11/8/01
Year 2		**Year 2**	
State of the Union 1	1/25/94	State of the Union 1	1/29/02
Haiti	9/15/94	Homeland Security 2	6/6/02
Haiti 2	9/18/94	9/11 anniversary	9/11/02
Iraq 2	10/10/94	Iraq	10/7/02
Middle class	12/15/94		
Year 3		**Year 3**	
State of the Union 2	1/24/95	State of the Union 2	1/28/03
Balancing the budget	6/13/95	Space Shuttle disaster	2/1/03
Bosnia	11/27/95	Iraq 2	3/19/03
		"Mission Accomplished"	5/1/03
		Terror	9/7/03
		Hussein's capture	12/14/03

economy, health care, Haiti, and Bosnia (see Table 2.1). Bush covered fewer domestic topics (e.g., stem cell research and the Columbia shuttle disaster), instead focusing primarily on the attacks of September 11, 2001, their aftermath, and the wars in Iraq and Afghanistan (see Table 2.1). However, rhetorical tone, not content, is the focus of this chapter.

Rhetoricians analyze and evaluate rhetoric for lines of argument, internal and external decorum, and a range of stylistic variables, including tone.[36] Roderick Hart created DICTION to evaluate political speech. In creating an enormous library of political and nonpolitical speech, Hart's program generates a baseline for each of his global variables. For each speech, DICTION provides a normal range of tone for each variable, complete with normal high and low scores. DICTION can reveal the variables in any given speech that fall within normal levels and those that are out of range for normal speech.

Clinton's national speeches, when viewed in total, averaged within the normal range for the five global variables analyzed by DICTION. However, when analyzed individually, there were aspects of tone that were out of the normal range. With the exception of one speech and one variable (the Commonality variable in his December 15, 1994, speech on the middle class), when Clinton was out of range, his variables were always higher. Clinton's speeches either exhibited a normal rhetorical tone or they exhibited *more* of a variable than normal: more Realism, more Certainty, or more Optimism.

George W. Bush was outside the range of DICTION's normal tone in less than half of his speeches. However, as with Clinton, when the speeches were out of range, they leaned toward more. Bush expressed either more Certainty or more Optimism. Only on two occasions was Bush less certain (9/11, September 11, 2001; Hussein's capture, December 14, 2003) and only once was he less universal, expressing lower Commonality (Homeland Security, November 8, 2001). Table 2.2 shows where Clinton and Bush deviated from the norms of ordinary speech established by DICTION.

Of course, analyzing the range of normal rhetorical tone reveals little about presidential leadership. Establishing or assessing the concept of a national presidential tone requires comparing the presidencies to each other rather than comparing them to generalized norms. H_1 predicts similar findings across the five global variables, which would indicate a universal presidential tone and thus a universal presidential audience. Using *t*-tests assuming unequal variances to evaluate the range of scores, I found that the Clinton and Bush administrations were statistically similar across three of the five variables: Activity, Optimism, and Certainty (see Table 2.3). H_1 articulates the notion of a public–president relationship determined by the inherent nature of the office. Upon taking the oath of office, a divisive candidate transmutes to a president for all. Thus, H_1 predicts similarity across all variables to reveal a nationalized presidential audience.

Therefore, my DICTION evaluation of national presidential speeches supports the notion of an institutionalized presidential voice. Even among these disparate and electorally challenged presidents, a norm for addressing the nation existed. The similarities across the variables of Activity, Optimism, and Certainty indicate that this norm involves action and motion as well as the projection of hope and assuredness when speaking to the mass public. The similarities across these variables suggest a universality in the role of national cheerleader. Because the bulk of these national addresses concerned incidents and difficulties both foreign and domestic, the tendency toward buoyant rhetoric reflects the component of leadership that rests on uniting disparate voices. Moreover, if the policy-centric

Table 2.2 DICTION Variables for National Speeches

Clinton						Bush					
Speech	*Activity*	*Optimism*	*Certainty*	*Realism*	*Commonality*	*Speech*	*Activity*	*Optimism*	*Certainty*	*Realism*	*Commonality*
Inaugural	50.48	50.08	51.29	52.63*	49.81	Inaugural	50.68	52.92*	50.42*	50.99	50.08
Econ. program	51.37	50.67	48.33	53.71*	50.53	Admin. goals	50.46	53.52*	48.97	50.87	50.36
Admin. goals	49.18	51.72	51.09	55.01*	50.03	Stem cells	49.28	51.75	48.76	46.21	47.85
Iraq	52.97	51.66	49.83	47.26	49.59	9/11	48.28	49.44	47.26	50.50	48.62
Econ. program 2	49.66	52.07	49.53	55.15*	50.27	Response to 9/11	49.07	51.08	44.80*	49.63	49.14
Health care	50.83	53.44*	51.25	52.05	49.85	Al Qaeda strikes	47.29	50.39	43.43*	46.84	49.54
SOTU 1	51.34	50.52	50.58	52.57	49.30	Homeland Sec.	51.59	50.93	50.39	50.66	46.52*
Haiti	49.39	51.46	50.48	51.91	50.13	SOTU 1	51.23	49.00	49.92	50.01	48.62
Haiti 2	49.91	50.56	49.23	50.08	50.76	Homeland Sec. 2	49.83	52.28*	51.45	50.54	50.64
Iraq 2	48.87	52.22	49.09	50.56	51.45	9/11 anniversary	49.70	50.21	53.55*	50.94	47.86
Middle class	51.67	50.81	51.24	53.10	52.77	Iraq	50.52	48.45	50.25	48.49	48.84
SOTU 2	50.48	49.32	49.79	51.78	52.11*	SOTU 2	50.32	47.57	51.47	48.88	47.10
Balancing budget	51.75	48.89	45.88*	52.79	51.09	Space Shuttle	49.07	49.84	47.96	50.07	50.55
Bosnia	48.92	50.96	50.33	51.36	50.41	Iraq 2	52.47	48.78	48.88	52.25	47.70
						"Mission"	52.37	49.55	50.85	51.42	47.80
						Terror	51.68	49.40	50.37	52.39	49.66
						Hussein	51.88	51.22	44.16*	49.55	47.08
Average	50.49	50.84	50.16	51.11	50.46	*Average*	50.34	49.83	49.71	50.01	48.84
Standard deviation	1.23	1.01	0.95	1.85	0.91	*Standard deviation*	1.46	1.18	1.34	1.67	1.21

Note: Speeches listed correspond to those in Table 2.1

*Falls outside of the DICTION variable's normal range.

Table 2.3 The National Voice in National Speeches

	Activity	*Optimism*	*Certainty*	*Realism*	*Commonality*
All speeches (Clinton and Bush)	0.76	0.21	0.28	**0.00**	**0.00**
Non-agenda speeches	0.70	0.20	0.14	0.16	**0.00**

Note: $p < 0.05$; figures in bold are significant.

speeches are removed and a *t*-test is performed on only the crisis- and event-driven speeches, the universality of presidential speechmaking increases, with four of the five tonal variables being similar (see Table 2.3).

The Commonality variable provides important insight into the leadership approaches of individual presidents and also the presidency. Table 2.3 demonstrates that the variable is not a part of the presidential voice. Even after removing the speeches whose context is strongly related to the individual president and his ideology, group values remain an area of difference in terms of rhetorical tone. The other four variables come from the same population of rhetoric, revealing a measurable national voice when speaking to a national audience.

An Electorally Supported President

President Obama rode into office on the wave of an extraordinary campaign buoyed by a high-turnout Democratic primary season and increased public attentiveness driven by the economic meltdown of 2008. In contrast to Presidents Clinton and Bush, President Obama won office with 53 percent of the popular vote, a bigger popular vote win than in all but three elections in the thirty years prior. Moreover, Obama's 133 million votes stemmed from 56.8 percent of the voting age population, the highest voter turnout since 1968. While his Electoral College percentage (68 percent) matched Clinton's, the number of votes cast for Obama would seem to suggest a larger and more stable majority—more of a national coalition to marshal than his predecessors could claim.

Despite a reputation for soaring rhetoric, President Obama gave fewer national addresses than his predecessors did. As Table 2.4 shows, Obama gave twelve national speeches in his first three years in office. In contrast, Clinton delivered fourteen and Bush gave seventeen over the same time frame. When comparing Obama's speech to the norms defined by DICTION, the president is within the norms most of the time in three of the five global variables. As shown in Table 2.4, Obama's use of Realism is statistically significantly higher

Table 2.4 Obama's National Speeches

		DICTION variable				
	Date	*Activity*	*Optimism*	*Certainty*	*Realism*	*Commonality*
Year 1						
Inaugural	1/20/09	47.65	51.43	48.97	53.34*	49.48
Economic stimulus	2/24/09	50.87	49.93	44.52	52.66	52.22
Health care	9/9/09	47.97	50.30	45.69*	49.30	50.10
Afghanistan	12/1/09	51.26	52.17	46.89	49.24	49.69
Year 2						
State of the Union 1	1/27/10	51.19	49.00	50.39	53.27*	51.59
Gulf oil spill	6/15/10	50.10	50.46	48.42	50.62	49.37
Iraq	8/31/10	52.16	54.55*	45.84	53.19*	50.76
Year 3						
State of the Union 2	2/15/11	48.85	49.49	47.95	53.24*	49.69
Libya	3/28/11	51.85	52.04	49.92	52.38	49.02
Afghanistan drawdown	6/22/11	51.02	53.60*	45.08*	54.31*	49.06
Federal budget	7/25/11	47.51	49.45*	49.74	52.24	51.37
Job growth	9/8/11	48.15	50.42	49.80	55.27*	49.60
	Average	49.88	50.58	48.24	51.07	50.16
	Standard deviation	1.74	1.10	1.95	1.57	1.06

*Falls outside of the DICTION variable's normal range.

than the DICTION norm. With the exception of his health-care speech of September 9, 2009, when President Obama diverged from the norm, he did so exhibiting more of a variable, not less. He employed more Realism in six national speeches and more Optimism in three speeches.

Interestingly, electoral support (or lack thereof) does not significantly affect the presence of a national presidential voice in national speeches. The rhetoric of Presidents Clinton, Bush, and Obama in national addresses is statistically similar in three of the five global categories of tone. Comparing the legislative agenda and event-driven speeches of President Obama with those of his electorally challenged predecessors produces the same similarity across the global variables. As summarized in Table 2.5, I find that these three presidents employed similar levels of Activity, Optimism, and Certainty. However, there was difference at the national level when portraying reality and when defining "us" versus "them" due to the emphasis on the agenda, which requires delineating the president's version of the world, why it needs to be changed, and who resists change. If the agenda speeches are removed, more similarity of tone emerges, but again, not within

Table 2.5 The National Voice, with Obama

	Activity	*Optimism*	*Certainty*	*Realism*	*Commonality*
Clinton and Bush	0.76	0.21	0.28	**0.00**	**0.00**
Clinton, Bush, and Obama	0.85	0.36	0.08	**0.01**	**0.00**
Clinton, Bush, and Obama (non-agenda)	0.85	0.16	0.31	0.16	**0.00**

Note: $p < 0.05$; figures in bold are significant.

Commonality. Thus, a national voice exists within national speeches regardless of content, with the exception of those that define the values of the group.

The National Voice Abroad

The president's role in foreign policy has long been considered a different animal than the president's role in domestic policy. Wildavsky argued that the differences are so vast as to produce a different model of behavior for each, what he termed the "two presidencies thesis."[37] Not only does the president have more constitutional tools in the foreign policy arena than he does on the domestic front, but also foreign policy activity influences public opinion and can influence reelection. War making, in particular, owing to the rally-around-the-flag effect, tends to produce stratospheric approval ratings. Traditional foreign policy making through diplomacy and treaty making also produces a boost in public opinion, though typically not as significant.[38]

The president abroad is perhaps the best example of Miroff's presidential spectacle.[39] Enormous pomp and circumstance follow the president abroad, from Air Force One landings and takeoffs to the efforts of host countries to welcome the President through state dinners and performances of local customs, all of which is televised. Moreover, the president is at his most presidential, standing before an American flag with other world leaders, clearly representing the nation as a whole. Presidential speeches abroad are similarly spectacle-filled events, given in great venues, articulating the president's foreign policy goals, ideals, and choices.

Foreign policy making offers greater latitude for presidents for a number of reasons, not the least of which is the inability of Congress to check most presidential behavior in this arena. Moreover, the public itself affords the president extensive latitude primarily due to lack of knowledge. On the domestic front, presidents who offer a view of events or circumstances that conflicts with citizens' own experiences often see that dissonance reflected in the polls. Painting a rosy scenario about the economy while citizens feel pain at the gas pump or in checkout lines creates discontinuity. The public's lack of knowledge on foreign policy allows the president to define and frame his choices as well as interpret events abroad. Even in the post-broadcast age of media in which information abounds, the president retains more knowledge about world events due to his control over the executive branch. Therefore, foreign policy speeches seem to offer more of an opportunity for a president to be individual rather than institutional.

At first glance, the DICTION data seem to reflect the freedom afforded to a president by the foreign policy arena. Table 2.6 displays no presidential voice, since three of the five global variables are from different populations. Specifically, Presidents Clinton, Bush, and Obama employed different levels of Optimism, Certainty, and Realism. Activity continued to be a key component of all presidential speech, however, with all three presidents demonstrating similar usage of language featuring change and action and lacking lethargy. Interestingly, in contrast to the domestic speeches, the foreign policy speeches reveal a consistent usage of Commonality in addition to Activity. Commonality, according to Hart, rests on group values and rejects characteristic or individualistic language.[40] Without doing a content analysis, it is impossible to tell whether the focus on the group was a focus on American-centric values or shared values among nations. Regardless, when abroad these three presidents shared an emphasis on group values that was lacking when they spoke domestically.

Given the time span of these administrations, I thought it necessary to do a more presidency-specific comparison of foreign policy speeches. Particularly, the Bush and Obama administrations were post-9/11 and the Clinton administration was not. Did the terror attack and the two wars that followed create a post-9/11 presidential voice?

Table 2.6 demonstrates that Bush and Obama used exactly the same tone abroad—on all levels. Despite their differences in party, policy, and rhetorical skill, George W. Bush and Barack Obama were similarly active, optimistic, certain, realistic, and group oriented in their tone. In contrast, Presidents Clinton and Bush had little similarity in rhetorical tone. Interestingly, Clinton and Obama, brothers ideologically but separated by 9/11, demonstrate a similar voice across the variables of Optimism and Realism. This suggests that the Bush rhetoric in the immediate wake of 9/11 was quite distinct from Clinton's foreign policy speeches but not so distinct from Obama's. I find that after 9/11 it wasn't just the content of presidential speeches that changed, but also the way in which the United States spoke to the world through its representative. The change in

Table 2.6 Comparing Foreign Policy Rhetoric

	All	*Clinton/Bush*	*Bush/Obama*	*Clinton/Obama*
Activity	0.25	0.52	0.30	0.11
Optimism	**0.00**	**0.00**	0.02	0.11
Certainty	**0.00**	**0.00**	0.29	**0.00**
Realism	**0.00**	**0.00**	0.04	0.08
Commonality	0.05	0.32	0.16	**0.01**

Note: $p < 0.01$; figures in bold are significant.

tone trumps party and ideology, suggesting in a different way the presence of a universal foreign policy presidential voice.

Employing a Universal Presidential Voice

Presidential leadership strategy does not exist in a vacuum. The context in which the president functions contributes mightily as a constraint on avenues for action. In the case of the president's utilization of the public to produce agenda success in Congress, I contend that the president's ability to act nationally and his management of the national role are the key determinants of his success. Moreover, I argue that presidents make strategically different choices based on their environment and on the avenues that the environment opens or closes. Thus, my investigation explores presidential intention as well as action.

To determine whether or not presidents in the changed media and political environment of the 1990s and 2000s similarly viewed their audience as national, I again used DICTION. With DICTION, I established that in the most national of settings, presidents from different parties existing in different contexts with different goals and ideologies spoke to the nation and the world similarly, in what I term a "presidential voice."

However, my interest in this book is not what presidents are doing when they speak in national settings, which occurs approximately 10 percent of the time. My focus is instead on whether presidents employ the same leadership strategies in the bulk of their rhetorical outreach—in local settings as they travel around the country. I illustrated in Chapter 1 that context influences the type of leadership strategies that are available to presidents. The next three chapters explore the cases of Clinton, Bush, and Obama and the corresponding cells of Figure 1.2. Chapter 3 begins with Bill Clinton, who entered office with a narrow media environment and a large Electoral College victory.

Chapter 3

A National President: Bill Clinton

And one of the most frustrating things about being President is, with 260 million people in this country and so many intermediaries between you and the White House and the people out where they live, it's hard to know sometimes—I mean, look, half the time when I see the evening news, I wouldn't be for me, either. [Laughter] So I'm glad to be back at a place where we can be directly involved and know the truth, right?

—William J. Clinton, Billings, Montana, May 31, 1995

Since FDR nationalized the presidency and introduced national appeals presented through a media that could reach the majority of citizens at the same time, expectations of presidential speech have become the norm. The first presidential speeches illustrated national problems, national crises, and international conflicts and solutions. In the time between FDR and Barack Obama, presidential responsibilities shifted from being tangential to policy making to being central to setting the nation's agenda. Moreover, the media began to judge presidents on how much of their stated agenda they had accomplished at various milestones: in the first one hundred days, in their first term, and in their presidency. By the time Barack Obama was elected, presidential policy activism had become the norm, and talking constantly about those goals, choices, and decisions had as well. As Han notes, speech activity increased substantially in recent years, particularly after the George H. W. Bush administration. John F. Kennedy, Lyndon B. Johnson, and Richard Nixon averaged about three hundred public activities a year, Jimmy Carter and Reagan about four hundred, George H. W. Bush about five hundred, and Clinton about six hundred.[1] The increase in public activity has all occurred at the local level, not from the Oval Office or the House of Representatives.

The emphasis on the national, from either the presidential or the public perspective, spurs the interesting question of what purpose local speeches serve. If all presidents represent the same national constituency, then there is a single audience for the speech. The existence of a single audience means the effectiveness of presidential leadership can be evaluated based on how responsive that audience is to presidential rhetoric. Moreover, with one national constituency, it does not matter where a president gives a speech. Local speeches serve as proxies for national speeches because the national audience exists in the local arena. The increase in local speeches must then be explain by other factors, such as poor national media attention or a shortened public attention span.[2]

As I articulate in previous chapters, media coverage and media fragmentation are only half the story, which is likely why presidential efforts appear ineffective. The effect of partisanship and coalition building must also be considered when evaluating presidential leadership strategies. The combined effects of electoral outcomes and media organization result in four potential strategic scenarios. In this chapter, I explore what used to be the standard scenario: a large Electoral College victory within a narrow, national media environment. President Clinton appears to have been the last president to govern within this context for leadership. The small changes in behavior by the Clinton administration heralded this change in context and the evolution toward a spectrum of public leadership.

A National President?

Bill Clinton entered office with an Electoral College victory over incumbent George H. W. Bush of 370–168, an extremely comfortable margin. He received 68 percent of the Electoral College votes, signaling what could be termed a national coalition. However, Clinton did not enter office with a mandate for action due to the disparity between his Electoral College victory and his popular vote totals. Ross Perot's participation as an independent third-party candidate did not influence the Electoral College total but did influence the popular vote outcome. Clinton earned only 43 percent of the popular vote in the three-way race.

Technically, then, the president-elect entered office with a pathway for leadership similar to that of his predecessors, according to the first quadrant of Figure 3.1.[3]

Figure 3.1 Systemic Influences on Clinton's Leadership

Electoral College victory	***Media environment*** Narrow	Fragmented
Large (>65% of total Electoral College vote)	Target a single audience Employ national rhetoric Less likely to travel	Target a single audience Employ national rhetoric Likely to travel
Narrow (<65% of total Electoral College vote)	Target multiple audiences Employ coalition base rhetoric Less likely to travel	Target multiple audiences Employ coalition base rhetoric Likely to travel

A narrow media environment and a large Electoral College victory yield what I term a national leadership strategy. My argument predicts that President Clinton, due to his environment, would target a single, national audience. Moreover, with a national audience, President Clinton would use the presidential voice, with the rhetorical tone described in Chapter 2. In addition, President Clinton would use the traditional going-public style whether speaking from the Oval Office or from a day care center in Tuscaloosa, Alabama. Furthermore, as Clinton continued working within a narrow, national media environment, travel would not be necessary to get his message to his national audience.

Targeting a Single Audience

The generalizability of the audience is the hallmark of the traditional view of rhetorical leadership; from this perspective, there is no practical difference between speaking to the nation, to partisan audiences, and to nonpartisan but area-specific audiences. What matters about the audience is its ability to influence the president's poll numbers. The substance of the rhetoric does not matter; only the effect matters, whether it be improving the environment for campaigning or actually influencing a vote outcome. In *Going Public*, Kernell argues that the strategy of presidential travel and the local event reflects the ultimate goal: influencing public opinion in order to influence Congress.[4] From this perspective, the audience serves as a mechanism to highlight the president's topic, as a photo op, or as a means to influence public opinion. Thus, there is no immediate difference between speaking to an interest group, at a day care center, at a state fair, or on national television, except scope. Size matters because the bigger the event, the more people who are affected and the greater the likelihood of national news coverage. According to this view, a changing media environment could significantly limit the president's ability to lead.

Bringing in the electoral component elevates the importance of understanding not only the audience in front of the president but also how and if presidents behave differently toward different audiences. A president who enters office with a comfortable Electoral College margin, like Bill Clinton, could conceivably claim a mandate. Most consider a presidential mandate to derive from policy positions: a mandate for health care or reducing the size of government, for example. However, since election results only reveal who won and by how much, not why (that is left to scholars and pundits), the mandate for action is actually much vaguer.[5] Nevertheless, though the specifics to claim a policy mandate are lacking, elections still reveal enough for presidents to claim an audience mandate. Whether an administration has chosen a national audience strategy or a single audience strategy will be evident in the president's travel itinerary as well as in what he says once he gets where he's going.

Finding the Presidential Audience

Questions might be raised about the quality of the logic of presidential decision making or the desired outcomes, but it is unlikely that presidential decisions are made heedless of strategy or achieving a goal. Consequently, presidential travel cannot be random. There are several ways in which travel relates to the presidential agenda: (1) improving the environment by improving public opinion polling, (2) improving the environment by getting more fellow party members elected to Congress, (3) improving the environment by improving media evaluations, and (4) improving the reelection environment. Goals one, two, and four all target citizens' attitudes. With goal one, the president seeks to influence attitudes in the near term, while with goals two and four, the president seeks to influence future behavior on a particular date in an election year. Goal three ignores the president's constituency in favor of a mechanism for influencing that constituency. None of these strategic goals relate directly to the president's agenda. Moreover, the goals of improving public opinion (goal one) and media evaluations (goal three) do not provide any means for the president to decide where to travel. There is no geographic component to improving national approval ratings or media commentary. Once the president is on the road, the opportunity to influence the media or citizens exists, but influence is an outcome, not a strategic plan. Moving the president around the country requires massive planning and institutional capacity and is not done on a whim.[6] While the goal of influence is sensible, it does not reveal how presidents decide which particular cities or towns to visit and how often.

Goal two (getting more fellow party members elected to Congress) and goal four (improving the reelection environment) place strategic thinking in the electoral and agenda realms. Goal two has presidents traveling in year two of their term to improve reelection outcomes for their party in order to improve agenda outcomes in subsequent Congresses. Goal four has presidents traveling in order to improve their own reelection outcomes. These are very sensible hypotheses, in essence testing the election imperative for presidents.

Unlike members of Congress, the president only seeks one reelection. However, it is logical to assume that, like members of Congress, presidents will structure their behavior to improve their chances for reelection.[7] Seemingly, traveling to all fifty states would improve electoral outcomes. Yet presidents do not travel to all fifty states, instead focusing on states they won, states in which they were competitive, and states that are more populous. Nevertheless, presidents do also travel to states where they lost, states that were not competitive, and states that are less populous.

Presidential Travel

In President Clinton's first three years in office, he stopped in 174 cities, averaging twenty-nine state visits a year (see Table 3.1).[8] Of the ten most populous states,[9] four were visited by President Clinton more than ten times (see Table 3.2). Clinton did not completely ignore the least populous states, although only Rhode Island and Hawaii received more than eight visits. At first glance, population appears to be a significant factor; populous states received visits while less populous states did not. However, exploring presidential travel in terms of the number of presidential trips per state reveals an addition to a simple population calculus. As shown in Table 3.3, the states receiving more than ten presidential visits were not merely the most populous. President Clinton paid more than ten visits to four states that were not the most populous. Table 3.3 lists the states visited most frequently by Clinton, which include Maryland, Virginia, and Washington, DC.

Table 3.1 Clinton's Itinerary

	Number of cities visited	*Number of states visited**
Year 1	53	31
Year 2	60	29
Year 3	61	28
Total	174	88
Average	58.0	29.3
Standard deviation	4.36	1.53

*Includes Washington, DC.

Table 3.2 Presidential Travel by Population: Clinton

Most populous states	*Number of visits*	*Least populous states*	*Number of visits*
California	34	Alaska	0
Florida	10	Delaware	3
Georgia	6	Hawaii	10
Illinois	7	Montana	1
Michigan	11	New Hampshire	2
New Jersey	6	North Dakota	3
New York	13	Rhode Island	10
Ohio	7	South Dakota	0
Pennsylvania	8	Vermont	1
Texas	7	Wyoming	2

Table 3.3 Most Clinton Visits

State	*Number of visits*
California	34
Florida	10
Hawaii	10
Maryland	12
Michigan	11
New York	13
Rhode Island	10
Virginia	22
Washington, DC	45

As discussed in Chapter 1, population is no longer the dominant factor in campaign strategy for presidential candidates. Instead, swing states, or battleground states, drive strategic campaign choices regarding the allocation of time, money, and effort. It stands to reason, then, that campaign competitiveness might also influence presidential travel. However, Maryland, Virginia, and Washington, DC, were not competitive in 1992 but were visited frequently by President Clinton in his first three years in office. There are some big states that were competitive in 1992, such as Georgia, Michigan, New Jersey, Ohio, and Pennsylvania. However, the most competitive states are smaller. Moreover, Table 3.4 demonstrates that competition in the election does not drive presidential travel. Of the less populated competitive states, Clinton traveled more than three times only to Colorado.

For presidential candidates, a state's competitiveness has a direct bearing on their chances of winning there. Scholars hypothesize that presidents travel to gain an edge in the next election. However, the outcome of the previous election could also play a role: Presidents might travel to states they won as a "thank you," or they might travel to states they lost to improve their chances there in the next election. The relationship between presidential travel and the prior election remains a bit murky.

Table 3.4 Competitive States in 1992

State	*Number of Clinton presidential visits*
Colorado	6
Georgia	6
Kentucky	1
Louisiana	2
Maine	2
Michigan	11
Missouri	3
Montana	1
Nevada	0
New Jersey	6
New Mexico	3
Ohio	7
Pennsylvania	8
Wisconsin	3

President Clinton won thirty-two states in 1992. Of those thirty-two states, Clinton visited twelve during his first three years in office (see Table 3.5). However, Clinton visited only five of those states ten or more times. In his first three years Clinton visited four of the nineteen states he lost in 1992, two of them ten or more times. President Clinton did prioritize by traveling to states he won and to states that were populous, but he also traveled to states that did not support any electoral imperative (i.e., Connecticut and North Carolina). President Clinton frequently traveled to states that did not provide an electoral boost from the myriad mechanisms suggested in the scholarship.

Although through a different mechanism, the data reveal what Cook, Sellers and Denton, and Doherty also demonstrate: A reelection imperative does not appear to dominate presidential travel decisions.[10] Population and competitiveness, the strategic underpinnings of the modern campaign, cannot entirely explain presidential travel. State outcomes in the election also do not clarify presidential travel choices. Maryland, Virginia, and Washington, DC, provide a substantial clue as to the other influences on presidential travel. At first glance, geography appears to be a significant factor. Perhaps proximity drives presidential travel due to the difficulty of moving the "flying White

Table 3.5 Presidential Visits to States Won and Lost

	Number of Clinton presidential visits				
State	*1993*	*1994*	*1995*	*Total*	*Won in 1992?*
California	10	9	15	34	Yes
Connecticut	1	4	3	8	Yes
Georgia	1	1	4	6	Yes
Hawaii	2	1	7	10	Yes
Maryland	4	3	5	12	Yes
Massachusetts	3	4	1	8	Yes
Michigan	2	8	1	11	Yes
Minnesota	1	5	1	7	Yes
New Jersey	2	2	2	6	Yes
Ohio	3	3	1	7	Yes
Pennsylvania	4	2	2	8	Yes
Washington, DC	21	15	9	45	Yes
Florida	3	4	3	10	No
North Carolina	1	1	1	3	No
Texas	1	2	4	7	No
Virginia	6	8	8	22	No

House." Costs escalate the further from the White House the president travels.[11] However, it seems unlikely that the most visited areas are chosen so often because they are cheap and easy, as the president does not prioritize like a family of four on a summer vacation.

The model put forth in Chapter 1 suggests that President Clinton should have traveled at the same rate as his predecessors, George H. W. Bush and Reagan. He did not; instead, he traveled more frequently. Given his national agenda leadership strategy and the assumption of national representation, an electoral imperative is a reasonable explanation. However, the increased travel might also relate to the changes in the electoral and media environments that were occurring during this period.

An Audience of the Whole

A president with a large Electoral College victory (I use 65 percent as the demarcation of "large") can claim a victory resting on a comfortable majority. Arguably, that victory, whose votes stem from the constitutional compromise, allows the president to claim to represent the nation and in turn appeal to the nation. Consequently, for the electorally comfortable president, there is no difference between speaking before an interest group, at a day care center, or from the Oval Office. The electorally comfortable president sells his policy employing a one-size-fits-all strategy applied in myriad venues across the nation. The absence of an electoral pattern in President Clinton's travel suggests that it does not matter where presidents go to sell their agenda, although it is not yet clear why presidential travel is occurring more frequently.

To determine whether presidents and their staffs believe that it does not matter where presidents travel since the local audience is a proxy for the national audience, I turned to the Public Papers of the Presidents. In addition to providing the text of all presidential speeches, the Public Papers of the Presidents also indicate the date, the location, and often the subject of presidential rhetoric.[12] Thus, it is possible to categorize presidential travel not only by locale but by audience type. I divided the president's potential audiences into ten distinct types in order to distinguish the various settings in which presidents speak and also to account for the types that can categorize presidential coalition partners. The potential audiences for the president are associations (interest groups, organizations, and volunteer groups, nonprofit and profit), businesses, farmers, government entities (federal, state, and local), the military, religious entities, partisans (attending fund-raisers or other clearly party-based activities), schools (from day care centers to universities), unions, and general audiences (with groupings classified by locale—to the community, at a state fair, etc.).

Table 3.6 reveals that initially, President Clinton's audiences reflected his national audience strategy. President Clinton spoke before general audiences in 37 percent of his first-year local speeches. His general audience appearances outstripped the next closest category by 7 percent in his first year. However, he did speak with associations 30 percent of the time. In his second year, a congressional election year, President Clinton spoke much more frequently before partisans and much less frequently before all other groups. General audiences remained his most common audience, making up a quarter of his appearances in his second year. In his third year in office, President Clinton spoke before general audiences just 18 percent of the time, with appearances before schools, the military, government entities, and associations all increasing.

There are also patterns to isolate in the audiences to whom President Clinton barely spoke. President Clinton infrequently spoke to farmers, religious organizations, and unions. President Clinton's lack of rhetorical outreach to these groups serves to further diminish the explanatory power of an electorally based argument, since farmers, unions, and religious groups have had immense influence during elections. Also, distinguishing farmers, unions, and religious organizations from purely partisan groups serves to highlight the differences between group and party behavior in governing and in elections. If reelection thinking dominated presidential strategy, these groups would receive the president relatively frequently due to their high level of participation. An appearance

Table 3.6 Clinton's Local Audiences (in percent)

Type of audience	*1993*	*1994*	*1995*	*Average*
Associations	30.4	21.1	30.1	27.2
Businesses	4.3	4.2	1.1	3.2
Farmers	0.0	0.0	0.0	0.0
Government entities	0.0	2.1	6.5	2.9
Military	5.4	8.4	18.3	10.7
Partisans	10.9	32.6	7.5	17.0
Religious entities	2.2	2.1	1.1	1.8
Schools	7.6	5.3	17.2	10.0
Unions	2.2	0.0	0.0	0.7
General	37.0	24.2	18.3	26.5

would certainly be an easy way to repay these groups for campaign service and votes. In addition, if the audience were only symbolically significant to going public, there would be no reason for such a clear pattern of avoidance—unless presidential appearances before these groups might depress approval ratings. The ignoring of Democratic electoral powerhouses coupled with the high proportion of appearances before general audiences suggest that Clinton viewed his audience nationally.

Rhetorical Tone as Leadership

The first prong of my analysis asserts that a narrow media environment and a large Electoral College victory yield a single audience strategy. On the surface, President Clinton's behavior supports this argument, though there are some concerns. President Clinton initially spoke with general audiences but became more partisan and group oriented in an election year. President Clinton's travel was more frequent than that of his predecessors, but it lacked an obvious pattern. The first quadrant of Figure 3.1 lists the targeted audience and the use of the national voice. Nevertheless, a national president could speak in specific group settings and remain nationally focused. To determine whether President Clinton used the national advantage of his media environment and his Electoral College victory, I now turn to rhetorical tone and rhetorical content. What did the president say and how did he say it?

To examine the tone of the plethora of local speeches, I evaluate both audience and presidential intent. If the nationalized presidency dominates, then the pattern of similar levels of the DICTION global variables of Activity, Optimism, and Certainty described in Chapter 2 should be present on the local level. Finding a national voice does not in any way preclude the divergence and differences obvious across the presidency due to individuality and partisan ideology. In fact, the patterns within that national voice underscore what is traditionally viewed as the national office. I contend that Activity, Optimism, and Certainty in tone reflect behavior, or an approach to the audience. Realism and Commonality, in contrast, reflect ideology, or an approach to the job, policies, or events of the day. Therefore, at the national level, divergence in rhetorical tone across Realism and Commonality is where national presidents distinguish themselves and their policies from their predecessors or the office itself. From this perspective, the audience is always national, but the president's worldview or policy ideology is not universal.

If a president distinguishes between his audiences, then the pattern of rhetorical tone will be different across presidents. By comparing local rhetoric within presidents' own rhetoric using DICTION, it is possible to determine whether the national voice exists on the local level. If a national voice does not exist and the tonal pattern at the local level is different, then DICTION also allows for distinguishing whether presidents are different within their own rhetoric. If a nationalized leadership style exists, then I expect when comparing local and national speeches that:

H_3: Presidential rhetorical tone in both local and national speeches, evidenced by DICTION's five global variables, will be statistically similar.

In comparing three different presidents—a Republican and two Democrats—there were areas of cohesion: They similarly employed Activity, Optimism, and Certainty across all national speeches (and Realism when considering just event and crisis national speech). Consequently, the national rhetorical style coalesces on action, hopefulness, and surety. The statistically significant differences in Commonality and Realism suggest that a national relationship disintegrates over what presidents want to do or want the nation to be in terms of group ideology, identity, and values. I argue that the pressures produced by the electoral context and media environment determine whether presidents employ national rhetorical norms or a two-tiered approach to public leadership, with the majority of their rhetoric targeted toward distinct audiences.

To evaluate whether President Clinton employed a consistent rhetorical tone across his speech, I used a *t*-test statistical comparison of local and national rhetoric. I compared President Clinton's national rhetoric with his local rhetoric and compared the national rhetoric of all three presidents (Clinton, Bush, and Obama) to Clinton's local rhetoric. Table 3.7 highlights how Clinton's rhetoric

Table 3.7 Comparing National and Local Rhetoric: Clinton

	Activity	*Optimism*	*Certainty*	*Realism*	*Commonality*
National vs. local, year 1	0.66	0.88	**0.00**	0.88	0.10
National vs. local, year 2	**0.01**	0.63	**0.00**	0.90	**0.05**
National vs. local, year 3	0.50	0.99	**0.00**	0.50	0.97
All presidents national vs. Clinton local	**0.04**	0.99	**0.00**	0.71	**0.05**

Note: $p < 0.05$; figures in bold are significant.

changed over time as he moved from a national, single-audience rhetorical tone to multiple voices and tones.

Table 3.7 relies on ANOVA testing, which evaluates whether two sets of data originate from the same population. The table illustrates the *p* value, which indicates whether the difference between the sets is significant. The DICTION results from a comparison of Clinton's national and local data reveal that the president did not entirely rely on a national voice. President Clinton was not statistically consistent in his application of his version of the national voice. In his first year, the *p* values are not significantly different from each other, with the exception of Certainty. Thus, President Clinton employed one voice across all DICTION variables except Certainty. His certainty varied depending on his audience. In year two, President Clinton was no longer employing a universal voice, as his usage of Activity, Certainty, and Commonality were no longer statistically similar across the local and national levels. In year three, President Clinton returned to using a singular voice, with only Certainty differing between the national and local levels.

For two of the three years investigated here, President Clinton employed almost the same tone at the national and local levels, differing only in how certain he was. However, the second year of his term revealed a different voice. President Clinton did not employ the same rhetorical tone. Using rhetorical tone as a proxy for leadership, President Clinton exercised a different style of leadership in his second year of office. The second year of a presidential term is when congressional midterm elections occur, so it is not surprising to find a more partisan or group focus, even for a president with a national audience.

Comparing President Clinton's local speeches with all of the national speeches given by Presidents Clinton, Bush, and Obama reveals a different picture, however. President Clinton's local rhetoric is not similar to the generic presidential voice produced by using the national rhetoric of three consecutive presidents. Thus, while President Clinton for the most part presented one voice and was consistent in his own rhetoric, he was not employing the universal presidential voice discussed in Chapter 2.

Rhetorical Content as Leadership

> During recent months many of you have asked what can you do to help make America strong again. I urge you again to contact your Senators and Congressmen. Tell them of your support for this bipartisan proposal. Tell them you

> believe this is an unequalled opportunity to help return America to prosperity and make government again the servant of the people. (Ronald Reagan, Address to the Nation on Federal Tax Reduction Legislation, July 27, 1981)

With this national address, Ronald Reagan activated the going-public model of leadership. The power of going public, asking the public for active participation, expands on the nationalized office created by FDR. The nationalized president leads through appeals to a constituency broader than his own party by way of media that reach an audience within approximately the same time frame (i.e., radio, television, and national newspaper coverage). The nationalization of the audience provides the president with the proverbial leg up on Congress as the audience exerts pressure directly ("Vote for the president's bill") and indirectly ("We like the president, so we want what he wants"). Reagan's first request of the public was stunningly successful: Citizens' letters and calls in support of the president's plan—millions more than normal—inundated members of Congress.[13]

As the first quadrant of Figure 3.1 shows, a national president, based on a national media environment and a national election, can go public nationally. President Clinton employed his own version of the national voice in two of three years of his rhetorical outreach. I contend that tone provides an understanding of leadership because of the understanding of audience, which yields a similar or different tone. However, there is another component to presidential outreach: the content of the rhetoric itself.

Using the bully pulpit as a policy leadership tool requires the president to move and motivate the public. Thus, public leadership requires the delivery of certain types of messages. In the wake of FDR's extraordinary presidency, expectations of subsequent administrations hinged on the adoption of both FDR's ends (the agenda) and his means (using the public). Neustadt argues that the rallying of the public provided indirect support for the true path to presidential power: bargaining and persuasion.[14] In contrast, Kernell argues that the public allowed for the avoidance of pluralistic politics in favor of individualistic politics.[15] Either way, FDR's reliance on the national audience to achieve presidential ends has remained a core component of presidential strategy.

Presidential efforts to use the public evolved in tandem with technology, particularly television and public opinion polling. Going public, according to Kernell, is "a strategic adaptation to the information age."[16] At its heart, going public is an attempt by the president to appeal to the public to pressure Congress to act rather than directly trying to persuade Congress to act. Since the target of going-public activity is Congress and not the public, the public remains an indirect resource, as public response is not enough to achieve the presidential agenda. In the going-public worldview, however, the public is the preeminent resource, since politicians are not willing to disregard an active public. Yet, the going-public model does not actually rest on an active public; rather, constituent pressure stems from public opinion polls. As Kernell notes, presidents and their pollsters "go so far as to ask the public whether the president should bargain with congressional leaders or challenge them by mobilizing public opinion."[17] The going-public calculus for the president and for Congress asserts that a correctly targeted message will produce high levels of support evident in public opinion polls, which will then prompt Congress to follow the president's prescription. Kernell's argument requires that Congress be unable to ignore public opinion. However, the argument rests on national opinion and not constituency opinion. Members of Congress are not universally receptive to national public opinion.[18]

The Pillars of Rhetorical Leadership

In Chapter 1 of *Going Public*, Kernell explains how going public is contrary to bargaining, and in doing so he also delineates the tenets of presidential oratory that define going public.[19] First, rhetoric may be meaningful or it may be fluff. Second, the president specifically asks for assistance with Congress: "Tell your senator that we must pass health care now." Third, the rhetoric fixes the president's position on the issue. A president cannot request assistance from the public if they do not know what he wants. This is the deal breaker in terms of bargaining and pluralism. A fixed public position prevents the normal give and take of bargaining, as a change in the fixed position represents a loss of face. Finally, going-public rhetoric is based on "undermining the legitimacy of other politicians"[20]; Congress is the problem in this scenario and is subject to rhetorical disparagement.

Therefore, if presidents are employing going-public leadership at the local level, then there are specific tasks the rhetoric must accomplish. First, a president seeking to achieve his presidential agenda through public pressure must apply that pressure in a way that influences the legislative process. Hypothesis four quantifies the going-public expectation that local rhetoric must be delivered in accordance with legislative battles:

H_4: There will be an increase in local rhetoric on a specific issue as Congress takes up the issue and another increase in local rhetoric as bills come up for meaningful votes.

A president seeking to go public will use rhetoric to influence his agenda's outcome by fixing his position, disparaging Congress, and asking the public to pressure Congress. Thus, I also expect the president to exhibit the following behavior when speaking to local constituencies:

H_5: Presidential rhetoric on specific agenda items will clearly delineate the president's issue position.

H_6: Presidential rhetoric on specific agenda items will clearly identify Congress as the problem in the policy process.

H_7: Presidential rhetoric on specific agenda items will clearly ask the public to contact members of Congress and indicate their support for the president's fixed position.

Timing Speechmaking

There is no predictable schedule or circumstance for presidential speeches given before a national audience beyond the State of the Union address. Ever since Woodrow Wilson returned it to the House of Representatives chamber, the State of the Union has been the grandest of the presidential speeches and the greatest opportunity for sheer spectacle. Moreover, it is a predictable event, given in January in non-inaugural years. Occasionally incoming presidents give speeches in January, and these are often accorded State of the Union status even though they are not official State of the Union addresses. Beyond the State of the Union, which is given inside the Capitol, and the inaugural, which is given January 20 on the steps of the Capitol, there is no predictable national speech. Instead, presidents deliver national addresses from inside the White House, in the Oval Office or other stately rooms. They also give national addresses on location. Typically, these speeches are given at 8 p.m. EST in order to maximize live audience viewership. The subject matter is the least predictable aspect of these national speeches, as events (e.g., the Gulf oil spill in 2010 and the Challenger shuttle disaster in 1986) often warrant national addresses. Kernell suggests that national addresses are a source of immense power but also danger, because they can backfire if they do not generate enough response to influence Congress.[21]

Table 3.8 lists the national speeches given by President Clinton in years one through three that were not event or crisis driven. Thus, Table 3.8 is somewhat smaller than Table 2.1, which lists all of the national speeches. The agenda speeches (which include the inaugural and State of the Unions, though it could

Table 3.8 Clinton's National Speeches on Domestic Agenda Items

Speech	*Date*
Inaugural	1/20/93
Economic program	2/15/93
Administration goals	2/17/93
Economic program 2	8/3/93
Health care	9/22/93
State of the Union 1	1/25/94
Middle class	12/15/94
State of the Union 2	1/24/95
Balancing the budget	6/13/95

be argued they are event driven) represent over 60 percent of Clinton's national speeches.

In order to detect patterns of behavior in local leadership efforts from a content analysis, rather than exploring all the presidential policy interests discussed in the local speech dataset, I chose four domestic agenda items for each president. These four issues were high priorities stemming from the incoming president's bid for office. The domestic priorities of President Clinton that are investigated here are stimulus/deficit reduction, health care, volunteerism (AmeriCorps), and welfare reform. AmeriCorps might seem an odd choice, since it was more of an individual presidential priority than a priority shared by the nation, as evidenced by public opinion polls. AmeriCorps was a relatively small issue that Clinton felt strongly about despite its low importance to the national public; Clinton emphasized the issue in the campaign and focused on it in his first year in office. It could be argued that these small issues of particular importance to the president and certain constituencies are the perfect comparative foil to the more obvious rhetorical leadership efforts, like health care.

In order to evaluate H_4, that the timing of local rhetoric will relate to congressional activity, I coded all the speeches in my dataset for the agenda priorities of the president. I first coded the speeches in terms of priorities: whether an agenda item was mentioned, and which agenda item was mentioned first. This coding scheme captures the president's focus on an issue in terms of breadth of coverage. Table 3.9 reveals the changing patterns of presidential priorities across issues and across years. Paul Light describes two patterns in the president's agenda that are also evident in this table: the cycle of decreasing influence and the cycle of increasing effectiveness.[22] Both cycles are factors of time spent in

Table 3.9 Agenda Items in Clinton's Local Speeches (in percent)

	Focus of speech				*Mentioned, not focus*		
Issue	*1993*	*1994*	*1995*	*All local speech*	*1993*	*1994*	*1995*
AmeriCorps	4	8	6	6	2	1	1
Health care	24	29	11	21	28	10	7
Stimulus/deficit reduction	33	3	0	12	2	1	0
Welfare reform	4	7	21	11	6	6	5
Non-agenda*	34	51	62	49	0	0	0

*Speeches whose focus was not the delineated agenda but in which agenda items were mentioned.

the White House—the longer the president occupies the office, the less capital, time, and energy he and his administration have. However, he and his staff also increase their expertise, specialization, and knowledge over time. What Light artfully describes is that presidents apply their increased skill in a declining environment for activity. Thus, rather than gaining ground in terms of issues, over time most presidents are simply treading water, trying to maintain positioning and effectiveness.

The president's campaign agenda dominated the first year of the Clinton administration. In keeping with Light's argument, local presidential rhetoric centered on these issues. Moreover, in keeping with Kernell's argument, the focus of rhetoric on the president's issues is a means to influence the congressional agenda with the presidential agenda: The president is talking about an issue, so Congress will talk about it as well. Clinton devoted more than 65 percent of his speeches to his priorities. The cycle of decreasing effectiveness, however, hit Clinton pretty hard when his party lost control of Congress in his second year. By 1995, President Clinton's local speeches dealt with more items that were not on his campaign agenda. Some of the change in emphasis was expected, since by 1995 Congress had already addressed three of the four agenda items (not all satisfactorily, as in the case of health care). Although President Clinton mentioned his campaign priorities in his first year in office, he did not keep those issues in his rhetoric throughout his remaining years in office.

The percentage of Clinton's speeches devoted to particular issues at first appears driven by some sort of scheduling, as H_4 anticipates. AmeriCorps averaged 4 percent in year one, with an increase to 8 percent in year two. Health care was a significant focus in years one and two, while stimulus/deficit reduction reached high levels in year one and dropped off in years two and three. Welfare reform did not emerge significantly within the president's speeches until year three.

The Kernell view of public leadership asserts that presidents "talk up" an issue in order to influence congressional action on that issue. As H_4 notes, if national going-public tenets govern presidential behavior, then a spike in issue mentions will occur around times of congressional activity (prior to, during, and subsequent to congressional action). Thus, the fluctuation in patterns observed in Table 3.9 should be related to congressional action if this rhetoric is indeed governed by a nationalized approach to communication.

President Clinton's Agenda and the Congressional Schedule

Table 3.9 suggests that President Clinton hardly focused on AmeriCorps; it was the focus of local speeches less than 10 percent of the time and present in the other 90 percent of local speeches less than 3 percent of the time. H_4 indicates that President Clinton would speak about AmeriCorps leading up to the introduction of the bill and around the time of the floor and conference votes on the bill. As Figure 3.2 shows, Congress passed the AmeriCorps bill on September 21, 1993. The bill was introduced in May and it passed both the House and the Senate easily. Figure 3.2 demonstrates that there was no spike in the number of speeches dealing with AmeriCorps before or after the bill was introduced. In fact, Clinton gave the most AmeriCorps speeches in a month (three) in his third year in office. Thus, there was no relationship between legislative behavior and presidential speeches to a local audience on this issue, but it was a relatively easy legislative victory. The president did not ask the public for assistance on AmeriCorps and he clearly did not need to do so.

An analysis of the larger agenda items reveals different patterns in terms of the timing of local rhetoric around legislative battles. Unlike AmeriCorps, the issue of health care was the focus of a national address in which President Clinton presented his plan to the American people. In a divergence from Kernell's going-public tenets, Clinton's September 22, 1993, speech did not ask the American people to do anything beyond listening. Clinton did fix his position by laying out his requirements for a health plan: "So tonight I want to talk to you about the principles that I believe must embody our efforts to reform America's health care system: security, simplicity, savings, choice, quality, and responsibility." Moreover, Clinton did not disparage the legislative process. In contrast, he was quite polite, acknowledging the honest differences within the political

Figure 3.2 Timing of Local, Agenda-Leading Speeches: Clinton

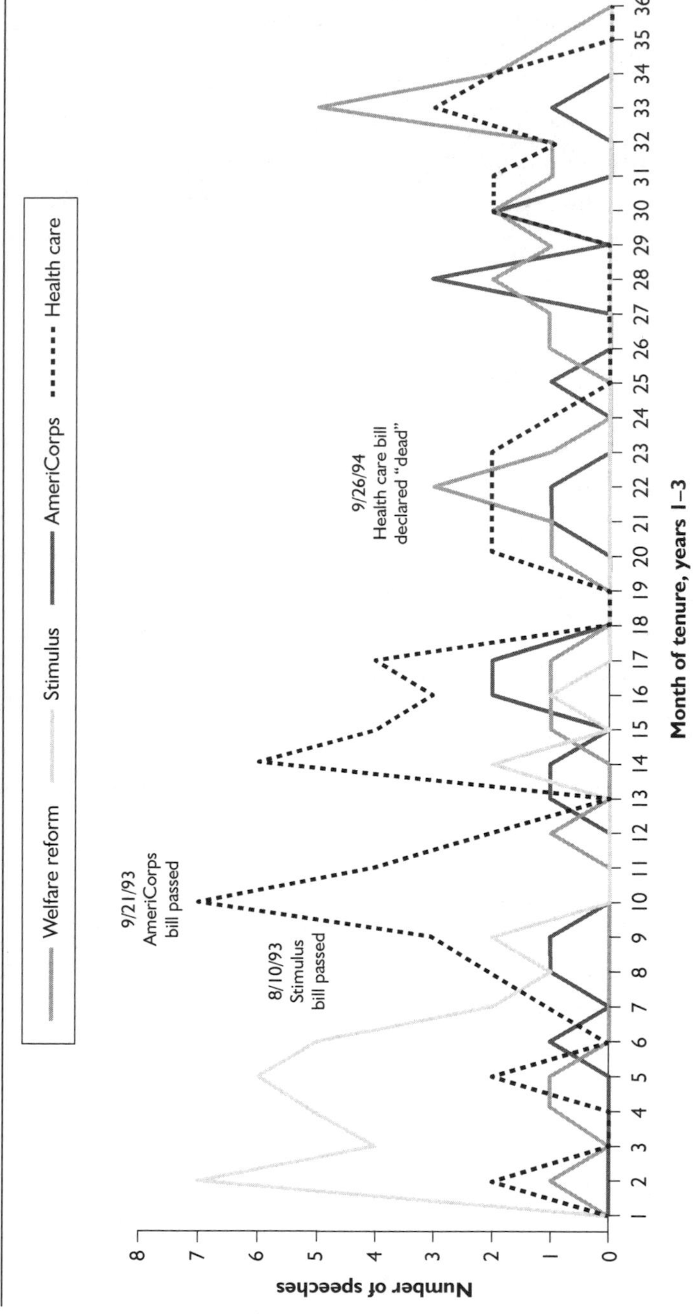

sphere. The speech was a heralding of the legislative process, as Kernell's theory would predict. Yet, the speech came after months of efforts by the White House to craft the Health Security Act through the Task Force on National Health Care Reform. The task force, headed by Hillary Rodham Clinton, met largely in secret, holding only one public hearing, in March of 1993. During the first six months of the Clinton administration, the president gave few local speeches focusing on health care; however, he did mention the subject frequently (in 28 percent of speeches in 1993 and in 10 percent in 1994).

West, Heith, and Goodwin consider the fall of 1993 as the critical period for health care legislation.[23] Thus, it is during this period that a national going-public campaign would have needed to occur. Clinton provided the opening national salvo, and Kernell's theory would expect this to have continued in local speeches to provide pressure on the legislative process. The timeline of Clinton's speeches that focused on health care appears to loosely support this premise. The bulk of the local speeches that centered on health care took place between August 1993 and August 1994. Clinton averaged only 3.5 health care-centric speeches a month in this time frame. However, Clinton averaged 5.5 speeches a month in October and November of 1993. Moreover, when the health-care-dominant speeches are combined with the mentions, health care becomes a meaningful component of the president's rhetoric in 1993 and 1994.

Considering this was the signature component of the Clinton campaign, however, less than four presidential health-centric speeches a month seems a bit paltry. This supports the contention that the Clinton health care plan failed because the White House lost the battle for definition, notably to the "Harry and Louise" television ads put forth by the Health Insurance Association of America.[24] More striking, however, is that Clinton's speeches on the road did not appear timed to coincide with particular legislative efforts (see Figure 3.2). The bulk of the legislative efforts occurred between April and August 1994, and the bill was finally declared "dead" on September 26, 1994. There is no correlation between the inside legislative behavior and the public presidential behavior. The president was not using local events to pressure Congress during the time that Congress was actually working on the Health Security Act.

The stimulus/deficit reduction plan was different, not in terms of difficulty—it was as contentious as health care—but because it was eventually passed by Congress and became public law. The president gave a national address on his stimulus/deficit reduction plan on February 15, 1993.[25] In this speech, as in his health care address, the president fixed his position regarding his plan and was critical of the process in Washington. However, in contrast to Kernell's going-public design, the president was not specifically critical of Congress, nor did he ask for the public's assistance. Six months later, the president employed classic going-public strategy. In his August 3, 1993, national address, President Clinton specifically accused senators of obstructing the process and specifically asked the public for help: "That's why the decision Congress must make this week is so terribly important. We cannot afford not to act. I need your help. I need for you to tell the people's representatives to get on with the people's business. Tell them to change the direction of the economy and do it now, so that we can start growing again, producing jobs again, and moving our country forward again." The stimulus/deficit reduction bill passed the House in a close vote, 218–216, and passed the Senate only after Vice President Gore cast the tie-breaking vote (51–50). The president signed the bill into law on August 10, 1993.

The six months between these two national addresses encapsulate the legislative process: the president introduced the bill, and the legislative battle ensued; Congress voted, and the president signed the bill into law. Leadership occurs in the story of the legislative battle. In the case of stimulus/deficit reduction, the president gave on average 4.28 speeches a month over the legislative timeline. However, between March and July he gave 5.4 local speeches a month on average, significantly more than on health care. As Figure 3.2 demonstrates, there is a clear spike in local speeches dominated by stimulus/deficit reduction immediately after the president's first national address. However, as the battle took place in committees and on the floors of both chambers, the president ceased taking the fight to local audiences. The intensity of the local effort coming at the beginning of the legislative battle rather than at the end suggests that these targeted appearances may have been less about pressuring Congress to pass the president's program and more about defining the legislative debate. Thus, the president's lack of local leadership on health care in favor of the task force's public leadership might have in effect demobilized his supporters.

Welfare reform was also part of President Clinton's campaign agenda, and he used the power of the executive branch to grant waivers to states wanting to try reform while the legislative process plodded along early in his term. In terms of local speeches, the president mentioned welfare reform in his first two years, but not with the same frequency as health care or stimulus/deficit reduction. That changed in 1995. As noted earlier, by year three a president should be more skilled in leadership efforts but will likely have a more challenging environment in which to work. The Republican takeover of Congress in 1994 should have presented a more challenging and conflictual environment for the president. The political arena did become more complex and rancorous, but oddly the president seemed to thrive on it.[26] In this environment, the president engaged the welfare reform debate. Because the bill was not introduced into the House until June 1996, passing the Republican Congress on August 22, 1996, any going-public effort surrounding this legislative battle is outside the scope of this study. Yet 21 percent of President Clinton's local speeches covered welfare reform in 1995.

On President Clinton's four campaign and administration agenda priorities, the extent to which the legislative calendar governed the delivery and focus of local speeches remains unclear. On AmeriCorps, there appears to be virtually no relationship. On health care, the issue waxed and waned within the president's local rhetoric during the legislative process but was not a factor during the planning by the task force. In contrast, on the stimulus/deficit reduction plan, local rhetoric took place at the beginning of the legislative process. On welfare reform, local rhetoric predated any effort by Congress by a year. There was almost no local rhetoric on these issues immediately prior to a legislative vote.

Fixing the President's Position

Kernell argues in *Going Public* that as a leadership style, rhetorical outreach rules out the possibility of bargaining by fixing the president's position.[27] Once his position is fixed, the president would risk damaging his reputation undertaking the give and take inherent in bargaining. The threat of going public and fixing the president's position is often as useful as actually going public. Therefore, it is not likely that a president would fix his position in every piece of rhetorical outreach. However, if the president were using these local events as nationalized going-public efforts, then it stands to reason that he would fix his position on the issues a good percentage of the time, as H_5 hypothesizes.

President Clinton did fix his position on agenda issues but nowhere near as frequently as a going-public strategy would allow. As shown in Table 3.10, Clinton never fixed his position on a single issue more than 40 percent of the time. President Clinton was most unmoving on his stimulus/deficit reduction plan in 1993. He was least fixed on AmeriCorps. This does not mean that Clinton was necessarily more flexible on the details of the AmeriCorps program; rather, it means that he was not specific and absolute in stating his requirements for passage. I discuss the difference below, as presidents are more likely to describe a problem than fix a position. On health care, President Clinton fixed his position almost 30 percent of the time; so, 30 percent of the time, he drew a line in the sand.

Table 3.10 Clinton's Pillars of Rhetorical Leadership (in percent)

Issue	*Fix position*	*Congress as problem*	*Contact Congress*	*Congress as solution*	*Describe problem*	*"What I have done for you"*
AmeriCorps	6	0	0	0	67	100
Health care	27	15	15	10	58	68
Stimulus/deficit reduction	38	26	24	44	65	71
Welfare reform	24	21	9	15	62	62
All speech	26	17	14	17	63	75

Note: The data for each pillar of leadership are percentages within each agenda category. The "All speech" category includes non-agenda speech, which is why no category totals 100%.

That also means that 70 percent of the time Clinton was not specific regarding what health care legislation must contain in order to get his signature. Fixing the president's position delineates for the public what the president's preferred legislative outcome is. President Clinton was only willing to fix his positions 25 percent of the time. Thus, the strategy of affecting Congress by motivating a national audience is simply not evident.

Congress as the Problem

Another pillar of the going-public style of leadership is the isolation of the parties involved in the process into the problem and the solution. The president becomes problem-solver-in-chief while Congress represents either the cause of the problem or at the very least a hindrance to solving the problem. As H_6 notes, a national going-public leadership style requires a demonization of Congress and members of Congress.

Despite the increasing partisanship of the time, President Clinton avoided truly demonizing Congress as an institution or its members. Instead, he preferred to demonize "Washington" or "special interests," or even the more generic "the other side" and "some people." Clinton was particularly fond of the term "the other side" in the post-1994 world: for example, "I heard the other side talk about economic growth." President Clinton faced a Republican-controlled Congress after the midterm elections; however, he was not that critical of the institution. Overall, Clinton was critical 17 percent of the time, and he was most critical when discussing deficit reduction.

"Contact Your Representative"

Kernell's final component of going-public leadership connects presidential behavior with public behavior to pressure Congress and force compliance. Public pressure would seem to be applied through letters and phone calls. However, it is a rare cohort of citizens who contact their congressperson after hearing a presidential speech. Most discussions of presidential public leadership rely on public opinion polls to gauge public pressure. The public behavior rests on the president asking for assistance from the public: "Please call, write, e-mail, or fax your Congress member in support of X, Y, or Z." The appeal to the public goes hand in hand with the fixing of positions; it is difficult to ask someone to do something if they do not know what you want them to do. Moreover, it is also related to the casting of Congress as the problem: They must be pressured to do what the president and the public know is right.

According to Jeremy Rosner, mail (paper or electronic), phone calls, and faxes are decreasing in importance as means of transmitting constituent opinions to Congress.[28] Even accounting for the upsurge in contact through e-mail, the amount of total yearly mail contact, as reported by individual Senate staffers, is the equivalent of receiving one letter from everyone in Wyoming, the least populous state in the union. Rosner also finds that Congress members and staffers are skeptical of mail, fearing automated mail and e-mail efforts by interest groups; however, mail and phone calls can be effective as early warning signs of shifting opinion and rising concern.[29]

The vagaries of constituent response, as well as the requirement that citizens who are moved by presidential rhetoric must change their couch potato behavior, lead most scholars to turn to a less dependent measure of citizen attitudes: public opinion polls. Moreover, the literature appears to assume that members of Congress have also turned to public opinion polls. Investigations of congressional interest in public opinion polls refute this argument.[30] Rosner notes that a statement from Senator John Warner—"I'm not one that follows the polls, but I'm not unmindful of the polls"—effectively illustrates the ambivalence of Congress members toward polling data.[31] Yet, when it comes to investigating presidential leadership of Congress or presidential success in Congress, there is little acknowledgement of the limitations of polls as constituent pressure. Since going public requires citizen pressure to influence members of Congress, there must be a measure of citizen pressure.

Table 3.10 demonstrates that of all of Kernell's national going-public requirements, direct calls for contact occur the least frequently. President Clinton specifically requested help 14 percent of the time on average, asking more often on the specific issues of health care (15 percent) and stimulus/deficit reduction (24 percent). President Clinton did not ask local audiences to pressure Congress very often. When he did ask, he tended to do so before specific groups regarding specific issues. More typically, the president asked for "help" and "your support" without specifically asking anyone to call, write, fax, or send smoke signals.

Congress as Part of the Solution

President Clinton's national approach to his audience was not put in service of traditionally defined going-public behavior, which puts Congress and the presidency at odds. In contrast, his presidential rhetoric was strikingly less divisive and appeared to serve a unifying purpose:

> Let me begin by saying how much I enjoyed flying down here with Congressman Clay and Congressman Gephardt and with Congressman Volkmer and Congresswoman Danner; they're here, too. They are part of the engine for change that you're going to see move through our Congress. (William J. Clinton, St. Louis, Missouri, February 18, 1993)

However, as shown in Table 3.10, President Clinton did not speak nicely about other political figures very often. On average President Clinton spoke of members of Congress in a positive light only 20 percent of the time; more than 80 percent of the time they either were cited as a problem or were not worth mentioning. More often than not, Congress and Congress members were not worth mentioning. After all, in an era where a single congressional vote can make or break key pieces of the president's agenda,[32] delegitimizing the opposition is a dangerous business. It is not surprising that on the local level, out of the harsh glare of the national press and pundit class, presidents avoid being specifically negative. It is the equivalent of a policy line in the sand; it is difficult to step back from, and it is likely to appear on video somewhere. Avoiding negativity, however, does not necessarily translate to bipartisanship or praising opponents. After all, there is the adage about choosing silence if you have nothing nice to say.

Describing Problems Rather Than Fixing Positions

Although President Clinton did not often fix positions on his agenda issues, a critical component of going public, he did exercise rhetorical leadership. Fixing a position for legislative leadership was not something that came naturally to the presidents discussed here, governing as they did in the post-"no new taxes" era. George H. W. Bush articulated a grandiose campaign promise, saying, "Read my lips: no new taxes." Eventually forced by circumstances and the congressional Democrats to break that pledge by not vetoing a bill that raised taxes, Bush Sr. was punished in the polls, and quite possibly in his 1992 reelection bid.[33] It could be argued that subsequent presidents learned a critical lesson regarding too much specificity and too little wiggle room. Opponents want presidents to fix their positions and produce a scenario like the one Bush Sr. encountered. The decline in fixed positions is the result a lesson learned rather than a new leadership style.

Fixing a position is essentially stating what a bill needs to do. Rhetorical stylings can make a request not sound like a request, but regardless of how it is phrased, fixing a position tells the audience the president wants something specific from Congress:

> Finally, I recommended—and this was difficult for me because I can't do anything as your President in the end without the support of the fine people in the Federal work force—but we recommended a freeze on Federal pay raises for a year and modest pay raises for the next 3, because that saves billions of dollars that we don't have to take out of the rest of the people in taxes to reduce the deficit. (William J. Clinton, St. Louis, Missouri, February 18, 1993)

Here Clinton clearly sought a freeze on federal wages; however, as Table 3.10 shows, he fixed his position in this way only 26 percent of the time. More than 75 percent of the time, Clinton avoided asking for a specific solution. Instead, he chose to describe his view of events, legislation, or needs.

The difference between fixing a position and describing a problem is significant. When fixing a position, presidents are drawing a line in the sand for both Congress and the public. This is what the president wants specifically. In contrast, the local rhetoric of President Clinton more frequently contained delineations of what was wrong coupled with only generic descriptions of what to do about it.

For example, when fixing his position on health care, President Clinton often sounded like he was reciting a list:

> The first and foremost thing is we have to have more health care security. . . . Second, this health care security plan will give you the help you deserve in paying for prescription drugs. This plan, for the first time, will make people on Medicare who are not poor enough to be on Medicaid eligible for help with their prescription drugs. It also will cover prescription drug benefits for working families. . . . The third thing that I want to emphasize is that this plan greatly

> expands your options for finding long-term care services in the home, in the community, in the hospital, not simply in a nursing home. (William J. Clinton, Culver City, California, October 5, 1993)

But he often did not specifically say we need *x*, nor did he say he asked Congress for *x*. He instead said what the problem was and generically how to fix it:

> Only in America—only in America do we spend over 14 percent of our income on health care. . . . Only in America do we have 1,500 separate insurance companies writing thousands of different policies, creating mountains of different paperwork and always, always looking for ways not to cover the people who bought their insurance. . . . Only in America are the doctors who hired out to keep people well and help people who are sick spending more and more countless hours. . . . Only in America have, in the last 10 years, we seen the work of clerical workers in the hospitals grow at 4 times the rate of new doctors and health care providers. That is not happening anywhere else. Why? Because while we have the finest doctors and nurses and technology and research in the world, we have a system of financing and delivering health care that is a nightmare. It is a nightmare for people who have lost their health insurance. It is a nightmare for people who don't get it. It's a nightmare for people who have to depend on the Government to get theirs, when not all the providers will cover Medicaid. It has been had. And guess what? It is the primary cause of the exploding Federal deficit. It is the primary cause of many of our biggest companies' inability to compete more overseas. It is the primary cause that millions of American workers will not get a raise between now and the end of the decade because all the new profits of the companies that are trying to cover their health care will go into the exploding cost of premiums. And only in America do we spend 10 cents on the dollar in a $900 billion health care bill on paperwork that no other country has. I say to you, my fellow Americans, it's time to give the American people health care that is always there, health care that can never be taken away, health care that is simpler and better. (William J. Clinton, Sacramento, California, October 3, 1993)

These two selections are from speeches that were given two days apart before two distinct types of audiences. On October 3 Clinton spoke to the community, and two days later he spoke before a specific (and powerful) interest group, the AARP. These two speeches were two days apart, yet they took two distinct approaches. In the first example, Clinton was using a national going-public technique on a small yet national group. In the second example, Clinton never asked for help; in fact, he ended the speech describing his technique: "That is what I'm dedicated to. And I thank you for being here today to support that. God bless you all. Thank you."

"What I Have Done for You Lately"

In contrast to the earlier hypotheses and the leadership style depicted in the shaded box of Figure 3.1, national going-public content was not present in President Clinton's rhetoric at the local level. Few of the traditional aspects of going public that are necessary for influencing legislative behavior dominated President Clinton's rhetoric. Although the president devoted a considerable amount of time to describing his view of the world, the most common pattern of rhetoric was the restating of what he was accomplishing in Washington:

> I want to help people on welfare, but I also want to reward people who, on their own, are off of welfare, on modest incomes, which is why we have dramatically expanded the earned-income tax credit. . . . We also tried to change the way the Government works. It's smaller than it used to be. There are 150,000 fewer people working for the Federal Government than there were the day I became President. We have dramatically reduced Government regulations in many areas. We're on the way to reducing the regulatory burden of the Department of Education by 40 percent, the Small Business Administration by 50 percent. We are reducing this year the time it takes to comply with the EPA rules and regulations by 25 percent and establishing a program in which anybody, any small business person who calls the EPA and honestly asks for help in dealing with a problem cannot be fined as a result of any discovery arising from the phone call while the person is trying to meet the requirements of Federal law. . . . The results of all this are overwhelmingly positive but still somewhat troubling. On the economic front, we have 7 million more jobs, 15 million more small businesses—the largest rate of small business formation in history—2.4 million new homeowners, record stock markets, low inflation, record profits. And yet—and a record number of new millionaires, which is something to be proud of in this country, people who've worked their way into becoming millionaires; they didn't inherit the money. (William J. Clinton, Burlington, Vermont, July 31, 1995)

The reiteration of accomplishments also explains the inconsistency of Clinton's speech with the theory regarding the timing of rhetoric. A significant portion of his presidential rhetoric on agenda items occurred after Congress had acted on those items. Clinton mentioned AmeriCorps more often after it became law than while it was becoming law. Thus, President Clinton kept talking about issues long after the legislative process was over—*if he could count them as wins.* In contrast, losing issues disappeared from his presidential rhetoric; those battles were over. President Clinton rarely discussed health care after 1994's legislative loss and the midterm election losses.

The Changing Face of Rhetorical Leadership

When President Clinton took the oath of office, it seemed that he faced the same national environment as his predecessors. A contentious electoral environment culminating in a big Electoral College win unites the country and offers the president a basis for national leadership. The president articulates his national message through a national press corps. Consequently, President Clinton should have traveled infrequently, speaking to audiences that reflected the nation as a whole and using a similar tone and similar content at the national and local levels.

In contrast with the traditional national president, President Clinton traveled far more frequently than his predecessors. He spoke primarily to national audiences in his first year but not in his second. His tone was primarily the same at the national and local levels, but his national voice was not universally present in his local speeches. President Clinton mostly, but not always, considered his audience a national audience. He did not use the content normally associated with national going-public efforts. President Clinton focused on his own efforts, his own leadership, and his own agenda and tried to avoid directly engaging in a negative tit-for-tat with Congress.

Thus, the model articulated in Chapter 1 is an approximate fit but not a perfect match for President Clinton's rhetorical outreach. The next two chapters focus on the model for electorally challenged and electorally supported presidents in a fragmented media environment. I will return to the inexactness of the fit of the Clinton presidency in Chapter 7 and explore how the Clinton presidency stood on the cusp of change, between increased partisanship and media fragmentation.

Chapter 4

A Constrained President: George W. Bush

Thank you all. Thank you for that very gracious and warm Cincinnati welcome. I'm honored to be here tonight. I appreciate you all coming. Tonight I want to take a few minutes to discuss a grave threat to peace and America's determination to lead the world in confronting that threat. The threat comes from Iraq. It arises directly from the Iraqi regime's own actions—its history of aggression and its drive toward an arsenal of terror. Eleven years ago, as a condition for ending the Persian Gulf war, the Iraqi regime was required to destroy its weapons of mass destruction, to cease all development of such weapons, and to stop all support for terrorist groups. The Iraqi regime has violated all of those obligations. It possesses and produces chemical and biological weapons. It is seeking nuclear weapons. It has given shelter and support to terrorism and practices terror against its own people. The entire world has witnessed Iraq's 11-year history of defiance, deception, and bad faith. We must also never forget the most vivid events of recent history. On September the 11th, 2001, America felt its vulnerability, even to threats that gather on the other side of the Earth. We resolved then and we are resolved today to confront every threat, from any source, that could bring sudden terror and suffering to America.

—George W. Bush, Cincinnati, Ohio, October 7, 2002

This address by President Bush illustrates the dichotomy of his rhetorical leadership style and highlights in an interesting way how contextual constraints on leadership influenced his rhetoric. Although President Bush was not known for his rhetorical facility, particularly with a teleprompter, by word and by deed, he was outspoken and irrepressible. He presented this side effectively in Cincinnati, using direct language like "grave threat [that] comes from Iraq." He reminds the world how "we resolved then and we are resolved today to confront every threat." This kind of language prompted critics to label George W. Bush's rhetorical leadership as cowboy diplomacy, characterized by its lack of equivocation.

Bush's bold language camouflages the strategic choices he made to cope with his contextual challenges. The Cincinnati speech was an address to the nation, yet it was not given from either the Oval Office or the House of Representatives, as is traditional for a prime-time speech. Instead, Bush spoke from the Grand Rotunda at the Cincinnati Museum Center at Union Terminal. Moreover, the introduction to the speech was strikingly different from what is typically national—for example, "Good evening. I appreciate you giving me a few minutes of your time tonight so I can discuss with you a complex and difficult issue" (address to the nation on August 9, 2001) or "Mr. Speaker, Vice President Cheney, Members of Congress, distinguished citizens and fellow citizens: Every year, by law and by custom, we meet here to consider the state of the union" (State of the Union address, January 28, 2003). The timing and topic of this speech guaranteed the president the most media coverage and the most public attention. Yet he eschewed the trappings of a national setting in favor of the setting of a local speech.

George W. Bush gave such a momentous speech—which detailed the rationale that ultimately led to the war in Iraq—in Cincinnati, Ohio, because the context of his constituency and media environment made local speeches the dominant form of rhetorical leadership during his presidency. Because of his popular vote loss and court-produced Electoral College victory in the post-broadcast-media age, President Bush could not employ a national approach to leadership. The shaded box in Figure 4.1 demonstrates how Bush represents the antithesis of the nationalized presidency within the least national environment. A nationalized environment is characterized by a national media capable of reaching a universal public built out of a healthy Electoral College victory, which serves to unite. In contrast, a president with a narrow Electoral College victory working within a fragmented media environment with multiple sources of information and an inability to guarantee transmission to a national audience is constrained. A narrow Electoral College victory constrains the ability of a president to appeal to the nation over the heads of Congress, since an electorally challenged president is speaking to as many people who did not vote for him as did. A fragmented media environment constrains the president's ability to reach coalition partners

Figure 4.1 Systemic Influences on Bush's Leadership

Electoral College victory	***Media environment*** *Narrow*	*Fragmented*
Large (>65% of total Electoral College vote)	Target a single audience Employ national rhetoric Less likely to travel	Target a single audience Employ national rhetoric Likely to travel
Narrow (<65% of total Electoral College vote)	Target multiple audiences Employ coalition base rhetoric Less likely to travel	Target multiple audiences Employ coalition base rhetoric Likely to travel

to spur congressional action because the fragmentation dilutes the president's message and inflates the number of contradictory and critical voices. Consequently, presidents who land in the fourth quadrant of Figure 4.1 due to their environment, like Bush, will behave differently than the nationalized president in the first quadrant. A constrained president, even one with the rhetorical predilections of a cowboy diplomat, will target multiple audiences, will employ different rhetoric with different audiences, and will need to travel to find those audiences.

A Fragmented Presidency

Like President Clinton, President Bush entered office with less than 50 percent of the popular vote, with approximately 50 million votes cast in support of the incoming president. Unlike President Clinton, for President Bush the lack of majority support continued into the Electoral College, where he earned the 271 minimum delegates necessary to secure victory. Bush achieved the necessary 271 only after a series of court cases, notably *Bush v. Gore*, 531 U.S. 98 (2000). The Supreme Court halted the recount of the disputed Palm Beach ballots and upheld the certification of the state's 25 electoral votes for Bush by Florida Secretary of State Katherine Harris. The Florida recount came to be a symbol of the incredibly close election and a divided nation. Thus, Bush took the oath of office on January 20, 2001, with half the voters believing that Chief Justice William Rehnquist swore in the loser, not the winner. The outcome was the antithesis of the unifying process the Electoral College normally provides.

Targeting a Fractured Audience

The presidential campaign and election seems on one level self-contained, and on another never-ending. The official nominating period begins with the Iowa caucuses and the New Hampshire primaries in January of a presidential election year. However, the unofficial, or invisible, primary begins much earlier, with candidates lining up endorsements and financing well before the election year. However, the continuation of public opinion polling and presidential fund-raising efforts and the continuous stagecraft associated with governing lead Sidney Blumenthal and others to bemoan the existence of a "permanent campaign" at the White House.[1]

The duality of the presidency emerges in the tension between a national office with national representation and campaign-like behavior. By definition, campaigns divide. A candidate cannot win without distinguishing himself or herself from the other candidate. A voter must have grounds on which to make a choice. The awkward truth inherent in the nationalized presidency is that a candidate must morph into a universal figure upon taking office. A large Electoral College victory provides a bridge between the "us and them" of the campaign and the "we are one" of a national presidency. A president-elect with a narrower Electoral College victory is immediately at a disadvantage, since those who are not satisfied with the outcome are not overwhelmingly drowned out by the tide of those who are satisfied. The small size of the electoral coalition coupled with media fragmentation make a different leadership style a necessary strategic choice.

Finding the Presidential Audience

President Clinton's efforts to exercise rhetorical leadership through travel were noteworthy as they significantly exceeded the efforts of prior presidents. However, President George W. Bush traveled even more extensively, visiting over 250 cities in his first three years and averaging thirty-five state visits a year (see Table 4.1). In his second year of office, a midterm election year, President Bush visited 103 cities in thirty-eight states. The number of visits in year two was significantly greater than the average number of city visits and his state visits that year were slightly higher than average. In contrast, President Clinton visited just sixty cities in twenty-nine states in his second year of office, only slightly higher than his norm. The challenged president (Bush) traveled much more frequently than the

Table 4.1 Presidential Travel: Clinton and Bush

	Number of cities visited		*Number of states visited**	
	Clinton	*Bush*	*Clinton*	*Bush*
Year 1	53	63	31	32
Year 2	60	103	29	38
Year 3	61	89	28	36
Total	174	255	88	106
Average	58.0	85.0	29.3	35.3
Standard deviation	4.36	20.30	1.53	3.06

*Includes Washington, DC.

national president (Clinton), despite the increased travel by President Clinton compared to previous presidents.

Although President Bush traveled much more frequently than President Clinton did, his pattern of travel is similarly lacking in overall electoral strategy. As Table 4.2 demonstrates, President Bush frequently visited all ten of the populous states. However, like his predecessor, Bush also visited states that were less populous, competitive, and non-competitive, as shown in Tables 4.3 and 4.4.

President Bush's travel to his winning states is evenly divided between repeated trips (more than ten) and less frequent travel, which was true of all three years (see Table 4.5). However, President Bush also traveled extensively (more than ten

Table 4.2 Presidential Travel by Population: Clinton and Bush

Most populous states	*Number of Clinton visits*	*Number of Bush visits*	*Least populous states*	*Number of Clinton visits*	*Number of Bush visits*
California	34	24	Alaska	0	7
Florida	10	22	Delaware	3	6
Georgia	6	12	Hawaii	10	1
Illinois	7	10	Montana	1	2
Michigan	11	14	New Hampshire	2	2
New Jersey	6	4	North Dakota	3	0
New York	13	11	Rhode Island	10	1
Ohio	7	11	South Dakota	0	0
Pennsylvania	8	19	Vermont	1	0
Texas	7	22	Wyoming	2	0

Table 4.3 Most Presidential Visits

State	*Number of Clinton visits*	*State*	*Number of Bush visits*
California	34	California	24
Florida	10	Florida	22
Hawaii	10	Georgia	12
Maryland	12	Illinois	10
Michigan	11	Maryland	12
New York	13	Michigan	14
Rhode Island	10	Montana	2
Virginia	22	New York	11
Washington, DC	45	North Carolina	11
		Ohio	11
		Pennsylvania	19
		Texas	22
		Virginia	22
		Washington, DC	62
		Wisconsin	13

Table 4.4 Competitive States in 1992 and 2000

States competitive in 1992	*Number of Clinton visits, 1993–1995*	*States competitive in 2000*	*Number of Bush visits, 2001–2003*
Colorado	6	Colorado	8
Georgia	6	Florida	22
Kentucky	1	Iowa	7
Louisiana	2	Maine	2
Maine	2	Michigan	14
Michigan	11	Minnesota	8
Missouri	3	Nevada	2
Montana	1	New Hampshire	2
Nevada	0	Ohio	11
New Jersey	6	Oregon	4
New Mexico	3	Pennsylvania	19
Ohio	7	Tennessee	9
Pennsylvania	8	West Virginia	4
Wisconsin	3	Wisconsin	13

Table 4.5 Presidential Visits to States Won

	Number of Clinton presidential visits			
States won in 1992	*1993*	*1994*	*1995*	*Total*
California	10	9	15	34
Connecticut	1	4	3	8
Georgia	1	1	4	6
Hawaii	2	1	7	10
Maryland	4	3	5	12
Massachusetts	3	4	1	8
Michigan	2	8	1	11
Minnesota	1	5	1	7
New Jersey	2	2	2	6
Ohio	3	3	1	7
Pennsylvania	4	2	2	8
Washington, DC	21	15	9	45

	Number of Bush presidential visits			
States won in 2000	*2001*	*2002*	*2003*	*Total*
Alabama	1	1	2	4
Arizona	1	3	3	7
Arkansas	2	1	2	5
Colorado	3	3	2	8
Florida	7	5	10	22
Georgia	3	6	3	12
Kentucky	1	1	3	5
Mississippi	1	2	2	5
Missouri	2	8	6	16
North Carolina	3	6	2	11
Ohio	1	4	6	11
Texas	8	5	9	22
Virginia	11	2	9	22

times over the three years) to states he lost (see Table 4.6). Three of the losing states that he traveled to—Connecticut, Maryland, and New Mexico—were not populous and not competitive.

The fact that both a national president (Clinton) and a challenged president (Bush) traveled extensively to speak in Maryland, Virginia, and parts of Washington, DC, reveals that governing and leadership strategies, not just media strategies, are at work in increased local travel. It could be argued that local travel represents the bridge between Neustadt's institutionalized and Kernell's individualized pluralism. Maryland, Virginia, and parts of Washington, DC, are inside the Beltway, in media parlance. These locales represent the epicenter of political, yet not governmental, Washington. In addition, these areas are not electorally strategic in the straight voting sense. Maryland, Virginia, and Washington, DC, were neither competitive

Table 4.6 Presidential Visits to States Lost

	Number of Clinton presidential visits			
States lost in 1992	*1993*	*1994*	*1995*	*Total*
Florida	3	4	3	10
North Carolina	1	1	1	3
Texas	1	2	4	7
Virginia	6	8	8	22
	Number of Bush presidential visits			
States lost in 2000	*2001*	*2002*	*2003*	*Total*
California	6	7	11	24
Connecticut	1	2	2	5
Illinois	1	5	4	10
Maryland	4	2	6	12
Michigan	3	5	6	14
Minnesota	1	5	2	8
New Jersey	1	1	2	4
New Mexico	2	3	1	6
New York	4	6	1	11
Oregon	1	1	2	4
Pennsylvania	4	9	6	19
Washington, DC	25	16	21	62
Wisconsin	5	6	2	13

nor electorally significant in 1992 and 2000. Therefore, the better explanation for presidential travel is the policy agenda, not the electoral agenda. Although Kernell argues that going public and bargaining are mutually exclusive strategies, the actions of differently driven presidents suggest a need to move beyond traditional conceptions of leadership targets. Since I contend that President Clinton could appeal to the masses without having to travel, yet President Bush could not appeal to the masses and thus had to travel, the fact that both *did* travel suggests a different governing style as an explanation. The common denominator between Bush and Clinton in terms of travel for their agenda is the need to reach those who are active, attentive, and willing to perform the public's role in public leadership.

An Audience of Parts

Like President Clinton, President Bush often spoke before associations and partisans (see Table 4.7). President Bush also frequently spoke at schools and before the military. Unlike his predecessor, President Bush increasingly spoke to businesses, most frequently in 2003 (14.5 percent). President Bush spoke before schools more frequently in years one and two, while Clinton spoke significantly more frequently before schools in year three.

More significantly, both presidents' appearances before general audiences declined over time. Presidents Clinton and Bush spoke most frequently to general audiences in their first years in office. President Clinton spoke to general audiences

Table 4.7 Bush's Local Audiences (in percent)

Type of audience	*2001*	*2002*	*2003*	*Average*	*Clinton average*
Associations	27.6	27.8	10.7	22.0	27.2
Businesses	5.1	8.3	14.5	9.3	3.2
Farmers	0.0	2.8	0.0	0.9	0.0
Government entities	6.1	5.6	3.1	4.9	2.9
Military	11.2	4.2	11.5	8.9	10.7
Partisans	18.4	23.6	43.5	28.5	17.0
Religious entities	0.0	0.0	3.1	1.0	1.8
Schools	15.3	16.7	7.6	13.2	10.0
Unions	2.0	0.0	0.0	0.7	0.7
General	14.3	11.1	6.1	10.5	26.5

much more frequently than did President Bush. President Bush paid the most attention to general audiences in year one, but even that was significantly less (in percentage and raw numbers) than President Clinton's attention to general audiences at its lowest. Among President Clinton's speeches in 1995, 18 percent were for general audiences; President Bush began his tenure speaking to general audiences just 14 percent of the time.

Like Clinton, President Bush barely spoke to farmers, other government entities, religious organizations, and unions. The infrequency of his appearances before religious organizations is quite startling given the electoral relationship between the religious right and the Republican Party. However, it does further weaken the explanatory power of an electorally based argument for presidential travel. As noted in Chapter 3, this evaluation distinguishes between partisan appearances and appearances before religious organizations. The difference between a right-to-life organization and a church exists in the tax code as well as in group and party behavior during governing and elections.

The decline in Bush's appearances before general audiences recalls the emphasis on the strategic use of the president's time. General audience appearances would not have declined if there had not been increased value in going somewhere else. Moreover, the bulk of activity occurred among groups that are typically part of active coalition building in Washington, DC: associations and partisans.

Rhetorical Tone as Leadership

The cornerstone of a national presidency is the connection between voting, audience, and leadership. Presidents cannot lead without followers. Because of the focus on a singular relationship between citizens and the president, that leadership strategy centers on the entirety of the nation. However, the electoral component of the process can either stabilize or destabilize the national arrangement depending on the extent of victory. Assessing the Electoral College margins from FDR to Obama suggests that threats to national representation are uncommon, as the margin of Electoral College victory tends to be quite large. However, periods of increased partisanship and dissension do occur, and when they do, they have a profound influence on the public leadership strategies available to a president.

To evaluate public leadership, I use rhetorical tone as a proxy for measuring public leadership strategies. Specifically, I evaluate whether presidents use the same tone at the local and national levels. Tone serves to determine whether presidents consider their audience as the nation or as the varied components that make up their electoral coalition. I encapsulate this into H_3, which I introduced in Chapter 3:

H_3: Presidential rhetorical tone in both local and national speeches, evidenced by DICTION's five global variables, will be statistically similar.

In addition, the DICTION analysis allows comparison not just within presidencies but also across presidencies. This offers the opportunity not just to evaluate individual presidential behavior but also to analyze patterns across administrations:

H_8: Presidential rhetorical tone in both local and national speeches, evidenced by DICTION's five global variables, will be statistically similar across presidents as well as between presidents.

As I did with President Clinton's rhetorical data in Chapter 3, I used a *t*-test statistical comparison of President Bush's local and national rhetoric in order to determine whether the tonal values originate from the same population. As I determined in Chapter 2, Activity, Optimism, and Certainty constitute the tone of what I call the presidential voice. This is the pattern of speech present in national speeches. The presence of the presidential voice at the local level is one sign that a singular presidential leadership style directed at a national audience exists. However, a slight step down from the universal presidential voice is the idea that a president may not be exercising the national voice but is speaking with one voice regardless of travel. In that case, the president would have one voice and one audience, but perhaps not the truly national audience. Based on the context faced by President Bush, described in the fourth quadrant of Figure 4.1, a one-voice or one-audience strategy seems unlikely.

Table 4.8 confirms the theoretical argument articulated in Figure 4.1: President Bush did not use one voice, nor did he use the presidential voice. Comparing all his national speeches with all his local speeches, President Bush employed differing levels of Optimism, Certainty, and Commonality. In comparison to President Clinton, President Bush employed different levels of Optimism, Certainty, and Commonality.

Breaking down President Bush's rhetoric by year demonstrates that he never employed a unified voice or the presidential voice, because Optimism and Certainty are consistently from a statistically different population. In all three years,

Table 4.8 Comparing National and Local Rhetoric: Bush

	Activity	*Optimism*	*Certainty*	*Realism*	*Commonality*
National vs. local, year 1	0.05	**0.00**	0.22	0.22	**0.00**
National vs. local, year 2	0.65	**0.00**	0.10	0.52	**0.01**
National vs. local, year 3	0.52	**0.00**	0.65	**0.03**	**0.03**
All presidents national vs. Bush local	0.27	**0.00**	**0.02**	0.35	**0.00**
Clinton local vs. Bush local	**0.00**	**0.00**	0.06	**0.00**	0.36
All Clinton vs. all Bush	0.81	**0.00**	**0.00**	0.96	**0.02**

Note: $p < 0.05$; figures in bold are significant.

President Bush employed the same level of Activity, and he is similar to the presidential voice in that category. With the exception of year three, President Bush employed the same level of Realism in his local and national speeches.

Fundamentally, President Bush was statistically inconsistent in his rhetorical leadership, speaking differently when talking to different audiences. In years one and two, President Bush was consistently active, certain, and real in national and local settings. However, his voice changed in year three, as he was no longer similar across those three variables. He employed different rhetorical leadership in year three when speaking in national versus local settings. The difference was so significant and significantly different from his first two years that it changed his overall pattern of rhetorical leadership from having one voice, albeit not the presidential voice, to having different voices.

Internally, then, President Bush employed different rhetorical strategies depending on the audience to which he targeted the rhetoric. However, comparing across presidents reveals even more disjunction and lack of a singular presidential voice. Presidents Clinton and Bush did not employ a similar rhetorical tone. Evaluating the variables across the first three years of Presidents Clinton and Bush as well as overall allows for H_8 to be easily rejected. Table 4.8 reveals that the two presidents' local speeches were less similar to each other than were their national speeches. Across all three years, three of the five categories demonstrate rhetorical differences: Activity, Optimism, and Realism. On the local level, Clinton and Bush did not express hope, conviction, or an understanding of the everyday with similar frequency. On Certainty and Commonality, Clinton and Bush are statistically similar when all three years are combined (although each had one year that was statistically different). When all the years are combined, almost 70 percent of the time Presidents Clinton and Bush did not employ a shared rhetorical tone. Statistically speaking, year three was the most significantly different of the three years, suggesting that as reelection looms, rhetorical idiosyncrasies and constituency differences increase.

Comparing Bush's local speeches to Clinton's demonstrates that in smaller venues the two presidents were less similar to each other and less similar than they were at the national level. H_8 operationalizes this proposition by articulating that a national voice necessitates a similar tone between a single president's national and local speeches and also similarity across administrations. As shown in Table 4.8, Presidents Clinton and Bush were statistically different from each other across all local and national rhetoric. The statistical analysis demonstrates that the DICTION variables across all local and national speeches did not come from the same population. Therefore, while a similar voice existed at the national level, that voice was not present in local speeches.

The Pillars of Rhetorical Leadership

The national president, with his national audience, is able to speak with one voice and essentially from one platform, regardless of locale. The national president applies his public platform in service of his domestic agenda as means to trump the parochial interests of legislators with the power of a unified coalition. The constrained president does not have the predetermined unified majority to deploy; therefore, he lacks the means to trump the parochial interests of legislators. Consequently, the speech of a constrained president should not have the verbiage of traditional going-public leadership.

As noted in Chapter 3, there are four tasks national rhetoric must accomplish if it is to pressure Congress to support the presidential agenda: (1) the timing of the local rhetoric must match the congressional calendar; (2) the president must draw a line in the sand, or fix his policy or issue position; (3) Congress must be identified as the problem; and (4) the public's assistance must be requested. If local speech serves the same purpose as national speech, then:

H_4: There will be an increase in local rhetoric on a specific issue as Congress takes up the issue and another increase in local rhetoric as bills come up for meaningful votes.

H_5: Presidential rhetoric on specific agenda items will clearly delineate the president's issue position.

H_6: Presidential rhetoric on specific agenda items will clearly identify Congress as the problem in the policy process.

H_7: Presidential rhetoric on specific agenda items will clearly ask the public to contact members of Congress and indicate their support for the president's fixed position.

Timing Speechmaking

When President Bush traveled around the country, he spoke at all manner of venues, from state fairs to military bases to medical conferences. Traditionally, the venue and the audience have served as a national substitute or as a mechanism to highlight a point. In this use of the audience as part of the public relations design, the public becomes a poster board behind the president: The president speaks about health care before nurses and doctors, to the elderly about a Medicare prescription drug program, or to the U.S. Chamber of Commerce about taxes—all to reinforce the message with the masses. While Presidents Clinton and Bush began their tenures speaking before general audiences, which do provide an approximation of the nation, both presidents abandoned that strategy. Figure 4.1 situates President Bush as less nationally oriented than President Clinton. However, despite the national context and environment, President Clinton did not employ the classic going-public, Reagan-type approach to public leadership. President Bush, constrained by his environment, exhibited even less national going-public leadership.

President Bush gave very few national speeches that were not event or crisis driven in years one through three. Table 4.9 lists President Bush's domestic agenda speeches, which represented only 29 percent of his national speeches (see Table 2.1, which lists all the national speeches). Foreign events and crises drove President Bush's tenure significantly. As with President Clinton, in order to evaluate President Bush's rhetorical content I chose four domestic agenda

Table 4.9 Bush's National Speeches on Domestic Agenda Items

Speech	*Date*
Inaugural	1/20/01
Administration goals	2/27/01
Stem cell research	8/9/01
State of the Union 1	1/29/02
State of the Union 2	1/28/03

items that were priorities in his campaign: tax relief, education reform (No Child Left Behind, or NCLB), Medicare reform/prescription drug benefit, and the faith based initiative.

One of President Bush's priorities was very different from the others. The faith-based initiative was comparable to Clinton's AmeriCorps in that it was an individual priority, a minority priority, and not a top national agenda item as evidenced by public opinion polls. Like Clinton did with AmeriCorps, Bush repeatedly focused on his faith-based initiative during his campaign and immediately upon taking office. Both presidents emphasized their respective issues in their campaigns and focused on them in their first year in office.

In order to evaluate H_4, that the timing of local rhetoric should relate to congressional activity, I used the coding scheme described in Chapter 3. Table 4.10 identifies the changing patterns of Bush's presidential priorities across his issues and across his tenure. President Bush's campaign agenda did dominate the first year of his administration, with 50 percent of his speeches at least mentioning these four priorities. The cycle of decreasing effectiveness hit President Bush, but not as significantly as his predecessor, since President Clinton's party lost control of Congress in the second year while Bush's gained control. President Bush, unlike President Clinton, gave more speeches on his campaign agenda items in year three than he did in year one. If the speeches that focused on an item are combined with the speeches that merely mentioned an issue, then Bush's consistent emphasis on his agenda over time is impressive. Both Clinton and Bush mentioned their campaign priorities in their first year in office; however, President Bush kept those issues within his rhetoric over his years in office, while President Clinton did not.

The timing of President Bush's speeches appears to have a pattern similar to President Clinton's rhetoric. President Bush's individual priority, the faith-based

Table 4.10 Agenda Items in Bush's Local Speeches (in percent)

	Focus of speech				*Mentioned, not focus*		
Issue	*2001*	*2002*	*2003*	*All local speech*	*2001*	*2002*	*2003*
Faith-based initiative	9	1	1	4	6	2	28
Medicare prescription drugs	2	3	8	5	2	0	32
No Child Left Behind	13	25	5	12	12	4	26
Tax relief	26	21	49	35	12	6	4
Non-agenda*	50	50	37	44	0	0	0

*Speeches whose focus was not the delineated agenda but in which agenda items were mentioned.

initiative, was small but present, making up 9 percent of the president's speeches in year one; it disappeared as a focus thereafter but was still mentioned. The Medicare/prescription drug issue was the reverse, receiving very little attention until year three. NCLB and tax relief followed the pattern of health care and stimulus/deficit reduction: two years of intensity with less in the third year. Interestingly, President Bush consistently devoted time to non-agenda items, though he focused on such topics less often than President Clinton did. President Bush stayed on message throughout those three years.

President Bush's Agenda and the Congressional Schedule

As H_4 notes, presidents seeking to influence congressional outcomes must time their leadership strategies to the congressional calendar. President Bush's pattern of local speechmaking appears similar to President Clinton's in that he did not initially stress all of his campaign agenda items. However, as Figure 4.2 demonstrates, President Bush did focus on three of the four agenda items from his campaign in his first two years: the faith-based initiative, tax relief, and NCLB. As with President Clinton's local speeches, President Bush's rhetorical efforts do not appear to have been driven by the legislative calendar.

The legislative pathway of President Bush's personal agenda item, the faith-based initiative, was more complex than that of President Clinton's personal interest, AmeriCorps. Immediately after taking office, President Bush created a White House advisory council to design legislation, which easily passed the Republican House in July of year one. However, the bill was pronounced dead in the Senate on November 15, 2002. Given these three areas of activity, Kernell's theory and H_4 would predict three spikes in speeches on the faith-based initiative. There was indeed a grouping of such speeches in June, July, and August of 2001—before, during, and after the House decision. However, there were almost no speeches at all around the time of the Senate decision in 2002. Furthermore, Bush said almost nothing about the initiative around the time of his faith-based executive order on December 12, 2002. As Table 4.10 shows, there were numerous secondary mentions of faith-based efforts subsequent to the Senate failure, particularly in 2003: 28 percent of Bush's speeches refer to faith-based programs. Thus, Bush continued to highlight the program but not in connection with any legislative action.

As with President Clinton, on the major campaign agenda planks, President Bush's local rhetorical style supported an aspect of H_4. As shown in Figure 4.2,

Figure 4.2 Timing of Local, Agenda-Leading Speeches: Bush

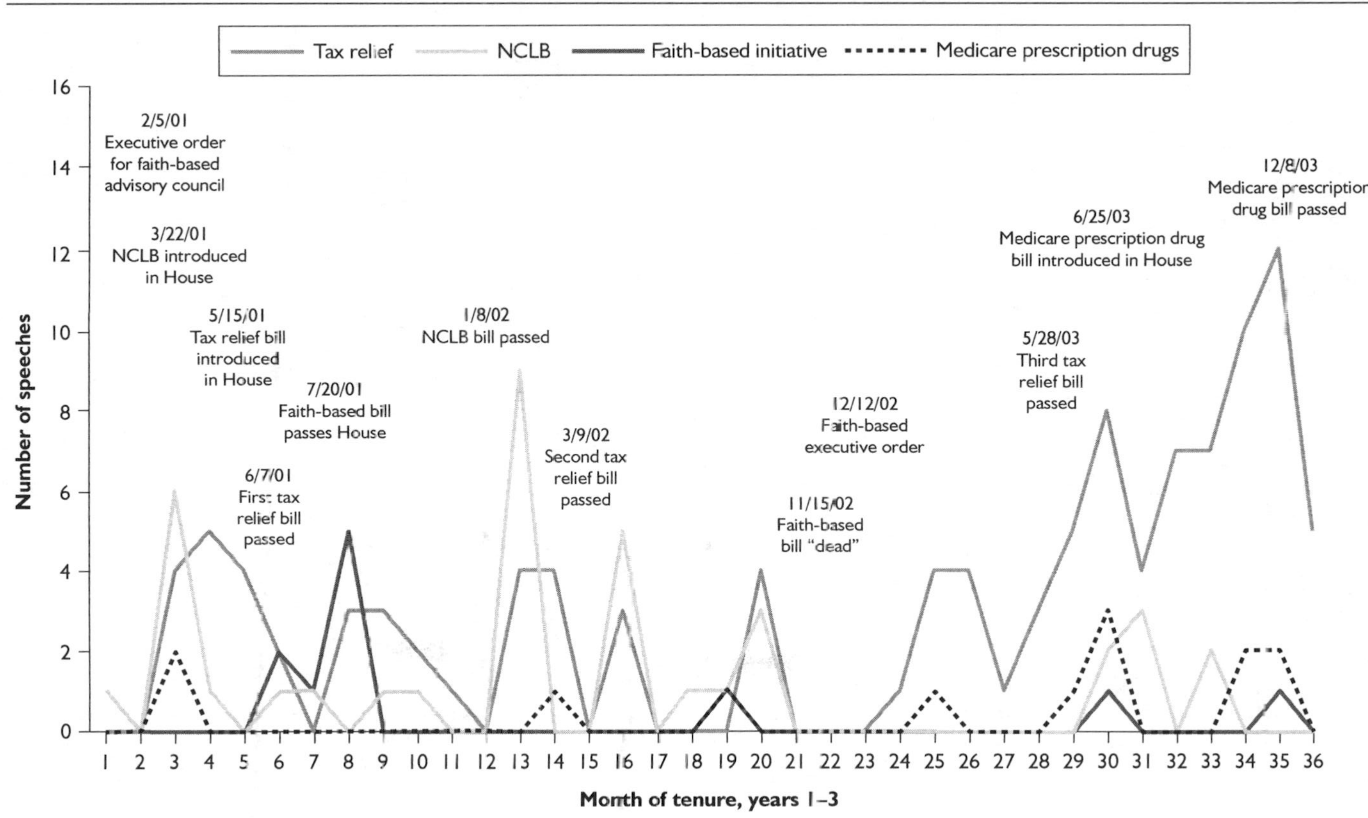

President Bush also tended to speak more frequently to local audiences regarding his agenda items when the bills were introduced in Congress. President Bush may have employed rhetoric to set the tone of the debate or to fix his position.

In President Bush's first two years in office, in keeping with Light's articulation and despite the refocusing effect of 9/11, he tackled three of his four main agenda items, including two large ones: tax relief and NCLB. The Economic Growth and Tax Relief Act passed Congress and the president signed it into law on June 7, 2001. As Figure 4.2 shows, the president spoke consistently, although not that frequently in local settings, on tax relief. In the five months between inauguration and the bill's passage, the president averaged 2.25 speeches a month on the topic. The average is so low because he did not speak about it as his main focus until May, when the bill was introduced in the House. In May and June of 2001, Bush gave nine local speeches on taxes. Thus, as predicted by $H_{4,}$ there is a spike in rhetoric relating to the congressional calendar. However, in contrast to H_4, the president continued to talk about taxes. Two more tax relief bills passed Congress, one in March 2002 and one in May 2003, which could explain the continuing rhetoric. However, in the last seven months of 2003, *after the last tax bill passed*, President Bush's local rhetoric on taxes increased to 7.57 times a month. The president's tax rhetoric doubled *in the absence of legislation.*

On the issues of NCLB and Medicare prescription drugs, the initial pattern—a spike upon bill introduction—persists. On NCLB, there is also a spike around the bill's passage, which by the numbers was relatively easy (House 384–45, Senate 91–8). However, between those two periods the president spoke about education in local settings once a month. The events of 9/11 fell within this period, so the president was not traveling as frequently, and when he did was not speaking as frequently about his domestic agenda. Therefore, it could be argued that once a month was quite a significant allocation of time and attention in the fall of 2001. As for the prescription drug addition to Medicare, after the spike in rhetoric when the bill was introduced, there was no follow-up surge around the time of the bill's passage despite its controversy (the bill passed the House 216–215 and the Senate 54–44).

Therefore, as was the case with President Clinton, President Bush's local rhetoric was not tied to the congressional schedule. President Bush constantly and consistently spoke about tax cuts, with an initial upswing, then stabilizing at about four times a month. Interestingly, after all his tax legislation passed, President Bush increased his tax-centric local rhetoric. With the first and third tax relief bills (but not the second bill), NCLB, Medicare prescription drugs, and the faith-based initiative, the president increased his local rhetoric around the time of the bill's introduction. On tax relief and NCLB there was an increase in local rhetoric in the month of the bill's passage. On the faith-based initiative and Medicare prescription drugs, the president's local rhetoric declined after the introduction of the bills. President Bush spoke locally more frequently on bills that easily passed Congress and was relatively silent during the difficult legislative battles.

Fixing the President's Position

President Bush's reputation is replete with references to line in the sand–type behavior, particularly in terms of terrorism. "You are either with us or against us" is an easier style to employ when you are the dominant figure in the relationship. However, in pursuing a domestic agenda, presidents garner the most media attention in the political arena but have few tools to guarantee outcomes. A line in the sand approach is hard to maintain because it curtails bargaining and makes compromise impossible. H_5 articulates that presidents will employ line in the sand rhetoric as a mechanism to use the public to force congressional compliance.

Despite a reputation for resoluteness and consistency, President Bush was no more of a position-fixer than President Clinton was. Table 4.11 summarizes how President Bush fixed his position most frequently on the Medicare prescription drug program and least often on NCLB education reform. Interestingly, on both Clinton's stimulus and Bush's Medicare prescription drugs (the most fixed issues), each president was dealing with his own party as the majority.

Table 4.11 Bush's Pillars of Rhetorical Leadership (in percent)

Issue	*Fix position*	*Congress as problem*	*Contact Congress*	*Congress as solution*	*Describe problem*	*"What I have done for you"*
Faith-based initiative	17	50	8	50	58	83
No Child Left Behind	13	8	0	66	55	79
Medicare prescription drugs	36	29	21	64	86	50
Tax relief	29	5	4	29	57	87
All speech	25	11	5	52	64	75

Note: The data for each pillar of leadership are percentages within each agenda category. The "All speech" category includes non-agenda speech, which is why no category totals 100%.

Fixing the president's position delineates for the public what the president's preferred legislative outcome is. The local rhetorical refutation of fixing a position suggests that presidents reject adopting a leadership style that precludes bargaining. Clinton and Bush were both willing to fix their positions approximately 25 percent of the time.

In contrast to the choice to go local as a means to get around the limitations of a hostile media, the choice between using and not using going-public tactics tracks with the shift in presidential audiences. A fixed position is much more powerful when it prompts action by general audiences or positively affects national public opinion polls, à la Ronald Reagan in 1981. Yet President Bush spoke more frequently to associations and partisans than to general audiences.

Congress as the Problem

The practice of demonizing your enemy is antithetical to the spirit of compromise forced on legislative partners by the constitutional design of the legislative process. Without a supermajority, Congress cannot ignore the president's negotiating power bestowed by the veto pen. Presidents cannot avoid negotiating with Congress because they cannot introduce legislation or compel congressional action. A campaign approach to governing, however, would depend on this contentious type of leadership, as a campaign requires identification of the enemy and rests on distinguishing one candidate from another. Demonizing the opposition resurrects a long-standing tradition in American politics: The revolutionaries demonized the king of England in order to make their position more appealing.

Like President Clinton, President Bush avoided demonizing individuals, preferring "Washington," "special interests," or the more generic "the other side" and "some people." President Bush demonized less often than President Clinton, but when he did, he was just as likely to say something nice about someone, as if seeking karmic balance. President Bush could be considered as an underlying cause of the discontinuity between citizens' support for their individual congressperson and lack of support for the institution. President Bush surrounded himself with local members of Congress whom he frequently praised, which stood in stark contrast to the generic berating of Washington and the process (see Table 4.11).

Of course, President Bush was unlikely to be as critical as President Clinton was simply by virtue of partisanship. When President Bush took office, Congress was Republican (although there was a tie in the Senate for the first two years); it became even more Republican after the midterm elections of 2002.

Consequently, Bush was critical of the institution only 11 percent of the time. In contrast, Clinton was critical of Congress 17 percent of the time after switching from a Congress controlled by Democrats to a Republican-controlled Congress. Clinton was critical across the board; Bush was not. Bush was strikingly critical in his rhetoric on the faith-based initiative and Medicare prescription drugs; on both issues, he was encountering a lack of support from his own party.

"Contact Your Representative"

Table 4.11 demonstrates that of all the hypotheses, H_7 is the most unfounded. Direct requests of the public by the president to contact Congress were rare. President Bush requested help only 5 percent of the time. On specific issues there were increases: In 21 percent of his rhetoric on Medicare prescription drugs, President Bush asked the public to reach out to their representatives. Like President Clinton, President Bush did not ask local audiences to pressure Congress very often. When he did ask, he tended to do so before specific groups regarding specific issues. More typically, both presidents asked for "help" and "your support" without specifically asking anyone to call, write, fax, or tweet.

Congress as Part of the Solution

Despite the intensity of the partisan environment under which President Bush governed, his local rhetoric was not specifically partisan or overtly confrontational. His rhetoric, however, was not universally presidential in tone, nor did it follow the traditional going-public format. The use of generic language like "other side," "some people," Washington," and "special interests" allowed the president to cast blame, shift responsibility, and fire up an audience without alienating anyone potentially useful. As a leadership tool, going public requires a response from the entire public in the form of polling data.[2] Thus, the president must reach the active and the non-active, the partisan and the nonpartisan. Yet, in the local arena, President Bush was not speaking to a national audience. The White House received thousands of invitations to events; they chose to attend events with partisan, association, or business audiences.

The audience in local settings, when not general, reflected active electoral and governing constituencies, interest groups, partisans, and business (although not farmers and unions). Consequently, Presidents Clinton and Bush spoke to individuals already active in the political system, whom national polls effectively mute. National polls offer a snapshot of the entire nation's attitudes, yet the entire nation is not politically active. Many do not vote, nor do they hold elected officials accountable for specific legislative actions the way active individuals do. Rhetorical strategy on the local level is not about motivating participation; the audience members are already motivated. The local strategy is about targeting that participation toward the president's preferred outcomes. President Bush could not hope to motivate a national presidential constituency he did not have and could not reach; but he could count on motivating the participatory citizenry.

As a result, at the local level, President Bush did not need to request that his audiences contact Congress. His audiences already understood how to participate in the political system. Instead of providing specifics ("Please write your Congress member and tell them to support this program"), President Bush, like President Clinton, chose to be more generic, confident these citizens did not require urging. "Help me" was enough.

As shown in Table 4.11 and the following excerpt, President Bush was frequently quite nice, to Democrats and Republicans alike:

> I'm particularly proud to be here with the Montana congressional delegation, fine Americans—fine Americans all, starting with the senior member of the delegation, the senior Senator [Democrat Max Baucus], who is a man who's got enormous power in Washington. He's the kind of man who has got enough power that if he likes what I have to say and you like what I have to say, I'm confident he'll get it done. We're counting on you. (George W. Bush, Billings, Montana, March 26, 2001)

President Bush was most effusive on NCLB. After the passage of the education reform, President Bush frequently praised the Democrats he worked with:

> And one of my traveling mates was Ted Kennedy, the Senator from Massachusetts. I've said good things about him. *[Laughter]* He nearly fell out. *[Laughter]* So did the boys at the Crawford coffee shop. *[Laughter]* But I said it because he worked hard to get a good bill; he worked with a Republican administration to get a good piece of education reform. We showed what can happen in Washington when you put your political parties aside and focus on what's best for the United States of America. (George W. Bush, New Orleans, Louisiana, January 15, 2002)

Part of the reason for this complimentary behavior is the setting. If the speeches are always nationally oriented regardless of setting, then it is possible to berate the unseen enemy. During a local presidential visit, the president includes the local congressional delegation. The delegation is generally made up of just the members of Congress from the president's party, but occasionally members of the other party are included as well. I suspect that the presence of "the problem" drives the president's decision not to be overly critical in specific.

Describing Problems Rather Than Fixing Positions

Like President Clinton, when President Bush drew a line in the sand, it was pretty clear what he wanted from Congress:

> And so in my budget, we ask Congress to increase the pay for the men and women who wear the uniform, to make sure they're better paid and better housed. A priority is a strong military. But it's one thing to spend more money. It's also important to have a Commander in Chief who sets a clear mission for the military of the United States. And the mission is this: Be prepared to fight and win war and, therefore, prevent war from happening in the first place. (George W. Bush, Billings, Montana, March 26, 2001)

However, Bush used that level of specificity in only a quarter of his local rhetoric. The majority of his rhetoric avoided asking for a specific solution. Instead, like President Clinton, President Bush focused on his worldview and his list of legislative wants and needs. President Bush described the problem 64 percent of the time and fixed his position in only 25 percent of his rhetoric. The timing of Bush's rhetoric potentially influenced this rejection of going-public language, as Bush's preference was for rhetoric at the beginning of the legislative process rather than nearing the voting. Describing the problem is an effort to control the understanding of an issue, its causes, and its solutions. In a sense, this is classic campaign behavior, not individualized pluralism—define your opponent before he can define you. In the case of an issue battle, the debate is primed by getting the "why" and the "what" out there first. In short, President Bush sought to define terms, define problems, and define solutions.

"What I Have Done for You Lately"

In addition to describing the environment, President Bush focused on demonstrating his accomplishments while in office. On the surface, this seems driven by electoral concerns; a president needs voters to believe he is upholding his campaign promises. In a very nationalized way, "what I have done for you lately" rhetoric represents a bridge between the past and future campaigns: "This is why you sent me and why you want me back." It is also an effort to remind citizens of the president's effectiveness and to provide a basis on which to answer the survey question, "Do you approve of the job the president is doing?" The fact that this rhetoric is overwhelmingly present in the local speeches of both Presidents Bush and Clinton suggests it is more than a campaign tool. The fact that it is targeted to groups and individuals active in the legislative process means this rhetoric is a leadership tool, not simply a campaign tool. President Bush frequently referenced his successes on taxes, as this excerpt demonstrates:

> And so I twice led the United States Congress to pass historic tax relief for the American people. We wanted tax relief to be as broad and as fair as possible, so we reduced taxes on everyone who pays taxes. I don't think it makes sense to penalize marriage in the Tax Code. We want to reward and honor marriage. And so we reduced the marriage penalty. We understand it takes a lot of—to raise a family and to educate a child, so we increased the child credit to $1,000. This summer I said the check would be in the mail, and it was. (George W. Bush, Manchester, New Hampshire, October 9, 2003)

This type of rhetoric was present in 75 percent of George W. Bush's local speeches (see Table 4.11). A president without a large electoral cushion lacks the ability to pressure Congress with that constituency. Thus, the president is continually marshaling the narrow coalition to work a "small ball" rather than a "moneyball" strategy, to use the baseball parlance where cumulative base hits are as valuable as home runs. The audiences before the president do not need to be reminded that he is working on their behalf, as would a large general audience, but that the president needs *the audience's* effort to succeed.

Leading When Not National

In keeping with the complicated environment that propelled him to the presidency, George W. Bush could not employ a national leadership approach. As elucidated in his signature speech on Iraq from Cincinnati, even when speaking to the nation, a national platform was not a comfortable fit. For the bulk of his oratory, President Bush did not employ a single voice when speaking before the public. Moreover, the White House particularly targeted audiences that were not representative of a national constituency. President Bush eschewed traditional nationalized leadership content in favor of content that emphasized his behavior, his goals, and his leadership while in office. In short, in speech after speech, President Bush focused on his immediate audience of partisans, associations, businesses, and schools in order to reach members of his electoral coalition.

President Bush exercised a categorically different pattern of behavior than what is depicted in portrayals of a national presidency. However, in his patterns of behavior he was not so different from President Clinton, who seemingly fit the criteria for employing national leadership. I turn next to President Obama, who represents an amalgam of his predecessors. President Obama earned a large Electoral College victory but faced a fragmented media. The next chapter considers how media fragmentation constrains a president's ability to reach the audience he can claim.

Chapter 5

An Obstructed President: Barack Obama

It is great to be here, great to be back in the "Show Me" State, great to be back in St. Charles. Some of you may remember, it was—that it was from this town that Lewis and Clark began their journey into a harsh and unforgiving landscape. And I can relate—[Laughter]—because the first time I came here, I was trying to get to Washington, DC, a harsh and unforgiving landscape. [Laughter]

—Barack Obama, St. Charles, Missouri, March 10, 2010

Presidents Clinton, Bush, and Obama all viewed the audiences before them on their local travels favorably. President Obama reiterated what his predecessors also stated: When out on the road, the president receives a warm welcome from constituents and gentle questions from the local press. In contrast, Washington events can be much less friendly and much more fraught with tension and politics. However, presidents do not travel so often, and give so many policy speeches, because they are in search of friendly confines from which to give a speech. Moreover, local travel is not merely a spectacle[1] designed to influence national public opinion through a well-staged photo op. Presidents use local travel as a means for exercising agenda leadership; however, the means and the mode of exercising rhetorical leadership depend on the environment in which a president governs. A large Electoral College victory coupled with a national media yields a national president who targets a single audience, employs national rhetoric, and does not need to travel to reach his audience. In contrast, a narrow Electoral College victory coupled with a fragmented, non-national media yields a constrained president who must target multiple audiences, use coalition base rhetoric, and travel frequently to reach his audience.

The shaded box in Figure 5.1 describes a president who exists between the extremes of national and constrained leadership. Particularly, this box reveals the effects of technological change on an electorally supported president. A large Electoral College win coupled with a fragmented, non-national media yields an obstructed president, a president who cannot reach his large single audience with national rhetoric without frequent travel. President Obama achieved a large Electoral College victory but confronted the challenges of the first wireless century. President Bush bore the brunt of advancing technological change coupled with electoral disunity. President Obama faced greater technological advances than Bush, but he enjoyed a comfortable majority. Consequently, President Obama represents an obstructed president, a president who wants to return to Reagan-esque national leadership but cannot do so when confronted with an increasingly fragmented media and technology environment.

National Leadership without a Megaphone

As noted in Chapter 2, President Obama's electoral results offered an optimal governing context. President Obama experienced an extraordinary battle with

Figure 5.1 Systemic Influences on Obama's Leadership

Electoral College victory	***Media environment***	
	Narrow	*Fragmented*
Large (>65% of total Electoral College vote)	Target a single audience Employ national rhetoric Less likely to travel	Target a single audience Employ national rhetoric Likely to travel
Narrow (<65% of total Electoral College vote)	Target multiple audiences Employ coalition base rhetoric Less likely to travel	Target multiple audiences Employ coalition base rhetoric Likely to travel

Hillary Clinton for the nomination. The general election took place during the economic meltdown of 2008, which drew increased attentiveness. In contrast to his predecessors, President Obama achieved a large popular vote victory as well as a large Electoral College victory while experiencing an increase in turnout. As a result, President Obama took office with a stable, large-majority, national coalition reminiscent of Ronald Reagan or FDR.

In order for President Obama to reach his stable, large-majority, national coalition, he did not have the luxury of disseminating information primarily through a stable, national press corps. Although Nixon, Reagan, and George H. W. Bush were all highly critical of the national press corps, they did not experience the fragmentation of the media environment or the resulting challenges that complicate rhetorical leadership.

Independent press critique of the president is over one hundred years old.[2] However, between President Clinton's tenure and President Obama's, the mechanism for delivering the presidential message and critiques of that message expanded in multiple directions and contracted in others. There are now numerous news outlets for a consumer to choose from. Cable providers offer hundreds of channels of programming, where three major plus two local channels used to exist. Talk radio and talk television grew in popularity in the 2000s, but the number of radio stations and newspapers is decreasing through consolidation and a decline in profitability. The rise of the Internet in politics over the course of the 2000s presents a new medium for presidents and further dilutes the control over the president's message. In the broadcast age, presidents were frustrated by the gatekeeping function provided by the Washington press corps. They challenged the president's ability to determine what was on the nightly news. However, the Internet undermines the Washington press corps' ability to control the political agenda; thus, the president now confronts a freer and more open environment, complicating agenda control.

During the 2008 presidential campaign, the Obama team mastered the use of the Internet as a campaign tool, especially in comparison to other candidates. Obama's web presence was head and shoulders above his competitors on both the Democratic and Republican sides. Obama's web page was very sophisticated, allowing users to do on the site what they did elsewhere on the web: buy, donate, join in, be social, and gather information.[3] In addition, the campaign created an impressive e-mail database, which they used to contact and update voters through texting and e-mail. The field of candidates never caught up with Obama's web and e-mail efforts, but Hillary Clinton's campaign came closest.[4]

A more sophisticated web presence coupled with massive sums of money used to buy TV and web advertising allowed the Obama campaign to bypass the gatekeeping effect of the traditional media. Early in 2007, the mainstream press anointed Hillary Clinton the presumptive Democratic nominee due to her party insider status and fund-raising capabilities. In the past, upstart campaigns like Obama's would have withered in the face of the invisible primary: No, or negative, media coverage led to less fund-raising, and less fund-raising led to little or negative media coverage. Money and media coverage traditionally went hand in hand as shortcuts for the pundit-ocracy's assessments of viability. The Obama campaign's use of the Internet to fund-raise and reach voters in primary states short-circuited the media's ability to declare the candidate unviable and thus limit the public's access to him. The Obama campaign's presence on Facebook, Myspace, and other social networking sites also allowed it to broaden its reach beyond the typical TV and newspaper audiences.[5]

The understanding of the value of web-based outreach continued once President Obama took office. On January 20, 2009, the George W. Bush White House home page disappeared and the new, multifaceted Barack Obama web page appeared. Borrowing from the campaign, the Obama White House website offered multiple ways for interested individuals to gather information and contact the administration, from e-mail to RSS feeds.[6] In addition, the White House continued Obama's campaign presence on YouTube, Facebook, Myspace, Flickr, LinkedIn, and iTunes. The president's web presence is exceptionally popular, boasting more than 152,000 friends on Myspace, more than 930,000 Facebook friends, more than 72,000 contacts on LinkedIn, more than 2.1 million followers on Twitter, and more than 45 million views on White House videos on YouTube.[7]

Targeting a National Audience

One of the fundamental premises of this book is that the size of the Electoral College victory matters for the president because it reflects the majoritarian nature of the president-elect's coalition. The large-majority victory mutes the inevitable failure-to-achieve critique that electorally challenged presidents endure.

Moreover, the sweeping nature of the victory is what generates the presidential honeymoon, with partisans giving partisanship a rest in the face of a majoritarian victory. In contrast, close races energize and embolden partisans while dismaying independents.

Based simply on audience factors, President Obama was a solidly national president. However, the contextual factor of the media influences his presidency much more significantly, and his behavior matches his predecessors much more than his electoral leadership scenario would suggest.

Finding the Presidential Audience

President Obama traveled to 199 cities in three years and averaged 29 distinct state visits. As Table 5.1 reveals, in comparison to his predecessors, Obama averaged fewer state visits and his total state visits were lower. The number of his city visits fell between Clinton and Bush, highlighting how Obama traveled less frequently than his predecessors but made more stops and met with more audiences per trip.

President Obama's travels reflect no discernable reelection strategy. In his first three years in office, President Obama visited all of the most populous states (see Table 5.2). He visited all but Georgia in 2009 but remedied that in 2010. By his third year, President Clinton had visited eight of the ten least populous states, while George W. Bush had only visited six. In his first three years, President Obama only visited four of the least populous states. In his first

Table 5.1 Presidential Travel: Clinton, Bush, and Obama

	Number of cities visited			*Number of states visited**		
	Clinton	*Bush*	*Obama*	*Clinton*	*Bush*	*Obama*
Year 1	53	63	63	31	32	27
Year 2	60	103	83	29	38	32
Year 3	61	89	53	28	36	27
Total	174	255	199	88	106	86
Average	58.0	85.0	66.3	29.3	35.3	28.7
Standard deviation	4.36	20.30	15.28	1.53	3.06	2.89

*Includes Washington, DC.

Table 5.2 Presidential Travel by Population: Clinton, Bush, and Obama

Most populous states	*Number of Clinton visits*	*Number of Bush visits*	*Number of Obama visits*
California	34	24	17
Florida	10	22	15
Georgia	6	12	3
Illinois	7	10	8
Michigan	11	14	9
New Jersey	6	4	1
New York	13	11	19
Ohio	7	11	15
Pennsylvania	8	19	12
Texas	7	22	5
Least populous states	*Number of Clinton visits*	*Number of Bush visits*	*Number of Obama visits*
Alaska	0	7	0
Delaware	3	6	1
Hawaii	10	1	3
Montana	1	2	0
New Hampshire	2	2	2
North Dakota	3	0	0
Rhode Island	10	1	3
South Dakota	0	0	0
Vermont	1	0	0
Wyoming	2	0	0

year, he visited 87.5 percent of states that were competitive in 2008 (he won fifteen of those battleground states; see Table 5.3). By 2010, Obama had visited all of the competitive states (see Table 5.3). In three years in office, President Clinton only missed one of the 1992 competitive states (Nevada) and President Bush missed none.

An Audience of Whole Parts

The second quadrant of Figure 5.1 predicts that as a president with a national electoral coalition, President Obama would seek a single, national audience.

Table 5.3 Visits to Battleground States in 2008: Obama

States	*Won by Obama in 2008*	*Lost by Obama in 2008*	*Total*
Battleground	15	1	16
Democrat leaning	13	0	13
Republican leaning	2	20	22
Total	30	21	51

Specific battleground states	*Number of Obama presidential visits*
Colorado	7
Florida	17
Iowa	8
Michigan	10
Minnesota	4
Missouri	11
Nevada	8
New Hampshire	4
New Jersey	6
New Mexico	2
North Carolina	2
Ohio	18
Oregon	2
Pennsylvania	14
Virginia	36
Wisconsin	7

However, Table 5.4 demonstrates that President Obama overwhelmingly spoke before partisans rather than general audiences. Partisans represented 30 percent of Obama's audiences. Schools were the second most common audience at 17 percent. Associations, businesses, and general audiences were the remaining significant portions of Obama's audiences. These audiences indicate that, despite his national victory, President Obama's rhetoric was not targeted toward audiences that served as proxies for the nation.

Moreover, according to Figure 5.1, President Obama's audiences should look more like President Clinton's than President Bush's, as Bush's narrow constituency encouraged targeting multiple audiences. Table 5.5 demonstrates

Table 5.4 Obama's Local Audiences (in percent)

Type of audience	*2009*	*2010*	*2011*	*Percentage of all local audiences*
Associations	15.46	6.02	20.91	12.87
Businesses	7.22	15.66	11.82	12.33
Farmers	0.00	0.00	0.00	0.00
Government entities	9.28	4.82	8.18	6.97
Military	10.31	4.82	4.55	6.17
Partisans	24.74	42.17	16.36	30.03
Religious entities	0.00	1.20	1.82	1.07
Schools	16.49	13.86	21.82	16.89
Unions	2.06	1.20	1.82	1.61
General	14.43	10.24	12.73	12.06

Table 5.5 Comparing Presidential Audience Types (in percent)

Type of audience	*Clinton*	*Bush*	*Obama*
Associations	27.2	22.0	12.9
Businesses	3.2	9.3	12.3
Farmers	0.0	0.9	0.0
Government entities	2.9	4.9	7.0
Military	10.7	8.9	6.2
Partisans	17.0	28.5	30.0
Religious entities	1.8	1.0	1.1
Schools	10.0	13.2	16.9
Unions	0.7	0.7	1.6
General	26.5	10.5	12.1

that Presidents Bush and Obama were almost equal in their percentage of partisan appearances. President Obama spoke before partisans almost twice as frequently as did President Clinton. President Obama spoke more frequently before schools than either Clinton or Bush, though Bush had No Child Left Behind as a key component of his agenda. According to Table 5.5, and in keeping with his campaign's rejection of "special interest groups," President Obama spoke much less frequently, approximately half as frequently, to associations than his did predecessors. Yet he spoke much more frequently to businesses—almost a third more than President Bush, a self-proclaimed pro-business president. Religious groups, farmers, and unions were rarely visited by President Obama.

A national presidential leadership strategy relies on the transmission of the president's goals and desires for his agenda through the public to Congress. The means of transmission can be actual contact through letters, e-mail, or phone calls, or it can be through improvement in public opinion polls. In either scenario, the audience is generic, determined by geography (the constituency of the member of Congress) or national opinion poll data. Yet, over almost twenty years of increased local rhetoric, the presidential audience looks less and less national. Presidents Bush and Obama entered office from entirely different electoral positions; consequently, their audiences should not have been similar, unless they were similarly national. Counterintuitively, Bush and Obama spoke before similarly non-national audiences. The commonality between the two, of course, is not electoral; rather, it is related to their media environment.

Rhetorical Tone as Leadership

The national president has one national audience, regardless of platform, speech locale, or media environment. The constrained president has multiple audiences and is dependent on speech locale and a fragmented media environment, which hampers the ability to reach these disparate audiences. The tone of the rhetoric employed by a national president will be different than the tone employed by the constrained president. The media environment propels an obstructed president toward multiple venues, while the large electoral coalition keeps the obstructed president nationally oriented. President Obama's travel and audience typology reflected the push/pull of this leadership style: He traveled less, as befitting a national president, yet he spoke before multiple audience types, which a national president has no need to do.

President Obama's rhetorical tone supported the national side of his orientation. As a president with a national constituency, President Obama relied on a singular national voice. Table 5.6 demonstrates that there is no statistical difference between the tone of Obama's rhetoric in national speeches and the tone of the rhetoric in his speeches presented locally. He employed the same rhetorical leadership whether speaking from the Oval Office or a day care center.

Table 5.6 also demonstrates how the different electoral components influence rhetorical leadership. President Obama presented the same rhetoric irrespective of

Table 5.6 Comparing National and Local Rhetoric: Obama

	Activity	*Optimism*	*Certainty*	*Realism*	*Commonality*
Obama national vs. Obama local	0.40	0.50	0.08	0.67	0.95
Clinton, Bush, and Obama	**0.00**	**0.00**	**0.00**	**0.00**	**0.00**
Clinton and Bush	**0.00**	**0.00**	0.06	**0.00**	0.36
Clinton and Obama	0.24	0.10	0.10	0.25	0.13

Note: $p < 0.05$; figures in bold are significant.

whom he was talking to and where he spoke. President Clinton, despite being a national president, was not as consistent over the course of his tenure. However, when comparing presidents, it is Bush who stands out as rhetorically different. He used a different voice dependent on his audience. Moreover, his rhetoric was significantly different from that of his peers. When Bush and Clinton are compared, there is no universal voice between the national and local speeches. However, when Clinton and Obama's rhetorical tones are compared directly, there is a presidential voice. When Clinton, Bush, and Obama are compared, the difference is enormous. The samples no longer come from the same population and they are more disparate than Clinton and Bush. Comparing Clinton's and Bush's national and local leadership shows that there was not a national voice that was consistent across presidents, as three of the five DICTION variables were from different populations. However, adding President Obama's rhetoric to Clinton's and Bush's yields not one component of tone that is similar: All five DICTION variables are from different populations.

The Pillars of Rhetorical Leadership

The hallmark of going public is the speech to the nation in the midst of a legislative fight with Congress, culminating in "the ask." The value of going public as a leadership tool is the use of the national megaphone to compel Congress toward the president's preferred outcome. The mechanism works because of the electoral connection between constituents and their representatives. The mechanism fails when a president cannot reach constituents, when he cannot make his case effectively, or when Congress has the means to resist his plea.

Going public as a leadership style assumes that the president has a link to the public that is distinct from congressional linkages. Exploring rhetorical tone as a measure of national leadership strategy demonstrates that a national tone exists in national speeches; however, it does not exist in the bulk of presidential rhetoric, the speeches given at the local level. As shown in Figure 5.1, using a national going-public strategy is related to the environment in which presidents function. President Clinton, as a national president, would be able to use his constituency to pressure Congress and thus could employ the traditional tactics of his predecessors. President Bush lacked that national audience, so he could not rely on a national constituency with which to pressure Congress to move toward his preferred option. Yet, neither president significantly relied on going-public behavior. Despite his larger and more stable constituency, President Obama did not consistently rely on the going public methodology, which requires a president to speak during legislative activity on his agenda, fix his position, disparage Congress, and ask the public to pressure Congress. However, he did use aspects of the national approach more often than his predecessors did.

Timing Speechmaking

As with the investigations of Presidents Clinton and Bush, I chose four domestic agenda items to evaluate President Obama's rhetorical leadership within his domestic agenda. The domestic priorities investigated here are the economy (the stimulus plan), health care, energy, and education. In terms of national speeches, President Obama gave more addresses from the Oval Office or House of Representatives than did President Bush and just slightly fewer than did President Clinton (see Table 5.7). The presidential campaign agenda dominated the first year of President Obama's administration. Of the three presidents investigated here, President Obama strayed the least from his campaign agenda, as shown in Table 5.8. Eighty percent of his local speeches focused on his four main agenda priorities.

President Obama's Agenda and the Congressional Schedule

Whereas his predecessors spread their attention around, President Obama's speeches remained narrowly focused (see Table 5.8). In years one and two, Obama devoted 58 and 67 percent of his speeches, respectively, to the economy. In year one, 32 percent focused on health care. In 2010, health care dropped

Table 5.7 National Speeches on Domestic Agenda Items

Clinton		*Bush*		*Obama*	
Speech	*Date*	*Speech*	*Date*	*Speech*	*Date*
Inaugural	1/20/93	Inaugural	1/20/01	Inaugural	1/20/09
Economic program	2/15/93	Administration goals	2/27/01	Economic stimulus	2/24/09
Administration goals	2/17/93	Stem cell research	8/9/01	Health care	9/9/09
Economic program 2	8/3/93	State of the Union 1	1/29/02	State of the Union 1	1/27/10
Health care	9/22/93	State of the Union 2	1/28/03	Gulf oil spill	6/15/10
State of the Union 1	1/25/94			State of the Union 2	2/15/11
Middle class	12/15/94			Federal budget	7/25/11
State of the Union 2	1/24/95			Job growth	9/8/11
Balancing the budget	6/13/95				

Table 5.8 The Focus of Local Presidential Speeches (in percent)

Clinton		*Bush*	
Issue	*Total*	*Issue*	*Total*
AmeriCorps	7	Faith-based initiative	3
Health care	23	Medicare prescription drugs	4
Stimulus/deficit reduction	13	No Child Left Behind	9
Welfare reform	12	Tax relief	26
Non-agenda	53	Non-agenda	33

Obama			
Issue	*2009*	*2010*	*All local speech*
Economy	58	67	61
Health care	32	9	11
Education	5	4	4
Energy	5	4	4
Non-agenda	15	23	20

Note: Non-agenda speeches are those whose focus was not the delineated agenda but in which agenda items were mentioned.

behind non-agenda items. Thus, in dramatic contrast to Presidents Clinton and Bush, President Obama largely spent the first year of his presidency on only one domestic priority.

The intense focus correlates well with congressional action (see Figure 5.2). Congress passed President Obama's stimulus plan, the American Recovery and Reinvestment Act of 2009 (ARRA), and both chambers passed versions of health care reform (although the president did not see a completed bill to sign in 2009). The House also passed the Clean Energy and Security Act in June 2009. Obama saw congressional action on three of his four campaign promises. Interestingly, the White House website (http://www.whitehouse.gov) claims credit for all the president's campaign promises, noting that ARRA included monies for the president's priorities on both energy and education.

The timing of President Obama's local speeches, however, does not reflect the going-public leadership style, where rhetoric is timed to coincide with congressional action. According to Figure 5.2, President Obama traveled around the country giving seven subnational speeches on the economy prior to the passage of ARRA. However, President Obama gave a national address *a full week after* signing ARRA into law, and 85 percent of his economic speeches around the country took place *after the bill passed into law*. In fact, the bulk of Obama's economic rhetoric occurred in the three months prior to the midterm elections.

On health care, arguably Obama's most significant legislative effort, there were more speeches prior to the second vote in the House of Representatives in March 2010. However, prior to the first vote in the House and the Senate, Obama was virtually silent. Thus, as with his predecessors, President Obama's local rhetoric was not targeted toward influencing the public in order to influence Congress.

Fixing the President's Position

President Obama represents a stark contrast to both of his predecessors as a position fixer. Where Clinton and Bush averaged position fixing approximately 25 percent of the time, President Obama drew a line in the sand across all four issues less than 10 percent of the time (see Table 5.9). Moreover, on no single issue was he above 5 percent. The heightened partisanship faced by President Obama produced an unusual type of position fixing. Obama drew lines in the

Figure 5.2 Timing of Local, Agenda-Leading Speeches: Obama

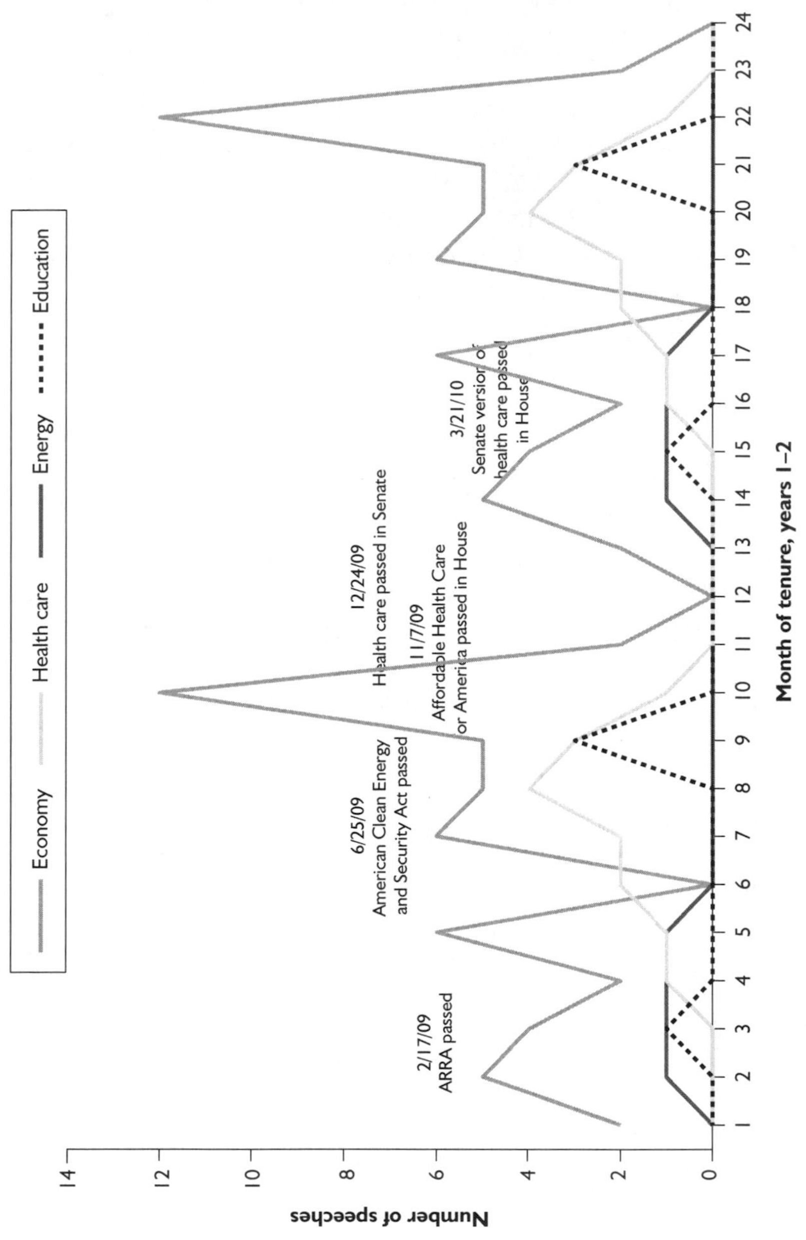

Economy
Health care
Energy
Education

2/17/09
ARRA passed

6/25/09
American Clean Energy
and Security Act passed

12/24/09
Health care passed in Senate

11/7/09
Affordable Health Care
for America passed in House

3/21/10
Senate version of
health care passed
in House

Number of speeches

14
12
10
8
6
4
2
0

1 2 3 4 5 6 7 8 9 10 11 12 13 14 15 16 17 18 19 20 21 22 23 24

Month of tenure, years 1–2

Table 5.9 Presidents and the Pillars of Rhetorical Leadership (in percent)

Clinton						
Issue	*Fix position*	*Congress as problem*	*Contact Congress*	*Congress as solution*	*Describe problem*	*"What I have done for you"*
AmeriCorps	6	0	0	0	67	100
Health care	27	15	15	10	58	68
Stimulus/deficit reduction	38	26	24	44	65	71
Welfare reform	24	21	9	15	62	62
All local speech	26	17	14	17	63	75

Bush						
Issues	*Fix position*	*Congress as problem*	*Contact Congress*	*Congress as solution*	*Describe problem*	*"What I have done for you"*
Faith-based initiative	17	50	8	50	58	83
No Child Left Behind	13	8	0	66	55	79
Medicare prescription drugs	36	29	21	64	86	50
Tax relief	29	5	4	29	57	87
All local speech	25	11	5	52	64	75

Obama						
Issue	*Fix position*	*Congress as problem*	*Contact Congress*	*Congress as solution*	*Describe problem*	*"What I have done for you"*
Economy	3	27	0	53	92	92
Health care	4	3	0	62	86	86
Energy	1	0	0	20	70	60
Education	1	0	0	20	90	90
All local speech	8	27	0	39	85	82

Note: The data for each pillar of leadership are percentages within each agenda category. The "All local speech" category includes non-agenda speech, which is why no category totals 100%.

sand about procedural actions rather than policy positions in response to Republican tactics, as demonstrated in the following excerpt.

> Now, today, for the second time in 24 hours, Senate Republicans unanimously blocked efforts to even begin debating reform. I'm not even asking them to vote for the bill. I just want to let them debate it. And you know—you've learned these Senate rules are complicated. So they won't even let it get on the floor to

> be debated. It's one thing to oppose reform, but to oppose just even talking about reform in front of the American people and having a legitimate debate, that's not right. The American people deserve an honest debate on this bill. It's been 2 years since the financial crisis became clear. I've been talking about it since 2007; before the crisis, I said we needed better rules on Wall Street. And you should not have to wait one more day for some of the strongest consumer protections ever. And I'm not going to let this effort fall victim to industry lobbyists who want to weaken it and water it down and kill it and snuff it out and stomp on it and whatever else they want to do to it. We can't let another crisis like this happen again. And we can't have such a short memory that we let them convince us that we don't need to change the status quo on Wall Street. (Barack Obama, Ottumwa, Iowa, April 27, 2010)

President Obama even drew a line in the sand over procedure alongside efforts to fix policy positions. The vote in the House of Representatives on March 21, 2010, should have produced, and did produce, the most policy position fixing by the president. In Strongsville, Ohio, on March 15, 2010, Obama demonstrated his rhetorical style. Two excerpts from that speech follow; the first passage denotes Obama's fixing of a position, while the second delineates his preference for describing policy. Also, note that the president did not ask for the audience to contact Congress.

> And I believe Congress owes the American people a final up-or-down vote. We need an up-or-down vote. It's time to vote. And now as we get closer to the vote, there's a lot of hand-wringing going on. We hear a lot of people in Washington talking about politics, talking about what this means in November, talking about the poll numbers for Democrats and Republicans. . . . And so I'm calling on Congress to pass these reforms, and I'm going to sign them into law. I want some courage. I want us to do the right thing, Ohio. And with your help, we're going to make it happen.

> So number one—number one is insurance reform. The second thing that this plan would change about the current system is this: For the first time, uninsured individuals, small businesses, they'd have the same kind of choice of private health insurance that Members of Congress get for themselves. . . . And what my proposal says is if you still can't afford the insurance in this new marketplace, then we're going to offer you tax credits to do so. And that will add up to the largest middle class tax cut for health care in history. That's what we're going to do. . . . So with this plan, we're going to make sure the dollars we make—the dollars that we spend on health care are going to make insurance more affordable and more secure. And we're going to eliminate wasteful taxpayer subsidies that

> currently go to insurance companies. Insurance companies are making billions of dollars on subsidies from you, the taxpayer. And if we take those subsidies away, we can use them to help folks like Natoma get health insurance so she doesn't lose her house. And, yes, we will set a new fee on insurance companies, because they stand to gain millions more customers who are buying insurance. There's nothing wrong with them giving something back. Now—so let me talk about the third thing, which is, my proposal would bring down the cost of health care for families, for businesses, and for the Federal Government. . . . We have incorporated most of the serious ideas from across the political spectrum about how to contain the rising costs of health care. We go after waste and abuse in the system, especially in Medicare. . . . Now—so, look, Ohio, that's the proposal.

Fixing the president's position delineates for the public what the president's preferred legislative outcome is. The local rhetorical refutation of fixing a position suggests that presidents, regardless of the connection to their coalition, reject adopting a leadership style that precludes bargaining. More interesting than all three of these presidents allowing for bargaining is the difference between the presidents. Clinton and Bush were willing to fix their positions 25 percent of the time, whereas President Obama did so only 8 percent of the time. Yet, the going-public model hinges on motivating the national audience by articulating a presidential position and strategy. Presidents Clinton and Obama entered office with the Electoral College support to try the strategy, yet neither consistently employed it.

In contrast to the choice to go local as a means to get around the limitations imposed by an electoral coalition or a hostile media, the choice between using and not using going-public tactics might relate more to partisanship. All three presidents, particularly President Obama, frequently spoke before partisans in a period noted for a particular brand of hyperpartisanship. It is possible that the audience itself delimits the use of fixed language in that flexibility encourages participation.

Congress as the Problem

Interestingly, the tactic that increases divisions, institutionally and politically, was the tactic on which President Obama diverged most from his predecessors. As Table 5.9 shows, Presidents Clinton and Bush averaged over 10 percent of negative rhetoric citing Congress as the problem. President Obama used negative rhetoric 27 percent of the time, equal to the combined disparagement of Clinton and Bush. Like his predecessors, Obama preferred to disparage the "other" or special interests, but on occasion he was willing to get quite explicitly negative about Congress and the Republicans in Congress. For example, in Madison, Wisconsin, during the heat of the congressional midterm elections President Obama blamed the Republican leadership directly and specifically:

> What we confronted was an opposition party that was still stuck on the same failed policies of the past, whose leaders in Congress were determined from the start to let us deal with the mess that they had done so much to create. Because their calculation was as simple as it was cynical. They knew that it was going to take a long time to solve the economic challenges we face. They saw the data. They were talking to the economists. They realized that Obama was walking in and we had just lost 4 million jobs in the 6 months before I was sworn in; 750,000 jobs the month I was sworn in; 600,000 jobs the month after that; 600,000 jobs the month after that. So before our economic policies could even be put into place, we'd already lost most of the 8 million jobs we would lose. And they knew that people would be frustrated. And they figured, if we just sit on the sidelines and just say no and just throw bombs and let Obama and the Democrats deal with everything, they figured they might be able to prosper at the polls. (Barack Obama, Madison, Wisconsin, September 28, 2010)

It is not clear that the choice to go negative relates to either the constituency or the media environment, since Clinton and Bush were more similar to each other in their negativity. If Clinton and Obama were more similar, then the constituency argument would carry more weight. However, if Obama and Bush were more similar, then the media argument would carry more explanatory power. The fact that Obama is the standout suggests that other factors are in play, particularly partisanship, since Obama visited partisans much more frequently. However, Obama's own majority controlled the House and Senate, albeit narrowly, in his first two years. President Clinton entered with a similar majority.

"Contact Your Representative"

On July 25, 2011, President Barack Obama did something he had not done since taking office. He asked the public for help:

> The American people may have voted for divided Government, but they didn't vote for a dysfunctional Government. So I'm asking you all to make your voice heard. If you want a balanced approach to reducing the deficit, let your

> Member of Congress know. If you believe we can solve this problem through compromise, send that message. (Barack Obama, Address to the Nation on the Federal Budget, July 25, 2011)

Despite his national constituency footing, prior to July 2011 and the battle with the House of Representatives over raising the debt ceiling, President Obama *never* directly asked his audience to contact Congress. Instead, Obama routinely asked for other kinds of help, as typified by these remarks in 2009:

> That's what we need to do right now, and I need your help. If you want a health care system that works for the American people as well as it works for the insurance companies, I need your help knocking on doors, talking to your neighbors, spread the facts. Let's get this done. (Barack Obama, Portsmouth, New Hampshire, August 11, 2009)

Even immediately prior to the House vote on the Senate version of the health care bill, President Obama did not ask his audience to contact their members of Congress as explicitly as his predecessors did. But he came as close as the English language would allow without actually using the terminology. It is striking, however, that a skilled orator and former lawyer who is very careful with words worked so hard to avoid the fundamental principle of individualized pluralism, and avoided it so fiercely that he actually tripped on the language: "you—we—and we":

> So the United States Congress owes the American people a final, up-or-down vote on health care. It's time to make a decision. The time for talk is over. We need to see where people stand. And we need all of you to help us win that vote. So I need you to knock on doors, talk to your neighbors, pick up the phone. When you hear an argument by the water cooler and somebody is saying this or that about it, say, "No, no, no, no, hold on a second." You—we—and we need you to make your voices heard all the way in Washington, DC. They need to hear your voices, because right now the Washington echo chamber is in full throttle. It is as deafening as it's ever been. And as we come to that final vote, that echo chamber's telling Members of Congress, wait, think about the politics, instead of thinking about doing the right thing. (Barack Obama, Glenside, Pennsylvania, March 8, 2010)

The reluctance to ask for help at all seems to be a fundamental rejection of the power of the national audience for the presidency. After all, both Clinton and Bush asked at times, although not as often as the legislative efforts suggest they could have. In contrast, President Obama did it once. He used the power of the office's national megaphone to ask the public to pressure the House of Representatives not to allow the U.S. government to default on its loan obligations. Thus, it could be argued that Obama restricted this tool's use to something of great significance. However, neither Clinton nor Bush used it so frequently as to provide an example of overuse.

Congress as Part of the Solution

As discussed in the previous chapters, if presidents are not using the traditional content of going-public leadership in their rhetoric, then they must be using other leadership approaches. Specifically, I found that Presidents Clinton and Bush were employing different rhetoric, they included Congress in their solutions, they explained their view of issues, and they touted their presidential accomplishments. Thus, despite his willingness to disparage Congress, President Obama applied the presidential model and frequently had something nice to say as well. As shown in Table 5.9, Presidents Bush and Obama had something nice to say about members of Congress much more often than did President Clinton. President Obama even went so far as to indicate to one crowd that their fabulous congressional delegation included Republicans, using the terms "this side" and "that side":

> I want to, before I start, acknowledge some people who have just done a wonderful job for this area, but also a wonderful job for the country: first of all, one of the best Governors that we've got in the United States of America, Governor Jay Nixon; one of my—not just my favorite Senators, but one of my favorite people and a great friend of mine who is fighting every day for the people of Missouri, Senator Claire McCaskill. We've got two outstanding Members of Congress, one from this side and one from that side, Congressman Emanuel Cleaver and Congressman Dennis Moore. And finally, I just want to acknowledge all the wonderful people at Smith Electric Vehicles and their energetic and outstanding staff. (Barack Obama, Kansas City, Missouri, July 8, 2010)

Describing Problems Rather Than Fixing Positions

Table 5.9 indicates that President Obama described problems much more readily (more than 20 percent more) than his predecessors. Obama's rhetoric contained a different quality in his description of the problem and process. In his rhetoric, President Obama was not content simply to relate his view of the problem; he often connected his view to the public view, sometimes even removing his view entirely. The following excerpt is from a speech on the economy that took place before a general audience in Missouri in 2009:

> You believed that after an era of selfishness and greed, that we could reclaim a sense of responsibility on Wall Street and in Washington, as well as on Main Street. You believed that instead of huge inequalities and an economy that's built on a bubble, we could restore a sense of fairness to our economy and build a new foundation for lasting growth and prosperity. You believed that at a time of war, we could stand strong against our enemies and stand firmly for our ideals, and show a new face of American leadership to the world. That's the change that you believed in. That's the trust you placed in me. It's something I will never forget, the fact that you made this possible. . . . Now, we've got a lot of work to do, because on our first day in office we found challenges of unprecedented size and scope. Our economy was in the midst of the most serious downturn since the Great Depression. Banks had stopped lending. The housing market was crippled. The deficit was at $1.3 trillion. And meanwhile, families continued to struggle with health care costs, too many of our kids couldn't get the education they needed, the Nation remained trapped by our dangerous dependence on foreign oil. Now, these challenges could not be met with half-measures. They couldn't be met with the same old formulas. They couldn't be confronted in isolation. They demanded action that was bold and sustained. They demand action that is bold and sustained. They call on us to clear away the wreckage of a painful recession, but also, at the same time, lay the building blocks for a new prosperity. And that's the work that we've begun over these first 100 days. (Barack Obama, Arnold, Missouri, April 29, 2009)

Problem definition represents a double-edged sword for a president, particularly when the problem is a lousy economy. FDR's inaugural address and fireside chats demonstrated the power of a positive call to action from the president in the midst of a crisis. President Obama similarly needed to rebuild confidence without ignoring the reality of the crisis, but he also needed to redefine the crisis and his solutions. Obama employed the classic campaign strategy of defining "us" versus "them" in service of problem definition. Interestingly, Obama used the beliefs of the audience—"you believed"—to outline the problems and link them to his solutions, rather than his own explicitly stated values.

In this way, Obama continued the national model he had begun before his campaign—that of a universal audience. The speech that brought him national media attention, and arguably earned him his Senate seat, is best remembered for its universal message:

> Now even as we speak, there are those who are preparing to divide us, the spin masters, the negative ad peddlers who embrace the politics of anything goes. Well, I say to them tonight, there is not a liberal America and a conservative America—there is the United States of America. There is not a Black America and a White America and Latino America and Asian America—there's the United States of America.
>
> The pundits, the pundits like to slice-and-dice our country into Red States and Blue States; Red States for Republicans, Blue States for Democrats. But I've got news for them, too. We worship an awesome God in the Blue States, and we don't like federal agents poking around in our libraries in the Red States. We coach Little League in the Blue States and yes, we've got some gay friends in the Red States. There are patriots who opposed the war in Iraq and there are patriots who supported the war in Iraq.
>
> We are one people, all of us pledging allegiance to the stars and stripes, all of us defending the United States of America. In the end, that's what this election is about. Do we participate in a politics of cynicism or do we participate in a politics of hope?[8]

Obama's rhetoric did not change from that perspective, regardless of where he spoke or to whom. It could be argued, then, that strangely his efforts to deliver this message primarily to partisans seem designed to mute partisan differences. This notion will be explored further below.

"What I Have Done for You Lately"

The largest component of presidential rhetoric and perhaps the antithesis of what going public seeks to accomplish is the continual restatement of successes before local audiences. President Obama's descriptive style was quite artful as he tied the campaign, public goals, and his own views together in a clear, logical line to make the case that something needed to be done. Of course, it is not enough to describe the problem, or even to offer to do something about the problem; presidents are elected to solve problems. The media, other politicians, other political actors, pollsters, and ordinary citizens constantly evaluate presidential efforts at problem solving. Therefore, particularly before audiences who want what the president wants, the national, constrained, and obstructed leadership all encourage the continual restatement of presidential accomplishments. Consequently, President Obama adopted the local rhetorical strategy employed by his predecessors quite quickly; the laundry list provided in this excerpt came after only three months in office:

> To jumpstart job creation and get our economy moving again, we passed the most ambitious economic recovery plan in our Nation's history. And already, we're beginning to see this change take hold. In Jefferson City, over 2,500 jobs will be created on Missouri's largest wind farm, so that American workers are harnessing clean, American energy. Across the State, roughly 20,000 transportation jobs will be supported by the Recovery Act, so that Missourians are rebuilding your roads, your bridges, your rails. To restore fairness to our economy, we've taken several steps with Congress to strengthen the middle class. We cut taxes for 95 percent of American households through a tax cut that will put $120 billion directly into your pockets. We finally signed a law long overdue that will protect equal pay for equal work for American women. We extended health care to millions of children across this country. We launched a housing plan that's already contributed to a spike in the number of homeowners who are refinancing their mortgages, which is the equivalent of another tax cut for them. And if you haven't refinanced, you might want to take a look and see if it's possible, because that can save people a lot of money. We've taken steps to unfreeze the market for auto loans and student loans and small-business loans. And we're acting with the full force of the Federal Government to ensure that our banks have the capital and the confidence to lend money to the families and business owners who keep this economy running. (Barack Obama, Arnold, Missouri, April 29, 2009)

"What I have done for you lately" rhetoric clearly represents a bridge between the previous and next campaign: "This is why you sent me and why you will want me back." However, given that there is no electoral rhyme or reason to presidential travel, leadership of the agenda is still the predominant mechanism for presidential travel.

Why would presidents need to remind their audiences of their presidential successes? The answer lies in who is in these audiences. During the presidential road shows, the bulk of presidential rhetoric occurs before partisans and members of associations. These audiences are not general audiences requiring motivation to enter politics and participate. These are active citizens who already do participate; thus, the presidential rhetoric is meant to get these citizens on board behind the president. It could be argued that this is the targeted version of national going public. The president reviews his successes with his local audiences, which shows these active citizens who want something from politics that support for this president works.

The Obstructed President

President Obama's electoral coalition provided maneuvering room with which to exercise national leadership. Analysis of President Obama's rhetorical tone indicates that he used the same voice at the national and local levels. However, he traveled frequently (not as often as his immediate predecessors, but much more than those prior to 1992), he spoke more frequently to partisans, he was more consistently disparaging to Congress, and he only once used the tool that belongs uniquely to a president with a national audience—asking for help. Thus, although he had the electoral support to employ a national audience approach, Obama did not consistently employ national tactics, nor did he consistently reject their usage. The debt ceiling debate suggests that the power of the moment yielded a reliance on the most powerful tool in the toolbox. However, the midterm election season of 2010 provided a different picture of how the partisan mood and quixotic media environment can stymie an electorally supported president.

Between June 2009 and September 2010, President Obama's national, majority-based, electoral coalition evaporated, on paper. Obama's approval ratings revealed the loss of independents and Republicans fed up with the Bush years.[9] If approval ratings are the representation of the electoral coalition, then President Obama changed, in slightly more than a year, from an electorally supported, moderately partisan president to a purely partisan president. Of course, public opinion poll results provide a different constituency than an electoral outcome. After all, the pollsters call individuals at home, put them on the spot to answer a question, and disregard levels of political activity. Election outcomes, in contrast, rely on the willingness of individuals to participate, the verve to do so, and thus reflect a different constituency. Interestingly, the consequence of the shifting approval ratings was a change not in rhetorical tone but in content.

The hallmark of *The Presidential Road Show* is demonstrating how different leadership strategies emerge based on the electoral and media environments. The 2010 election season revealed the push/pull of a president who achieved a national electoral coalition but faced a challenging media environment. President Obama continued to employ his singular voice, but he altered the content of his speech and his use of going-public tactics based on his audience. The result was two distinct patterns of speech and thus two distinct patterns of leadership.

During the fall of 2010, President Obama alternated between speaking to general audiences at town hall–style meetings and partisan rallies. The town hall meetings received poor media coverage reflecting the strangeness of the approach. The town halls were not large meetings in a school gymnasium as one might expect.[10] Instead, the president of the United States appeared in the backyards of ordinary citizens. The events did not play well on television, ironically showcasing the president as a candidate drawing few supporters. More significantly, the question-and-answer format seemed to highlight President Obama's problems with independents. As Stolberg noted in the *New York Times*, "When Mr. Obama appeared . . . earlier this week for a question-and-answer session, he got an earful from supporters who expressed deep unease about the economy, and in some cases, discontent with his performance. . . . One complaint that many Democrats . . . have about Mr. Obama is that he often comes off looking professorial and distant."[11]

The following excerpts come from speeches given on the same day in 2010 in Seattle, Washington, to two different types of audiences. The first speech is to a general audience, while the second is before partisans

Backyard Version of "What I Have Done"

And so with, again, the help of Patty and Jim and others, we've been able to shift billions of dollars that were going to these unwarranted subsidies to banks and now put them directly into the student loan programs and to Pell grants so that more and more people are able to get the kind of higher level training that they need to compete in this new global economy. So here's the bottom line: Where the economy was shrinking by 6 percent when I took office, the economy is now growing again; where we were losing 750,000 jobs a month, we've now seen 9 consecutive months of private sector job growth. So we've made progress, and we're moving in the right direction. But we've still got a lot of work to do. (Barack Obama, Seattle, Washington, October 21, 2010)

Partisan Rally Version of "What I Have Done"

And over the last 2 years, as difficult as things have been, as big as the problems that we inherited were, I have been so inspired because I've had the opportunity to work with people—like Patty Murray—to make sure that every American

> has decent health care, to make sure that an economy that was shrinking is growing again, to start putting people back to work, to make sure we've got equal pay for equal work, to make sure that we've got a couple of wonderful women on the Supreme Court, to make sure that young people can afford a college education, to make sure that we brought back 100,000 troops from Iraq, to make sure that we're respected around the world once again, to start investing in research and development so that our economy can thrive, to make sure that we're investing in clean energy so that we're at the forefront, not only of growing our economy, but of saving the planet. (Barack Obama, Seattle, Washington, October 21, 2010)

Granted, there is a difference in approach between a rally and a town hall meeting, but on the same day in the same city before two different types of audiences, the same president chose not only to shorten his list of accomplishments but also to shorten that list to only one group. It is not surprising that partisans would be more enthusiastic about the president's efforts on their behalf in Washington, DC; he actually told them what he did! In contrast, the list provided to the independents in the backyard was much shorter and designed to focus on the future rather than the immediate past.

Not only did President Obama more explicitly promote his administration's accomplishments with partisans, he was also much more explicit regarding the behavior of his opponents. For example, at a backyard question-and-answer session in Des Moines, Iowa, the president gently explained the difference between himself, his party, and his opponents prior to taking questions:

> And I just want to say—and then I'm just going to open it up for comments and questions—when you look at the choice we face in this election coming up, the other side, what it's really offering is the same policies that from 2001 to 2009 put off hard problems and didn't really speak honestly to the American people about how we're going to get this country on track over the long term. And I just want to use as an example the proposal that they put forward with respect to tax policy. They want to borrow $700 billion to provide tax cuts for the top 2 percent of Americans, people making more than $250,000 a year. It would mean an average of a $100,000 check to millionaires and billionaires. That's $700 billion we don't have, so we'd either have to borrow it, which would add to our deficit, or we'd have to cut, just to give you an example, about 20 percent of the amount of money that we spend on education. We'd have to cut investments we've made in clean energy. We'd have to cut investments we've made in Head Start. We'd have to cut improvements in terms of student loans for kids

> going to college that would affect about 8 million kids. So that's an example of where you've got a choice to make. You can't say you want to balance the budget, deal with our deficit, invest in our kids, and have a $700 billion tax cut that affects only 2 percent of the population. You just can't do it. And so I hope that as you go forward, not just over the next 6 weeks before the election, but over the next 2 years or next 6 years or next 10 years, as you're examining what's taking place in Washington, that you just keep in mind that we're not going to be able to solve our big problems unless we honestly address them. And it means that we've got to make choices and we've got to decide what's important. And if we think our kids are important and the next generation's important, then we've got to act like it. We can't pretend that there are shortcuts or that we can cut our taxes, completely have all the benefits that we want and balance the budget and not make any tough choices. That's, I think more than anything, the message that I want to be communicating to the American people in the months and years ahead. (Barack Obama, Des Moines, Iowa, September 29, 2010)

In contrast, when speaking with partisans, President Obama distinguished between himself, his party, and his opponents vigorously and repeatedly. Right before the midterm elections, in Charlottesville, Virginia, President Obama said:

> And when Tom and I went to Washington, we both hoped that Republicans and Democrats would take some time to put politics aside because we had a once-in-a-generation challenge, because although we are proud to be Democrats, we are prouder to be Americans. And there are plenty of Republicans around the country that feel the same way. But Republican leaders in Washington, they made a different decision. They realized—they looked around, they said, "Boy, we really made a big mess out of this economy, and it's going to take a long time to fix it, and in the meantime people will probably be angry and frustrated. So maybe if we just sit on the sidelines and say no to everything and don't lift a finger to help, knowing that unemployment will still be high, maybe we'll—maybe, just maybe, people will blame the Democrats instead of us." That was their basic strategy. And so now in this election the other side is betting on amnesia. They're betting that you forgot who caused this mess in the first place. So, Charlottesville, it is up to you to let them know that we have not forgotten. It's up to you to remember this election is a choice between the policies that got us into this mess and the policies that are getting us out of this mess. Let me tell you something. If they win this election, the chair of a Republican campaign committee has promised, quote, "the exact same agenda" as before Tom and I took office. In other words— [*Audience members:* Boo!]

> No, no—now, this is the agenda that resulted in the worst economy since the Great Depression, an agenda of cutting taxes mostly for millionaires and billionaires. You cut the rules for special interests and big corporations. You cut middle class families loose to fend for themselves. It's the same agenda that turned a record surplus into a record deficit, the same agenda that allowed Wall Street to run wild, the same agenda that nearly destroyed our economy. Now, look, this is not as if we had not tried their agenda. Charlottesville, we tried it for 8 years. It didn't work. And so I bring all this up not because I want to reargue the past. I just don't want to relive the past. We've been through it before. We're not going back there. We're not going back. Think about what has happened over the last 20 months. Because of the steps—because of the steps we've taken, we no longer face the possibility of a second depression. The economy is growing again. Private sector jobs we've seen increase 9 months in a row. Now, look, nobody knows better than Tom that we've still got a long way to go. We've still got a lot of work to do. There are too many people hurting here and all across the country. There are families who are still hanging on by a thread. That's what keeps me up at night. That's what keeps Tom up at night. How can we help families who got hit hard during this recession? How can we make sure that they're back up on their feet? But you know what, we've got a different idea about what the next 2 years should look like, what the next 10 and 20 years should look like. It's very different from what the Republicans are thinking. (Barack Obama, Charlottesville, Virginia, October 29, 2010)

The differing language and content of the speeches underscores how leadership strategies change due to the changed environment for leadership, even for presidents with excellent incoming support. When speaking to the backyard participants, Obama was general, drawing simple comparisons and relying on the unwillingness to cut popular programs. The rhetoric, whether read or viewed on television, was tentative. In contrast, when speaking to partisans, Obama was fiery (for him), drawing clear distinctions between himself, his party, and his opponents.

Performing a statistical analysis on the DICTION variables just from Obama's 2010 local speeches provides support for the differences present here. As noted earlier, President Obama used the same rhetorical tone across his years in office. However, when comparing his rhetoric from the speeches made during the midterm election season (September 1 through November 2, 2010) with the rhetoric from the rest of the year, a slight but significant change emerges.

Table 5.10 reveals that the tone of Obama's rhetoric shifted in just one variable: Commonality. The shift is not enough to argue that his overall rhetorical

Table 5.10 Obama's Local Tone in 2010

	Activity	*Optimism*	*Certainty*	*Realism*	*Commonality*
Midterm election season vs. rest of 2010	0.46	0.19	0.23	0.94	**0.03**

Note: $p < 0.05$; figure in bold is significant.

tone or leadership approach changed. However, it is noteworthy that during the campaign season, Obama altered his use of language designed to highlight the "agreed upon values of a group and rejecting idiosyncratic modes of engagement."[12] President Obama clearly distinguished between "us" and "them" within this time frame. The DICTION analysis supports the textual evidence presented above. The president was "sort of" applying the same approach to each setting, yet something about either the backyard style or the not quite supportive audience altered the president's language and thus his rhetorical effort.

National Leadership in a Fragmented Environment

The days following President Obama's election and inauguration were filled with media references to FDR and Reagan. The comparisons primarily reflected the economic crisis but also focused on the president's rhetorical skills. As Matt Bai noted in the *New York Times*,

> No American president since Kennedy . . . or maybe Roosevelt . . . or perhaps Lincoln . . . has inspired such a tide of historical comparisons. Obama is a walking analogy; if he were a punctuation mark, he'd be a colon. . . . Which analogy fits best depends largely on which of two overlapping story lines you're more inclined to embrace. First, there is Obama as crisis president—the kind of leader who emerges at a dire moment and rallies the nation to prevail. This is what the Lincoln buffs and the F.D.R. boosters see when they hark back to 1861 and 1933, moments when earlier generations of Americans faced existential tests and ultimately surmounted them. . . . If there is an especially useful historical parallel for what Obama seeks to achieve in these early weeks, it may not be Roosevelt or Kennedy or Lincoln, but Ronald Reagan. . . . Reagan understood the need not only to address the anxiety in American life but also to explain it. . . . Speaking to the nation from the Capitol terrace, Obama handed up his own powerful indictment of a generation of American leaders whose "collective failure to make hard choices" had imperiled the nation's economic health;

> it was time, the young president lectured, to heed the Scripture and "set aside childish things." This is the kind of rhetoric that even some of Obama's allies might find insulting, but like Reagan, Obama seems to understand that in order to lead people out of crisis, you first have to make clear how they got there. History demands its sacrifices—and also its unpleasant truths.[13]

The implication in these comparisons is the classic Neustadtian view of leadership: Leadership success derives from individual skill. Presidents successfully lead through effective rhetoric, personal charisma, and the willingness to chart a course. However, the ability to lead is not entirely individual; it is also institutional and contextual. The ability to succeed through the exercise of leadership is challenged by a poor individual skill set. However, the environment in which the president functions challenges the approach to leadership much more than a president's effectiveness in reading a teleprompter. In the fragmented media environment, even a national, electorally supported president seeks out support through travel to local, active participants. Obama was almost as hindered as the constrained President Bush, and he employed a similar leadership strategy to deal with the muffling of his national voice. The next chapters turn to questions of effectiveness and representation for national, constrained, and obstructed presidents.

CHAPTER 6

CHANGING TACTICS, IMPROVING OUTCOMES?

All politics is local.

—Thomas O'Neill Sr., 1936

Former Speaker of the House Tip O'Neill famously learned from his father after losing his only election (Cambridge city council) that no politician can ignore their base and survive.[1] The base must be nurtured. Core support sustains candidates and protects them from the fair-weather nature of the rest of their coalition. During elections, candidates typically appeal to the core during the nominating phase and tack to the center during the general election to pick up supporters of varying degrees of strength. At the presidential level, the difference between core and peripheral support in terms of ideology, attentiveness, and participation is stark. Core supporters participate in primaries, donate more money, and are active volunteers. Peripheral supporters range from individuals who ignore politics almost entirely to those who are attentive but not affiliated, and sometimes even disaffected supporters of the other party. Presidents with large Electoral College victories managed to attract both the core and the periphery. Conversely, electorally challenged presidents were unable to motivate, activate, or appeal to citizens beyond those already on their ideological side.

This state of leadership continues once the candidate becomes president, but the focus shifts from turnout on Election Day to the passage of legislation. The relationship between president and citizen during the governing period is not as effectively delineated as the relationship between candidate and voter. During a campaign, the candidate seeks to motivate and activate through various public activities. The activities are designed to encourage the citizen to vote for the candidate and not his or her opponent. The citizen receives the messages through free media (press coverage) and paid media (advertising) and then acts by voting or not voting for the candidate. In contrast, the public activities of the president serve to influence indirectly—either by influencing the environment, which influences Congress, or by influencing the voter, who then directly influences a member of Congress. Nevertheless, the activities still rely on the public receiving the message and responding to it. Thus, the president's agenda has always been vulnerable to changes in, or impediments to, the relationships between the president, the public, and the press as well as the relationship between the president, the public, and members of Congress.

Presidents who are more affected by the changed environment require an additional mechanism or methodology to compensate for the resulting vulnerability. I argue that to compensate, presidential leadership strategy and tactics change, driven by the electoral and media environments. However, questions remain as to whether the new strategies work, and whether the two-pronged strategy improves the opportunities for leadership or opportunities to pass the presidential agenda. Local travel is costly and time consuming; therefore, the value added for the president must meet a relatively high threshold. This chapter focuses entirely on what presidents get out of the increased travel. The local rhetoric and outreach to specific audiences has the potential to improve leadership opportunities by affecting both the environment and individual members of Congress. Specifically, local events receive much better press coverage from local press than from the national media. More significantly, these events reveal a correlation between local presidential appearances and support for the presidential agenda by the local members of Congress. However, in an unexpected finding, presidential visits appear to depress state approval ratings measured around the time of legislative efforts. Presidents appear to achieve short-term legislative goals while sacrificing short-term approval ratings.

Influencing the Environment

A multitude of factors influence the environment in which the president functions. This book argues that the electoral outcome and the type of media environment specifically influence the president and the strategies he can employ to influence the outcome of his agenda. While the previous chapters focused entirely on the behavior of the president and his White House as a result of the static factors yielded by his election, this chapter's focus explores the more dynamic features of the presidential environment. A president's Electoral College outcome is an unchanging fact of life; however, media coverage, approval ratings, and congressional voting are much more fluid and potentially influenced by presidential behavior.

Effectiveness from Local Media Coverage

In 1981, an exploration of the press corps asserted that the media provided a friendly or at least neutral environment for presidential communications.[2] In fact, the most commonly used descriptor of the relationship between the press and the presidency was *mutual dependency*: Presidents needed to disseminate information and media organizations needed information to disseminate.[3] By 1992, media organizations were no longer as friendly, nor were they as dependent. While the president continues to be a focal point, the need to fill 24 hours of cable news programming engenders creative efforts to produce news. The White House no longer controls news about the president. Instead, "talking heads," or pundits, set the tone and tenor of debate.[4]

These changes in the media yielded the changes in the presidency.[5] Although presidents since George Washington have complained about their treatment in the press,[6] Jeffrey Cohen finds a pervasive increase in negativity and cynicism after 1992, what he terms the post-broadcast age.[7] Moreover, the increased pervasiveness of cynicism and negativity alongside the increased number of media outlets limit the potential of a communications strategy that needs to reach a national audience.[8] A president can no longer count on a large national audience for a presidential speech, not when there are so many cable channels and web pages offering alternative content.[9]

The Bush White House actually documented their view of their problems with the national press in the post-broadcast age. In a letter to NBC News, Counselor to the President Ed Gillespie challenged the language, tone, and intent of their coverage of the president:

> This deceitful editing to further a media-manufactured storyline is utterly misleading and irresponsible and I hereby request in the interest of fairness and accuracy that the network air the President's responses to both initial questions in full on the two programs that used the excerpts.[10]

Gillespie's concluding attacks on the network demonstrate the frustration of the White House with this new media environment:

> Mr. Capus, I'm sure you don't want people to conclude that there is really no distinction between the "news" as reported on NBC and the "opinion" as reported on MSNBC, despite the increasing blurring of those lines. I welcome your response to this letter, and hope it is one that reassures your broadcast network's viewers that blatantly partisan talk show hosts like Christopher Matthews and Keith Olbermann at MSNBC don't hold editorial sway over the NBC network news division.[11]

The reason this matters to the president is that media coverage does influence the environment. The media can affect public opinion about the president; however, they rarely bolster a president's approval rating. If media coverage did not influence public opinion polls, which then potentially influence congressional behavior, it would not matter that there was an increase in the negativity, cynicism, and perceived bias of the national press.[12]

The national press and local press both cover the president's rhetorical outreach while he travels the country. The tone, quality, and quantity of the coverage, however, are quite different between the national and local press. Part of the problem for the president at the national level is the "been there, done that" approach taken by the national press corps. It is particularly evident in presidential campaigns, when presidential candidates are covered by the same reporter because that reporter is traveling with the campaign. Campaign stump speeches tend to be similar, reflecting changes in style rather than substance. Candidates will add references to local sports teams, local events, even local foods. The tendency toward repetition encourages campaign reporters to focus on what is new—changing tactics, changing poll numbers—in short, the game coverage, which citizens despise.[13]

Once in office, presidents continue to recycle rhetoric. Consider George W. Bush in 2002:

> And there's another reason. Every life matters in America. Everybody counts. Everybody has worth. And these killers don't think that way. They're willing to take innocent life in the name of a hijacked religion. And so my job is to do everything we can to protect our homeland—it's to make America more secure. (George W. Bush, Louisville, Kentucky, September 5, 2002)

> We also value life in America. Everybody counts. Everybody has worth. Everybody is a precious soul. And the enemy we—the enemy doesn't regard life the way we do. You see, they hijack a great religion and kill innocent people. They don't

> care, but we do. And so long as we hold those values dear, which we will, the enemy will try to strike us. (George W. Bush, Alcoa, Tennessee, October 8, 2002)

Reporters traveling with the president will hear a reasonable facsimile of the same speech over short periods of time. The first time the president gives the speech, it receives honest coverage from national reporters, while the second, third, and fourth instances lead to negative and cynical coverage.

Public attitudes toward the press reflect the changes in style and coverage. The changes in public attitude vis-à-vis the national press have been a boon for local media. In 2004, 60 percent of the public regularly read a local newspaper, 59 percent regularly watched local television, and only 34 percent regularly watched network nightly news broadcasts.[14] Local media, then, represent an opportunity to reach individuals not watching national news media as well as an opportunity for citizens to receive coverage not driven by national organizations' imperatives. The Clinton, Bush, and Obama White Houses understood that local "newspapers have credibility with their readers, they have relatively large readerships, and . . . believe[d] that they will generally garner better and more positive coverage from them than from the national news media."[15]

Analysis of local media coverage of the president from various sources supports the strategic choices of all the presidents investigated here: Increased local travel garners an increase in positive press coverage. Using a random sample of newspapers and a random sample of days from a single calendar year (2000), Cohen finds that presidential activities effectively influence the volume of news coverage: Local news coverage increases when the president speaks. Interestingly, there is a limit to positive local press coverage; presidential omnipresence in the news erodes coverage.[16] In other words, presidents can actually speak too frequently.

The effect of presidential public activities on local coverage is separate from the national news; the national news does influence local news but does not determine it.[17] Presidential activities influence the quantity of local news coverage independent of national news sources.[18] Of course, content matters as much as if not more than volume of coverage. Cohen finds that newspaper characteristics are not significant.[19] A Democratic president does not receive negative coverage from Republican-leaning newspapers (as determined by ownership, endorsements, and op-ed pages) and vice versa. Eshbaugh-Soha and Peake and Barrett and Peake disagree and contend that ownership does affect the quality of coverage.[20] However, if ownership and not context determined tone, presidential travel would not aid presidential efforts to improve the environment for leadership when the point is to receive positive coverage.

The more active a president is locally, the better the local coverage he receives. An active president decreases the likelihood of negative coverage in local newspapers.[21] However, very high levels of activity decrease not only the likelihood of negative news but also the likelihood of any coverage at all. Therefore, there is a fine line of news management at the local level, but presidential travel still affords the president a good chance of positively influencing citizens through local news coverage of events.

Effectiveness of Approval Ratings

Since Cornwell's focus on presidential approval ratings in 1965, they have become the de facto means for measuring and delineating change in presidential leadership efforts via the public. Despite the intense media and scholarly interest in public opinion polls, the president's ability to influence his own ratings have proven remarkably limited.[22]

The consequences of not being able to influence the presidential approval rating are significant, so long as it is the means to achieve presidential goals. For bargaining within an institutionalized pluralistic system, the approval rating provides pressure as an indirect measure of the power of the president's position. A popular president achieves more because the public provides a bulwark for the presidential preference, based on the assumption that the president is popular because of his choices. The consequences of a dip in approval are significant but not debilitating, as it does not ultimately control bargaining. However, if public attitudes are the mechanism by which Congress is threatened, then popularity cannot be left to chance or circumstances: Presidents must seek to control or influence their approval ratings.

At first glance, presidents appear able to influence their popularity via events and activities.[23] However, a significant number of studies, particularly when media effects are factored in, demonstrate the inability of the president to influence his own approval rating. As a result, a cottage industry developed trying to explain the value of the presidential approval rating. Two phenomena occurred between 1992 and 2008 that relate to the changes in media environment and also affect the approval rating as a presidential tool. First, the presidential approval rating reflected an uncoupling of job approval from personal approval thanks to Presidents Clinton and George W. Bush. President Clinton received high job approval ratings and low personal ratings, while George W. Bush initially received the reverse.[24] Second, media outlets multiplied. As a result, George Edwards argues, the president's rhetorical efforts do not influence the public, and thus the approval rating does not reflect effective exercising of presidential power.[25]

Rottinghaus contends that presidents can in fact influence national opinion polls through speeches, both national and local. However, Rottinghaus also notes that the ability to do so is quite conditional.[26]

Although I argued earlier that presidents are actually talking to the audience in front of them, local rhetorical leadership activities could still reflect the desire to manage public opinion. The national going-public approach employs the cumulative effect of local visits on national polls—national polls move in response to individual experiences in the presidential audience or citizens connecting through media coverage of local events. Nevertheless, the effort could also be more narrowly focused on the state level: moving state public opinion ratings with local rhetoric. The rationale for a state approach is typically electoral in nature, setting up for the reelection race; however, it could also be legislative in nature, attempting to influence congressional delegations through state opinion. Unexpectedly, the effect of local rhetoric on local opinion is quite negative.

Local Visits and National Polls

The ability to measure the public's response to presidential rhetoric has become more sophisticated and more constant.[27] Nevertheless, the increased ability to poll has not necessarily produced a better environment for presidential leadership. The president is not getting improved national public opinion polls when giving national addresses to national audiences, nor is he getting better national polls through local rhetoric.

Rottinghaus terms presidential travel around the country to give speeches "barnstorming."[28] Along with major presidential addresses and press availability, barnstorming represents a communication strategy designed to "persuade as many people as possible."[29] Rottinghaus compiles an impressive database of local speeches alongside pre- and post-speech public opinion data beyond the approval rating. For example, he isolates support for Clinton's assault rifle plan prior to a February 10, 1995, speech at 67 percent. After the speech, 69 percent of the public supported the plan.[30] At first glance, a 2 percent increase in public approval is hardly meaningful. However, this is a 2 percent increase in national approval after one local speech. Thus, the barnstorm effort is in a sense an additive leadership approach: Put together enough local speeches producing a minor change and you have significant national change. While the approach might appear strategically sensible, Rottinghaus ultimately finds no effect from barnstorming: "The barnstorm tactic never has a positive and significant effect on national public opinion."[31] Rottinghaus speculates that using local events to affect national polls does not work because of time. In fact, he argues that the effects of local travel to move opinion are "glacial."[32] If the intent is to influence local media and pressure Congress members, then the "effect may not be present in national public opinion polls."[33]

Local Visits and State Polls

If presidents travel to influence opinion, which in turn influences Congress, then the lack of effect on national polls from local travel would be devastating to a president. However, as Cohen finds, local rhetoric does influence local media in a manner that is beneficial to the president.[34] Increasing local rhetoric has a more beneficial effect on local media coverage than it does on public opinion.

There are numerous challenges to determining the influence of presidential rhetoric on state opinion polls. First, there must be consistent measures of state opinion. Second, there must be measures of approval before and after local presidential rhetoric. Third, there must be enough of these data points to produce a data set. Cohen and Powell attempt to compensate for these three problems with a normed baseline model that uses the president's popularity when no visit has occurred.[35] Cohen and Powell find that "a presidential visit boosts state-level support by about 1.3 percent on average, which is statistically significant."[36] Moreover, they find a greater effect on state-level approval from large state visits as opposed to small state visits. Travel in election years does not influence state-level approval, but travel in non-election years influences it significantly.[37] Cohen and Powell argue that "presidents appear more presidential when they are not campaigning."[38]

Cohen and Powell accept the limitations of their model, admitting that their measurement "is quite blunt."[39] The problem partly stems from lumping all local speeches together regardless of their relevance to the presidential agenda. For example, if Cohen and Powell found approval ratings before and after a speech on Labor Day at a fair, it would weigh as much as a significant presidential policy address. To capture presidential influence from local speeches on state approval ratings more effectively, I use a modified application of Rottinghaus's pre- and post-speech approach, using local polls instead of national polls. However, as Cohen and Powell note, a complete set of local polls is difficult to find. Like Cohen and Powell, I used the State Job Approval Project's (SJAP) assembly of available state-level opinion, with "available" being the operative word. Complicating the effort further, I attempt to match the approval data with presidential agenda items in the local speeches cited in earlier chapters.

Table 6.1 reveals the limitations inherent in trying to link local approval data with local speechmaking. As I note in earlier chapters, presidential effort prior to a congressional vote is necessary to influence Congress members. Correspondingly, this analysis requires evidence of state-level approval before and after each local speech. The availability of state-level approval is limited, however, so Table 6.1 can provide only a few examples of effect on state approval. For example, President Clinton gave thirty-three local speeches on the stimulus in 1993, thirty prior to its passage in August 1993. However, in only four cases does SJAP provide pre-speech and post-speech approval ratings; the incomplete data set handicaps a full measurement of the direct effects of speeches on approval. A larger set of data exists for President Bush's Medicare prescription drug plan and for President Obama's stimulus bill. Still, the variability in availability unfortunately means that the data provided here fall somewhere between anecdotal and quantitative.

The cornerstone of going public and all notions of rhetorical leadership is the idea of responsiveness. Presidents speak, citizens' opinions move, and Congress responds. The average change column in Table 6.1 demonstrates that presidents can and do move citizen opinion. However, these micro-level findings are much larger than the macro-level average affects found in previous studies; the smallest change—2 percent—is significantly larger than the 1.3 percent average change found by Cohen and Powell. In fact, the average of the average change is 6.3 percent—a relatively dramatic change. An opinion shift by virtue of a public appearance may explain why presidents commit so much time, money, and attention to local rhetorical efforts.

Unfortunately, percentage change masks the most important aspect of tracking approval ratings—they go down as well as up. On four of the six agenda issues with available approval rating data, after a presidential visit, the president's state approval rating goes down! The downward movement of approval is quite significant (see Table 6.1). On the macro level, after manipulating the variables, Cohen and Powell find that presidents influence their rating 1.3 percent.[40] On the micro level, the presidential appearance, the height of pomp and circumstance, diminished what citizens thought of the president over 60 percent of the time since 1992.

The negative response reflected in the state approval rating draws attention to what the approval rating measures and, more significantly, to what the president does in these rhetorical efforts. In Chapters 3, 4, and 5, I delineate how Presidents Clinton, Bush, and Obama devoted the bulk of their local rhetoric to describing problems and what they had been doing in Washington. Describing problems

Table 6.1 Changes in State-Level Job Approval after Presidential Visits

Legislative action	*State*	*Date of visit*	*Percent change in approval rating*	*Average change*
Clinton stimulus bill passed, 8/10/93	CA	2/21/93	1	−2.0
	OH	5/10/93	−8	
	WI	6/1/93	−16	
	IL	7/26/93	14	
Bush NCLB bill passed, 1/8/02	CA	10/24/01	32	29.5
	OH	1/8/02	27	
Bush tax relief bill passed, 6/7/01	NJ	3/14/01	−6	19.0
	CA	5/29/01	32	
Bush Medicare prescription drug bill passed, 12/8/03	MI	1/29/03	−1	−5.6
	WV	2/9/03	−5	
	IL	6/11/03	−11	
	CT	6/12/03	−6	
	NJ	6/16/03	−5	
	GA	6/20/03	−5	
	CA	6/27/03	−6	
	TX	7/18/03	−8	
	CO	8/11/03	−15	
	AL	11/3/03	−4	
	NC	11/7/03	−7	
	FL	11/13/03	−5	
	AZ	11/25/03	18	
	NV	11/25/03	−18	

and touting accomplishments could elicit negative responses, particularly from individuals outside the president's constituency. After all, the White House communications staff design and target these rhetorical efforts toward a specific, mostly partisan audience. The state-level approval rating captures more than that favorable audience; it also captures the unfavorable and apathetic audiences. Several combinations of support for the president yield diminished approval ratings after a local speech. The most common combination of the approval rating comes from supporters and independents who voted for the president, with little support from the other party or the ambivalent. In dire times, the rally effect typically emerges when the other party, independents, and the ambivalent join supporters in a moment of national unity. On the president's top agenda items in a partisan period, the approval rating after a local speech reflects the negative movement of independents who voted for the president, not partisans.

Table 6.1 *Continued*

Legislative action	*State*	*Date of visit*	*Percent change in approval rating*	*Average change*
Obama stimulus bill passed, 2/17/09	FL	2/10/09	0	
	VA	2/11/09	–8	
	CA	3/18/09	–3	
	CA	3/19/09	–3	
	NM	5/1/09	–1	
	CA	5/27/09	–7	
	NJ	7/16/09	–11	
	VA	7/29/09	–5	–2.0
	VA	8/3/09	–5	
	VA	8/6/09	6	
	VA	8/6/09	6	
	VA	8/6/09	6	
	NY	9/14/09	–2	
	PA	9/15/09	–6	
	CA	10/15/09	0	
	CA	10/15/09	0	
Obama health care bill passed, 12/24/09	MI	4/29/09	7	
	WI	6/11/09	–4	
	VA	7/1/09	–12	
	MT	8/14/09	0	–1.0
	MN	9/12/09	10	
	PA	9/15/09	–6	
	MD	9/30/09	2	

Note: This table only lists visits for which there are approval ratings before and after the visit.

Source: Based on data from the State Job Approval Project directed by Thad Beyle, Richard Niemi, and Lee Sigelman and funded by the NSF (grant SES9974176).

When presidential rhetoric serves to influence the environment for presidential action, producing a positive change, no matter how minor, is useful. A negative change would seemingly influence the potential congressional environment to a greater degree, allowing for more independence of action by members of Congress. However, since the president does not intend for these speeches to reach a wider nationalized audience and does not expect to receive coverage significant enough to move polls, even at the state level, these negative results are not damaging and may even indicate the success of the strategy.

The decline in state-level approval ratings after presidential rhetoric also supports the coalitional nature of these speeches. Presidents are talking locally to partisans, groups, businesses—all those who might assert themselves in the political sphere. Simple cost–benefit analysis underscores why: It requires considerably more effort to move opposition partisans and apathetic non-partisans toward the president's preferred option. On any political issue, notably the president's agenda, there are partisans willing and able to exert pressure for the president's preferred position. Additionally, using direct persuasion, the president can move unaffiliated but active and interested groups and individuals much more easily than the uninterested or opposed. Not only is it a waste of resources to try to move the opposed and uninterested, but also the evidence suggests it is quite ineffective.

The anecdotal picture of state-level approval shown in Table 6.1 captures the movement of independents who had previously supported the president, abandoning the formerly centered presidential candidate due to his shifting either to the center-right or center-left. If the goal is to lead through a nationalized effort, influencing national polls by affecting results state by state, which also sidesteps the national media, then these results reveal alarmingly ineffective leadership. However, if the goal is partisan, coalitional leadership, whereby presidents attempt to influence a national audience at the national level or a nationalized constituency at the state level, then these findings are unsurprising, perhaps even expected.

Influencing Congressional Voting

The president successfully influences local media, but he only influences local approval on the macro level. Nonetheless, the main reason for attempting to influence the media or approval rating at either the national or local level is to ultimately influence Congress and thereby achieve passage of the presidential agenda. From the congressional perspective, the factors that influence legislative outcomes—the size of the majority, institutional factors, and constituency factors—are beyond the reach of the president.[41] The power of the Neustadtian president stems from the role of the president as a player with which Congress must bargain. National going-public theory rejects the idea of the president as part of the institutional relationship and places presidential power outside the chambers of Congress. However, the targeting of active audiences and important legislative players suggests that presidents design their rhetorical leadership in order to create a successful legislative coalition that can bargain effectively.

There have been numerous efforts to understand how speaking nationally influences congressional outcomes, specifically testing how powerful going public is as a tool to achieve the presidential agenda. Andrew Barrett contends that the more presidents speak about presidential initiatives, the more success they have in Congress.[42] However, Barrett explores legislation from 1977 through 1992, the period prior to the changes in the media environment. Powell and Schloyer correctly note that in contrast to Kernell's work, most explorations of the effect of going public are at the institutional level, not the individual level.[43] Using the same era as Barrett, Powell and Schloyer find virtually no evidence of the power of "implicit electoral threats. . . . In both the House and Senate, there is no discernable relationship between a member's support for the president and either the total number of speeches on an issue, or those speeches in the member's home state."[44] Interestingly, Powell and Schloyer find that cross-pressured members of the president's party are least likely to support the president, less likely than cross-pressured members of the opposition.[45]

Presidents Clinton, Bush, and Obama did not target Congress as an institutional enemy in local speeches, according to the data in Chapters 3–5. Nor did these presidents employ the line-in-the-sand tactics equated with going public, rarely asking their audiences to contact members of Congress directly. Fundamentally, these local speeches were for those who heard the speech—meaning the partisan or active audience. However, the audience often also included the same elected officials whom the president hoped to target. The presence of members of Congress on the dais with the president during these local events likely contributed to the lack of enmity but also potentially influenced voting.

Local speeches might influence individual members of Congress in several ways: directly, by virtue of being in attendance and feeling pressure from the president and the audience, or indirectly, from the audience at election time or from the local media and local opinion coverage of the event. Table 6.2 outlines the congressional voting on the presidential agenda items explored earlier. Only one of President Clinton's agenda items is included, as none of his other agenda items received a floor vote in his first three years. President Obama achieved two floor votes on his agenda items in his first year. President Bush dominates Table 6.2, as four of his agenda items became law between 2001 and 2003. The voting patterns of the congressional delegation present during the president's travels indicate the relative power of a presidential appearance.

Table 6.2 reveals that in six of the fourteen floor votes on the seven agenda items, these three presidents reached more than 20 percent of the chamber's membership by sharing the stage at local events.[46] President Bush's local rhetoric reached half the Senate on tax relief in 2003 and Medicare prescription drugs, also in 2003. Of those votes in which the president visited more than

Table 6.2 Votes in Congress after Presidential Visits

			Congress members visited				
Legislative action	*Chamber*	*Vote*	*Voted "yes"*	*Percentage of total "yes" vote*	*Percentage of total "no" vote*	*Percentage of total "yes" vote from opposition*	*Percentage of total "no" vote from own party*
Clinton stimulus, 1993	House	218–216	16	7	2	0	0
	Senate	50–50	19	38	14	0	4
Bush NCLB, 2002	House	381–41	24	6	5	7	1
	Senate	87–10	31	36	20	40	2
Bush tax relief, 2001	House	230–197	8	3	8	1	0
	Senate	62–38	18	29	24	18	0
Bush tax relief, 2003	House	231–200	34	15	20	17	0
	Senate	50–50	23	46	54	4	0
Bush Medicare prescription drugs, 2003	House	220–215	24	11	14	2	0
	Senate	54–44	29	54	55	54	6
Obama stimulus, 2009	House	246–183	1	0	2	0	0
	Senate	66–38	5	8	3	0	0
Obama health care, 2009–2010, first vote	House	220–215	25	11	2	1	0
	Senate	60–39	29	48	18	0	0
Obama health care, 2010, second vote to reconcile with Senate	House	219–212	4	1	0	0	13

20 percent of the membership, the president received more "ayes" than "nays" in all but two cases. Interestingly, the two cases where the president visited and received a greater number of "no" votes were those with the most visits: tax relief and Medicare prescription drugs, both in 2003. Thus, exploring visits to a member's state or district reveals more positive votes than negative votes for the president's agenda after numerous visits. For the cases in which less than 20 percent of the membership were visited, the results are beneficial for the president in three of the eight cases. Strikingly, in this limited data set, 62 percent of the times that the president reaches less than 20 percent of the membership, the result is a "no" vote for the president's preferred outcome. Therefore, frequency of travel appears important for positive floor outcomes, but there may be thresholds for minimum effectiveness and diminishing returns.

The frequency factor suggests potential strategic considerations. The president achieved passage in all the agenda items presented in Table 6.2. With divided government, a president needs his own party's support as well as support from the majority. In unified government, a president needs his own party's support and only needs opposition support if their majority is slim or if the vote is a tough one for his party. In all but one of the cases considered in Table 6.2, the president's party controlled both chambers. In 2001, the Senate changed party majority three times while President Bush was in office, from 50R–50D to 50D–49R to 50R–48D. As noted above, cross-pressured members of the president's party are least likely to support the president. For these three presidents who faced unified government with slim margins in a highly partisan era, travel was more likely aimed at holding their majority rather than converting members of the opposition.

Of all the agenda items covered in Table 6.2, only one received significant support from the opposition party. No Child Left Behind was President Bush's crowning achievement in bipartisanship. The bill received 198 ayes in the House from Democrats, more ayes than from Republicans. No other bill from Bush, Clinton, or Obama received more than 16 opposition votes in the House. In the Senate, where there is more individualism, these presidents received more than their majority only once: NCLB passed 87–10.

Table 6.2 reveals two different strategies based on partisanship. Democratic Presidents Clinton and Obama received virtually no benefit from Republicans after visiting their states or districts. The Republicans who received these presidents in their state or district did not vote for the presidents' agenda items. In contrast, President Bush received enormous benefit from traveling to areas with Democrats in office. Of those Democrats who received President Bush in the state, 36 percent said yes to NCLB. The twenty Democrats who received visits and voted yes represented 40 percent of the Democrats in the Senate. With twenty-seven separate visits, the president was able to influence 40 percent of the opposition party to support his program. On Medicare prescription drugs, President Bush visits produced support from 54 percent of Senate Democrats. On tax relief, President Bush received the support of almost 20 percent of House and Senate Democrats, not as many as with NCLB or Medicare prescription drugs, but still significant.

On Medicare prescription drugs there was a cost, with President Bush losing 6 percent of his own party in the Senate. A review of Table 6.2 shows that a 6 percent Republican defection over Medicare prescription drugs was the second largest loss from the president's own party. Only President Obama exceeded this amount when he lost 13 percent of his party after visits on the health care bill. The two Democratic presidents were unable to convert the opposition, and their visits to opposition localities did not alter that outcome. Interestingly, the largest losses crossed party lines but covered the same issue area: the American health care system.

The most interesting example of the beneficial effect of travel on critical pieces of the presidential agenda lies in the three votes on President Obama's health care bill. The Democrats knew health care would be an exceptionally close vote, as many conservative Democrats voiced some of the same concerns as Republicans. There were three non-reconciliation floor votes on health care—two in the House, one in the Senate. The first House and Senate bills were different, and rather than forcing the two very different bills to the conference committee, the House leadership decided to bring the Senate bill to the floor. As shown in Table 6.2, President Obama visited twenty-five Democrats, all of whom voted yes in the first House vote. He visited only four of the 215 who voted no. In order to make this historic legislative achievement, President Obama and the Democratic leadership needed 219 votes. In the final tally of the second vote, five Democrats who had originally voted no voted yes, while eight Democrats switched from no to yes. Of those thirteen "in-play" members of Congress, President Obama visited five. President Obama visited only one Congress member who originally voted yes and then voted no. The other four visits, to Congress members who voted no originally, all produced "yes" votes. Thus, President Obama achieved an 80 percent success rate in his effort to apply pressure to these critical members of Congress.

Measuring Leadership

The bulk of this book has focused on determining presidents' leadership strategies, since I argue that presidents' behavior remains rooted in the environment in which they function. I explored a president's leadership strategies by dissecting his language in terms of tone and content and also by focusing on the president's audience. Traditionally, the method is less interesting to students of politics than the outcome. However, the outcomes summarized in this chapter also reveal much about the presidential methodology.

The national mythos under which presidents labor also weighs down determinants of presidential success. National presidents try to move national public opinion polls with their rhetoric and influence the national media in order to engender agenda success. Since 1992, the environment in which presidents function has increasingly limited the ability of presidents to employ a national strategy. The contentious media environment faced by Clinton, Bush, and Obama undoubtedly increased presidential travel. However, the effect on national media does not emerge from national or local opinion poll changes. Moreover, the positive effects from local media coverage do not translate to state-level public opinion change. Nevertheless, the congressional results demonstrate that the changed tactics work, at least in terms of winning tough congressional battles.

Chapter 7

Alternate Models of Leadership

I think a thesis . . . which identifies broad historical patterns in presidential leadership and explains the political dynamics at work behind them—is most interesting in pointing up contemporary expressions of difference and potentially significant deviations from the rule.

—Stephen Skowronek, *Presidential Leadership in Political Time*

In most considerations of leadership, the evaluation of success primarily centers on skill. President Reagan was more rhetorically skilled than either Ford or Carter, thus he was more successful. Alternatively, as Skowronek notes, leadership evaluations become anecdotally or historically contextual.[1] Ford and Carter were not successful because they had to lead in the wake of Watergate. In contrast, my analysis argues that context can be a structural determinant, particularly that the electoral and media environments shape the choices presidents make when exercising rhetorical leadership.

In Chapter 6, I discussed the effectiveness of this altered presidential leadership style. Since 1992, presidents have responded to their changed environment by going local: targeting their speech toward specific coalition partners rather than the nation at large, generating more positive local media coverage, and influencing congressional voting patterns. These responses, however, have not positively influenced national approval ratings.

This chapter considers the effectiveness of the model rather than the effectiveness of the leadership effort. How effectively does it explain presidential behavior?

How effective are the contextual determinants in explaining presidential behavior? Correspondingly, is this model time-bound to the period under consideration here (1992–2012)? In particular, I focus on alternative constraints: using the popular vote or public opinion poll results and a measure of the power of constituency rather than the Electoral College, or using media coverage style rather than the proliferation of the media. I also consider the end of the narrow media environment and whether there will be future presidents who are faced with a narrow media environment and a narrow Electoral College victory, shown in the first and third quadrants of my model.

Evaluating the Model

The model I describe in Chapter 1 delineates the parameters that influence presidential behavior. The environment influences three facets of public leadership: (1) the type of audience presidents target, (2) the tone and type of rhetoric they employ when targeting their audience, and (3) the amount of travel they need to employ to reach their audience. Specifically, I assert that media environment and the extent of the Electoral College victory determine the method through which presidents exercise leadership. However, there are other measures or descriptors of the same environmental factors that warrant consideration. I consider first using the popular vote rather than the Electoral College outcome to evaluate constituency constraints. Then, I consider whether the quality of media coverage rather than the number of media outlets influences presidential leadership by providing a barrier to communication.

Electoral College vs. the Popular Vote

In Chapter 1, I argued that the electoral outcome affects the type of public leadership a president can exercise. In particular, a narrow electoral outcome inhibits the ability of the president to exercise national leadership. A president will have difficulty leading an audience he cannot claim to represent. Constitutionally speaking, no matter how contested a process, the candidate certified by the Electoral College is, after taking the oath of office, the president of the United States. American history demonstrates the formal acceptance of the process and its outcomes. There have been no riots, assassinations, or other expressions of political upheaval and outrage. However, there is a world of difference between acquiescing to an outcome and supporting the leadership of the individual who takes office after the contested outcome. In fact, the separated system actively courts the massing of coalitional opposition in response to electoral outcomes.

The connection between support and the formation of a coalition is underscored by the outcome of elections following contested elections. In 1800, Thomas Jefferson won after losing to John Adams in the hotly contested election of 1796. In 1828, Andrew Jackson won after losing the 1824 contested race in which Henry Clay sided with John Quincy Adams. Samuel Tilden did not win in 1880 after the contested 1876 race with Rutherford Hayes, but the deal struck to withdraw troops from the South was probably worth more to the Democrats than winning the presidency. Richard Nixon won in 1968 after losing a disputed election to John F. Kennedy in 1960 (the election of 1964 might have been contested had Kennedy lived). Al Gore chose not to run in 2004 after winning the popular vote yet losing the Electoral College outcome in 2000. However, there were many calls within the Democratic Party for Gore to run, "to get his office back." It is impossible to argue that Gore would have certainly unseated the incumbent president based on historical precedent, but the pattern is meaningful. Electorally constrained presidents do not convert supporters and do not add supporters over the course of their presidential term, thus they cannot govern as if they have earned a national constituency.

The Electoral College itself gets a lot of flak when considered as a democratic entity. A web search on the Electoral College as unfair, undemocratic, and outdated produces 2.7 million hits, 78 percent of which relate to its undemocratic nature.[2] Opponents to the Electoral College consider the institution an archaic mechanism to counter a problem that no longer exists. The framers were concerned that ordinary citizens would not have enough knowledge to select an out-of-state candidate. In contrast, voters now have an abundance of information at their fingertips. Opponents are also concerned about the potential for conflict, which can emerge when the popular vote recipient does not win the Electoral College; a constitutional crisis has not occurred recently, but the 2000 election certainly came close. Moreover, as Han and Heith note, "Some states benefit unduly from this system. . . . Different states use different methods for selecting electors, and there is no guarantee that electors will abide by the popular vote in all states. . . . And because of the winner-take-all system in most states, some popular votes are nullified."[3] What the Electoral College does in the modern era is attempt to merge "elements of popular democracy with representative democracy . . . [by expanding the notion] that the president has the mandate to lead the country (for example, Ronald Reagan won 51 percent of the popular vote in 1980, but 91 percent of the electoral vote)."[4]

The complaints raised about the Electoral College also emerge because of the political strategy that it engenders. Presidential candidates do not campaign equally in all fifty states. Presidential elections occur in all fifty states, but presidential campaigns do not put resources into all states. Most states use a winner-take-all system to allocate their Electoral College votes, meaning the candidate with the most votes wins all of the state's Electoral College votes. Thus, most candidates strategically allocate their time and resources to states in which the race is contested, virtually ignoring states that they are likely to win or lose. As noted in Chapter 1, in states that are contested, more voters participate. Moreover, when candidates focus only on states in play, it potentially disenfranchises citizens in consistent and populous states.

Given the non-constitutional tie created between the Electoral College outcome and the popular vote outcome, the perception that the popular vote and the Electoral College outcome are the same dominates. The Bush–Gore outcome in 2000, where Bush received the requisite number of Electoral College votes but did not win the popular vote, dramatically emphasized the illusory nature of the linkage: It is possible to win enough Electoral College votes without having received the most popular votes.

Furthermore, popular vote totals without the additive factor of the state congressional delegation can present a slightly different picture of a presidential election. As noted in Table 1.1, the margins of victory in the Electoral College are significantly larger than the margins of victory in the popular vote. Even in landslide elections, the differential does not match up. In 1972, Richard Nixon won 96 percent of the Electoral College vote but only 60 percent of the popular vote. As I articulated in Chapter 1, 60 percent of the popular vote is clearly a majoritarian victory, but it does not imply the overwhelming sense of victory that 96 percent suggests.

Swapping out the Electoral College outcome for the popular vote outcome slightly alters the placement of presidents in the original formulation of constraints on leadership presented in the 2 × 2 table in Chapter 1. In Figure 1.2, the first quadrant represents presidents with large Electoral College victories. In Figure 7.1, the first quadrant is for large popular vote victories. When shifting

Figure 7.1 Analyzing Presidents by Popular Vote and Media Orientation

Popular vote victory	***Media orientation***	
	Neutral	*Confrontational*
Large (>53% of total vote)	FDR (1932) Nixon (1972) Reagan (1984) Bush I (1988)	Obama (2008)
Narrow (<53% of total vote)	Carter (1976) Reagan (1980)	Clinton (1992, 1996) Bush 2 (2000, 2004)

from Electoral College votes to popular votes, the first victories of Presidents Reagan and Clinton no longer fall into the coveted "large" category (although Reagan's reelection victory in 1984 does still qualify as "large.") Presidents Reagan and Clinton did not achieve more than 53 percent of the popular vote in their first elections.

Shifting from the Electoral College to the popular vote is also interesting in that it links presidents who are not thought to be similar in the domain of public leadership. As shown in the third quadrant of Figure 7.1 (narrow and neutral), Presidents Carter and Reagan both had a narrow popular outcome within their media environment. President Reagan's enormous Electoral College victory in 1980 obscured the narrowness of his popular vote outcome. President Carter won office with just 50 percent of the popular vote, reflecting the perception of his dearth of communication skills. However, the "great communicator," Ronald Reagan, won office four years later with only 51 percent of the popular vote. The similarity in popular vote totals suggests that these presidents should have shared a similar inability to marshal a national audience. However, when using the Electoral College outcome, Ronald Reagan should have enjoyed the options produced by a mammoth victory, while the lack of a large Electoral College victory should have limited the leadership options of President Carter. The behavior of both presidents while in office suggests that the Electoral College margin provides a better representation of the constraints generated by the public. The movement of President Clinton's first victory from the first quadrant (large and neutral) to join President Bush in the fourth quadrant (narrow and confrontational) will be discussed separately.

Media Orientation vs. Media Organization

In a widely discussed 2010 op-ed in the *Washington Post*, the venerable journalist and former host of ABC's *Nightline*, Ted Koppel, summed up the "narrowcasting" or targeted news and opinion business model produced in the post-broadcast age with a lament:

> Broadcast news has been outflanked and will soon be overtaken by scores of other media options. The need for clear, objective reporting in a world of rising religious fundamentalism, economic interdependence and global ecological problems is probably greater than it has ever been. But we are no longer a national audience receiving news from a handful of trusted gatekeepers; we're now a million or more clusters of consumers, harvesting information from like-minded providers.[5]

Koppel nicely sums up the changes to the media that have been highlighted by many, notably Jeff Cohen in his two works on the presidency and the news media.[6] Media outlets have multiplied and the news standard, categorized by objectivity and neutrality, no longer represents the dominant form of reporting.

In the model for *The Presidential Road Show*, I focus on the decline of gatekeeping and the multiplication of media options. As shown in Figures 1.1 and 1.2, the media environment that presidents faced was either narrow or fragmented. Presidents in the narrow era disseminated their message via three major networks, a few national newspapers, and the Associated Press wire service. In contrast, in the fragmented era, presidents faced network news reporters, pundits for those networks' cable stations, newspaper reporters, op-ed writers, radio pundits, bloggers, online news organizations, and myriad smaller newspapers and magazines. I argue that the fragmentation of the media environment made it more difficult for the president to reach a national audience. Presidents could not count on relationships with a few key reporters or on simply doing three television interviews. There were so many more voices in the system that the "line of the day" approach created by the Reagan administration would prove difficult to replicate. Consider the example of the Reagan administration, which set the standard for news management through the implementation of a seven-point approach. As described by Lori Cox Han, it sought to "plan ahead, stay on the offensive, control the flow of information, limit reporters' access to Reagan, talk about the issues the White House wants to talk about, speak in one voice, and repeat the same message many times."[7] The "line of the day," in which the

Reagan White House decided in its morning meeting what the White House and administration would highlight during the course of a day, was the logical culmination of this approach.[8] Han notes that Reagan's strategy tempered aggressive press management of the Washington press corps with wide availability to the local press and effective understanding of the visual needs of television.[9] As a result, Reagan received relatively positive press coverage despite his relatively poor relationship with the Washington press corps. The "repeat the same message" strategy is harder when so many voices are talking to each other rather than simply disseminating presidential information or talking to the president.

Fragmentation is not the only media change that differentiated this era from the previous one. Figure 7.1 shows how tone, language, and what constitutes a story also meaningfully changed this era. By the time Bill Clinton took office in 1992, it was the norm to ask presidential candidates about extramarital affairs, drug use, underwear, and all manner of topics that were previously off the table and deemed irrelevant to leadership. Consequently, the presidents taking office after 1992 faced a different style of reporter and a different type of coverage. Figure 7.1 reveals how the media constraints determined by the manner in which the media covered the presidency: neutrally or confrontationally. Focusing on style of coverage rather than ability to disseminate consistently reveals changes only to the placement of President Clinton. All the presidents prior to 1992 faced neutral press coverage. This in no way reflects an easier relationship between press and president; rather, the relationship was characterized by less confrontation and less charged language.

The Clinton Case

The electoral and media constraints delineated in Figure 1.2 and discussed throughout the book pretty effectively predict the behavior of both President Bush and President Obama. George W. Bush took office after earning one of the closest Electoral College victories in history within a fragmented media environment. I predicted that to manage this constraining environment, Bush could not employ a national audience approach to public leadership and instead would target multiple audiences, employ coalition-based rhetoric, and travel frequently. President Obama faced a luxuriously large electoral coalition in comparison to Bush, yet he also confronted the same fragmented media environment. Whereas the constraints faced by President Bush encouraged a singular leadership approach, Obama's contextual obstructions were in conflict. Obama took office with a victory that could support a national leadership approach. However, a fragmented media environment encourages a communication style that does not reach a national audience.

In keeping with the model and supported by my evaluation of his rhetorical efforts, Bush did not use the same voice when speaking from the Oval Office and local events, he did not speak before a representative sample of the nation in his local appearances, and he traveled frequently for local appearances. Moreover, he did not employ traditional going-public leadership tactics in his local speeches. Obama's behavior and strategy also matched the outline from the model. Obama used the same voice at the national and local levels, yet he did so before specific groups rather than a nationally representative audience. He also traveled frequently to seek his audience and local coverage. More interestingly, though he used a single voice, Obama did not exploit the breadth of the going-public model available to a president who can call on a national audience. His tactics were similar to those of his constrained predecessors.

In contrast, President Clinton does not fall neatly into the model outlined in this book. Unlike his peers, President Clinton is affected by altering the model to include the popular vote and media orientation. Presidents Bush and Obama both had Electoral College outcomes that matched their popular vote outcomes. President Bush won with a squeaker of a victory in the Electoral College coupled with a loss of the popular vote by 500,000 votes. President Obama won with a comfortable margin in both the Electoral College outcome and the popular vote. President Clinton won with a comfortable Electoral College outcome, but he won only a plurality of popular votes, not a majority, in his three-way race with George H. W. Bush and Ross Perot.

Using the popular vote rather than the Electoral College, then, moves Clinton from the first quadrant and the strategy and tactics of a national president to the fourth quadrant, where he would be expected to employ the strategy and tactics of a non-national coalition. Clinton does not just shift down the column from the first to the third quadrant, like President Reagan does. President Clinton shifts from the first to the fourth quadrant, from a national president to a constrained president by virtue of the media environment.

President Clinton's two-term tenure spanned the massive change undertaken by the media in the political system. When Clinton took office in 1992, vertical and horizontal mergers were occurring with frequency and the Internet was about to emerge as a significant transmitter of political information. Thus, the narrow versus fragmented media environment was in flux but was still dominated by the major players in political news. If we shift the focus to media orientation, the way politics was covered, rather than the sheer number of people covering politics, then Clinton is not poised on the cusp of change but rather is situated within it. The change in tone and approach in the coverage of presidential campaigns and then the presidency was significant and dramatic, and it spawned an array of scholarship. President Clinton notes in his autobiography that reading Thomas Patterson's *Out of Order* in the summer of 1994 helped him to understand the coverage, take it less personally, and accept that there was nothing he could do to change it.[10]

Considering both the popular vote and the change in media behavior moves Clinton into the constrained arena with George W. Bush. As Figure 7.2 illustrates, the change in quadrants changes leadership strategy. From this perspective, Clinton would be expected to travel frequently seeking friendlier media, to speak before audiences that are not nationally representative, and to use a different tone depending on his audience. Table 7.1 demonstrates how Clinton's actual behavior within the changing context compared to Bush and Obama.

President Bush was clearly not exercising a national strategy; President Obama vacillated between a national and a non-national strategy, which follows from the tension created by his inability to consistently reach the national audience yielded by his Electoral College victory. President Obama was consistent within categories: When selecting his audiences he was all not national, while in rhetoric he was all national. In contrast, President Clinton presents a mixed bag within the categories. He did not always appeal to a national audience and he did not always use the same rhetoric, but he did travel and he did reject the language of

Figure 7.2 Modifying the Model: Substituting Different Configurations of Constituency and Media Change

Popular vote victory	***Media orientation***	
	Neutral	*Confrontational*
Large (>53% of total vote)	National audience strategy National rhetoric Less likely to travel	National audience strategy National rhetoric Likely to travel
Narrow (<53% of total vote)	Base audience strategy Two-tiered rhetoric Less likely to travel	Base audience strategy Two-tiered rhetoric Likely to travel

Table 7.1 Comparing Presidential Media Strategies

	Clinton strategy		*Bush strategy*		*Obama strategy*	
Observed behavior	*National*	*Not national*	*National*	*Not national*	*National*	*Not national*
Travel		✓		✓		✓
Audience characteristic						
Year 1	✓			✓		✓
Year 2		✓		✓		✓
Year 3		✓		✓		✓
Tone of rhetoric						
Year 1	✓		✓		✓	
Year 2		✓		✓	✓	
Year 3	✓		✓		✓	
Going-public content		✓		✓		✓

going public. Interesting are the points of comparison with Bush and Obama. Clinton was more national than both Bush and Obama in terms of his audience: He was more apt to speak before a general audience and traveled less. Also interesting is that Clinton writes that "Thomas Patterson's book helped me to see that there might be nothing I could do to change the press coverage. If that was true, I had to learn to handle it better."[11] This may have been when Clinton drifted from the national approach and attempted a nascent version of what Bush and Obama consistently did to escape the national press corps.

Approval Ratings

I began this study interested in why it seems so hard to capture a benefit from presidential rhetorical success. To be sure, there have been rare occasions where presidents moved a nation and in turn moved Congress, or where they received a significant bump in approval ratings without going to war. Nonetheless, the majority of presidential rhetoric seems wasted—as George Edwards argued, "falling on deaf ears."[12] Potentially, the inability to discern a benefit from presidential rhetorical leadership, whether in opinion polls or in Congress, stems from the incessant focus on a national constituency through the approval rating.

In this analysis, I avoid the use of approval ratings (with the exception of comparing national and state poll results in Chapter 6) because of the limited information they provide. As Page and Shapiro note in their seminal work, *The Rational Public*, poll results are a single snapshot in time; only the long-term collection of data provides a reliable picture of opinion.[13] In *Polling to Govern*, I argued that if the approval rating provided enough information for decision making, there would be no need to spend millions of dollars on the private presidential polling apparatus.[14]

The public opinion polling apparatus gives the president insight into how the public views him and his decision making, while also allowing for the crafting of language to encourage support for presidential appeals.[15] Public opinion polls, particularly approval ratings, provide a comparative, dynamic measure across administrations. However, the ratings are not systemic measures; they are mutable, malleable reflections of the mood of the entire presidential constituency. Thus, they are only marginally useful to the president and marginally reflective of presidential success.

The Gallup organization began regular tracking of measures of presidential performance during the Truman administration. On April 12, 1945, 88 percent of those polled approved of the job President Truman was doing.[16] Over time, few presidents achieved the glorious rating earned by President Truman on opening day of continuous polling. Since 1945, Gallup finds that only seven presidents have averaged approval ratings above 50 percent, and of those, only three averaged above 60 percent.

Of more concern than the inability of presidents to achieve high ratings is what approval ratings represent. Elections clearly indicate who won and who lost; the message or meaning behind that victory is much murkier. Often presidents seek to claim a mandate for action based on the outcome of an election; however, it is often difficult to determine if individuals are voting *for* something or someone rather than *against* something or someone. Similarly, presidential approval ratings indicate in a given three-day period the percentage of a representative sample that approves of the job the president is doing. Like the mandate, the meaning behind approval ratings and the significance for presidential leadership is obscure.

The approval rating generates a lot of scholarly and pundit attention regarding what influences the rating and what presidents can do to influence their ratings. In 1973, John Mueller argued that there are three identifiable patterns of approval change present across presidencies.[17] First, Mueller determined that approval declined over time in each presidential term due to the buildup of disgruntlement stemming from presidential decisions. Second, Mueller identified the "rally around the flag effect" where approval ratings increase in response to foreign events or crises. Third, Mueller argued, "an economy in slump harms a president's popularity but an economy that is improving does not seem to help his rating."[18] From Mueller's perspective, the approval rating (and thus the public) reacts to the president; it does not constrain the president. In contrast, Neustadt suggests that the approval rating does constrain the president because elites pay attention to it, and elites anticipate public reaction to the president.[19] Canes-Wrone takes the argument further, contending that presidents constrain themselves in their attentiveness to the rise and fall of approval ratings and that presidents choose their leadership strategies based on policies the public already likes.[20]

All the connections between the approval rating and outcomes are based on the idea that the people whose opinions are measured by the approval rating matter to politicians. Vice President Dick Cheney gave one of the balder answers to the question of whether opinion polls matter in an interview with ABC's Martha Raddatz in 2008:

> RADDATZ: Let me go back to the Americans. Two-thirds of Americans say it's not worth fighting, and they're looking at the value gain versus the cost in American lives, certainly, and Iraqi lives.
>
> THE VICE PRESIDENT: So?
>
> RADDATZ: So—you don't care what the American people think?
>
> THE VICE PRESIDENT: No, I think you cannot be blown off course by the fluctuations in the public opinion polls. Think about what would have happened if Abraham Lincoln had paid attention to polls, if they had had polls during the Civil War. He never would have succeeded if he hadn't had a clear objective, a vision for where he wanted to go, and he was willing to withstand the slings and arrows of the political wars in order to get there. And this President has been very courageous, very consistent, very determined to continue down the course we were on and to achieve our objective. And that's victory in Iraq, that's the establishment of a democracy where there's never been a democracy, it's the establishment of a regime that respects the rights and liberties of their people, as an ally for the United States in the war against terror, and as a positive force for change in the Middle East. That's a huge accomplishment.[21]

Cheney, and his president, George W. Bush, overtly considered public opinion polling as anathema to leadership. Leadership from this perspective is about decision making and choices. Regardless, using public opinion polls as a measurement of leadership or even as a tool of leadership ensures that presidential leadership is about the national constituency. Members of Congress reject the use of public opinion polls for precisely this reason; Jacobs et al. find that members of Congress outside the leadership do not rely on public opinion polls, as they believe they have better measures of constituency opinion.[22] National measures are not relevant for members of Congress because their electoral connection stems from district voter behavior.

Few politicians and even fewer presidents would be as bold as a second-term vice president in articulating complete support for Edmund Burke's "trustee" form of representative.[23] Of course, few representatives are true delegates, either, as most politicians fall into the "politico" category, which allows for elements of both doing what is in the constituency's best interest and doing what the constituency wants.[24] The trustee representative represents the district. It is not clear that a delegate or the politico represents the same grouping. As a result, the approval rating assumes an orientation belied by the campaign behavior that outlined a path to office.

The Evolution of the Model

There has been no investigation into the third quadrant of the original and modified models. Figure 1.2 identifies Gerald Ford and Jimmy Carter as the only two presidents with a narrow, national media environment who earned a narrow Electoral College victory. President Ford lacked any constituency because he was appointed to office, and President Carter was unable to garner more than 55 percent of the Electoral College votes. A president in this category could reach the nation through a national media but lacked the connection with the public to spur much in the way of response to leadership. Anecdotal and scholarly views of these two administrations support the hardship imposed by the absence of a large Electoral College majority. It is hard to use rhetorical leadership as a tool without an electoral basis on which to build.

The intensity of the partisanship between 1992 and 2012 suggests that there will be presidents, like Ford, Carter, and George W. Bush, who take office without what can be considered nationwide support. President Obama demonstrates, however, that even within this partisan environment, support, which can buoy leadership, can be achieved. What is clear, however, is that it is unlikely the environment will return to the narrowed, national media era that reigned between 1972 and 1992. That is not to say that the current media environment could not consolidate into something less freewheeling than what existed for President Obama. With a consolidation of the fragmented media environment, presidents could exercise leadership with less frequent travel, making direct appeals once again to a national audience.

Chapter 8

Presidential Leadership for the Twenty-First Century

Hello, Ohio! Ah, it is good to be back in Ohio. It is good to be back in Shaker Heights, home of the Red Raiders. . . . I want to thank your mayor, Earl Leiken, for hosting us today; your superintendent, Mark Freeman; the principal here, Mike Griffith. Well, and I know—I'm pretty sure we've got a couple of Congresspeople here, but I don't see them. Where are they? The—okay, we got Marcia Fudge. Marcy Kaptur is here. Dennis Kucinich, Betty Sutton in the house. Outstanding Members of Congress, doing the right thing every day, so we thank them all for being here. . . . I want to wish everybody a happy New Year; 2012 is going to be a good year. It's going to be a good year. And one of my New Year's resolutions is to make sure that I get out of Washington and spend time with folks like you. Because folks here in Ohio and all across the country, I want you to know you're the reason why I ran for this office in the first place. You remind me what we are still fighting for. You inspire me.

—Barack Obama, Shaker Heights, Ohio, January 4, 2012

In local speech after local speech, Barack Obama, like George W. Bush and Bill Clinton before him, celebrated his audience. In his first sentences to the exuberant Ohio crowd, Obama highlighted the underlying premise of *The Presidential Road Show*: find your people, speak to your people, listen to your people, and work for your people. The variation in leadership strategy across presidents stems from the variation in the challenges that presidents confront. Obama enjoyed a large constituency, but a hostile, fragmented media marketplace limited his ability to reach his audience without travel. Bush faced a narrow audience and a hostile, fragmented media marketplace, which encouraged the use of a different voice along with travel to reach his audience. Bill Clinton's audience reflected both his large Electoral College victory and his narrow popular vote total, which allowed the exercise of mostly national leadership within a changing media marketplace.

While presidential rhetorical outreach is hardly new, the local nature of the leadership is. Traditionally, presidents exercised national public leadership rooted in their ownership of a national audience. As the relationship between the president and a national electoral constituency frayed, so too did the leadership strategy dependent on a national audience. For the presidential domestic agenda, leadership dependent on the support of independents or those not active in the political sphere remains out of reach in the post-broadcast age. In its place, a series of new leadership tactics emerged. An era of partisanship and media fragmentation relegated leadership through the national address to times of crisis, national tragedy, and war. The dearth of a national constituency from which to draw power and the influence of media fragmentation on the presidential audience has consequences for the president, the public, and the political sphere. The narrowing of the electoral coalition and the resulting presidential audience profoundly affects the ability to use rhetorical leadership to pressure Congress. Moreover, the cynicism, negativity, and inconsistency across mediums dramatically influences the quality of presidential rhetorical outreach. As the environment surrounding the president shifted, the behavior and strategy of the president and his advisors adjusted accordingly. Given the continued evolution of the media marketplace, presidential tactics will continue to adapt as well. The basic premise of using public leadership in lieu of constitutionally derived power will continue to flourish, but in ever-changing guises.

The Nature of the Presidential Constituency

The Presidential Road Show rests on understanding what the president's constituency is, not what myth and ideology would like it to be. Reimagining the president's audience naturally influences the understanding of his corresponding leadership strategy. Almost all scholarship on the presidency considers the president's audience to be the national audience, full of voters and non-voters, partisans and non-partisans, regardless of the president's electoral coalition.[1] The insistent focus on the pool of available citizens rather than the pool of participatory citizens represents the source of the failure to explain presidential rhetorical behavior and its effect on outcomes. Amid the fragmentation of the media marketplace, presidents (in the absence of war, crises, or natural disaster) rarely attempt to mobilize the entirety of the nation.

Neustadt argues that there are five distinct constituencies: Congress, executive officialdom, partisans, citizens at large, and those abroad.[2] The public in Neustadt's model is the national public—separate from partisans. Neustadt distinguished the public from partisans by following FDR's lead. FDR designed his fireside chats to be above partisanship. Arguably, FDR's audience itself was above partisanship; his victory in 1932 was so complete that it is possible to consider his audience non-partisan, as his electoral coalition was almost the entire nation. Nevertheless, the idea of a constituency that belonged entirely to the president was new. Partisanship and partisan voting characterized presidential audiences prior to FDR. As Laracey articulates, presidents did speak in the nineteenth century, but they did so through the partisan press, so their audience was by definition of partisan design.[3] Thus, Neustadt, by seeking to explain the success of FDR, separates the presidential audience from partisanship and elevates the mass audience produced by voting.

The evaluations that followed Neustadt's seminal work, *Presidential Power*, continued on this path, using the approval rating to identify the attitudes of the nation at large. Using public opinion polling data contributes to the nationalization of the president's constituency, as opinion polls group motivated, participatory, and partisan citizens together with those who are undecided, independent, and uninterested. Consequently, it is hardly shocking that scholarly tests of the presidential ability to move public opinion reveal trouble garnering the attention of all citizens and trouble moving a majority of citizens within these samples. In 2010, the mandate for smaller government arising from Tea Party victories rested on a voter turnout of 37.8 percent. Since over 60 percent of the nation did not participate, the mandate for action stemmed from participants, not the nation as a whole. As the 2010 midterm elections demonstrated, the focus on the national audience when evaluating presidential leadership strategies and their effectiveness represents a static view of the president, his environment, and his audience.

Consider what presidents, as candidates, had to do to gain office. Candidates need to persuade their base, citizens of similar political persuasion, to turn out to vote. They need to persuade enough independents, members of the other party, and uninterested, non-participatory individuals—in any combination when added to their base to win a plurality of votes in each state in the union. Presidential candidates never need a majority of the nation to do anything. Former Vice President Al Gore won a majority of the popular vote but ultimately did not become president because those are not the rules laid out in the Constitution. Electoral College voting and strategy determine outcomes; therefore, presidential candidates never need to think of the whole nation as their audience.[4]

In addition to their campaign successes and their campaign staffers, presidents bring their campaign skills and tactics to the White House. For constituency development and rhetorical leadership, presidents bring the campaign poll apparatus to bear on presidential decision making. Polls disaggregate the public into meaningful mechanisms to marshal. The polling apparatus showcases this understanding, as presidents use polls to design rhetoric and to monitor their electoral constituency in order to make sure their constituency is still with them for reelection.[5] Even after taking office, presidents continue to think about the public in terms of who supported them, who continues to support them, and who does not support them and why.

The president's governing constituency evolves out of the presidential candidate's winning electoral coalition, which serves to further deemphasize national leadership. The president's political party anchors his base of electoral support. Victory in a presidential election requires producing a coalition that encompasses the base and enough "floating voters" to win enough states to achieve 270 votes in the Electoral College. Therefore, the president's winning coalition stems from the votes of partisans, independents, and, for a few presidents, partisans from the other side of the aisle. Thus, the presidential governing coalition often reflects dichotomous positioning, since candidates need to appeal to the most ardent of partisans during the primary and then also to low-information, floating voters in the general campaign. The media and pundits often refer to this change in strategy as "tacking back to the center." Interestingly, the focus on the masses as the president's audience elevates the behavior to win the general election as more significant to leadership than the effort to win the nomination. While governing, however, the reverse is often true.

The core of the president's electoral coalition reflects participation in the primary as well as in the general election. Voters from the primary period are often financial donors as well. Presidential primary voters are loyal and strongly supportive of the candidate's agenda. In contrast, voters picked up in the general election period are much less loyal and generally much less attentive to the process, and they typically choose between the candidates based on short-term decision making.[6] Ironically, then, voters, donors, and participants remain in focus for the entirety of the presidential campaign, but a winning outcome often hinges on the number of ordinary citizens who participate.

Yet, the governing coalition appears to be focused away from the core of the electoral coalition and toward Neustadt's Washingtonians. Seligman and Covington contend that the presidential constituency results from translating the electoral coalition to a governing coalition. Their governing coalition, similar to Neustadt's, includes Congress, staff and appointees, interest groups, the bureaucracy, the media, and the general public.[7] Seligman and Covington, like the Reagan administration (which termed it core and peripheral support), considered the coalition in terms of strength of support, meaning the depth and breadth of commitment to the president and his policies.[8]

Viewing the presidential audience from the perspective of strength of support changes the array of available leadership strategies. The audience in the national view essentially distinguishes two categories of support by position in the political sphere: There are insiders and outsiders. Insiders are either bargained with or pressured for outcomes. Outsiders are the leverage, either by influencing the environment or by directly compelling compliance. In the aftermath of the election, the motivated, active supporters who worked tirelessly as volunteers, the small donors who contributed, and the members of interest groups who got out the vote are minimized in importance, as they are theoretically submerged in the mass of the public reflected in the president's approval rating.

The aggregation of strong participants, weak participants, and nonparticipants into the mass known as the public does not accurately portray political reality. In comparison, the focus on strength of connection by Seligman and Covington allows for the continuation of patterns established during the campaign. During the campaign, candidates are incredibly attentive to individuals who participate through dinners, appearances, e-mails, and updates. Candidates are also attentive to the issue positions of the active citizenry, particularly during the primary period. The careful dance candidates do during the nominating period to balance the competing goals of groups emphasizes the relevance of participatory activity by citizens.

A number of presidential actions encapsulate the rejection of a purely national audience. In *Polling to Govern*, I found that a major application of the presidential polling apparatus is the monitoring of the president's constituency.[9] Not only do presidents and their staffs track the national audience's view of the president and his issues, but they also group the president's audience by strength of attachment to the campaign. The White House polling apparatus helps track how the individuals who supported the candidate view the president's issue positions, decisions, and leadership.[10] The polling apparatus serves to maintain and potentially expand the electoral coalition for the inevitable reelection run, as a president could not be elected without the groups who supported his initial run for office.[11] Thus, the polling apparatus reveals that presidents since Nixon acted under an election imperative, much in the way Mayhew illustrated for members of Congress.[12]

The findings of *The Presidential Road Show* offer further evidence not only that presidents operate under a modified election imperative (as they can only run for reelection once) but also, as with members of Congress, that the election imperative translates to constituency behavior. In 1977, Richard Fenno argued that members of Congress view their constituency as a series of concentric circles in which the furthest circle, the geographic district, encompasses the broadest view of constituency, those individuals the member is obligated to represent.[13] The smallest circle contains friends, family members, and trusted advisors. As the circles decrease in size, the importance to the member of Congress increases. Fenno argued that the relative importance of sectors of the district predictably determined the allocation of resources, notably the Congress member's time.

Similarly, the changed rhetorical tone indicative of a different leadership strategy, combined with rhetorical tactics that highlight service to specific groups, represent the president's constituency-driven behavior. Figure 8.1 illustrates a presidential model that focuses on the allocation of time and attentiveness. Modeling presidential behavior in this fashion articulates the

Figure 8.1 Comparing Congressional and Presidential Constituencies

Fenno's congressional model		*Presidential model*
Personal (e.g., friends, family)	**Core**	Personal (e.g., friends, family)
Primary (e.g., early donors and voters)	↓	Primary (e.g., early donors and voters)
Reelection (e.g., continuing voters)	↓	Issue (e.g., supporters based on policy alignment)
Geographic (e.g., people living in the district)	**Periphery**	National (e.g., citizens of the United States)

strength of connection between the president and an individual, dependent on that individual's level of participation in the political sphere. Moreover, the closer the individual is to the president (meaning the core supporters), the more intense the expectations of support are between the individual or group and the president. The closest to the president, the personal and primary supporters, are those individuals and groups who were there from the beginning. The beginning may be the beginning of a political career or the beginning of a run for the presidency. In either case, the president does not have to work terribly hard to motivate those individuals to support him or work on behalf of his agenda once in office.

For those in the outer layers of support, the conditions placed on support for the president's agenda increase and the presidential effort to obtain that support also increases. Moreover, the farther away individuals are from the core, the less present they are in the political system. Issue supporters are not with the president across all issues, but they are there for the particular issues that motivate them to participate. The national audience is there by constitutional design. However, for the president, the national audience's support is the most conditional, the least trustworthy, and the hardest to motivate.

The findings in this book illustrate how the constituency context challenges presidential allocations of time and attentiveness. The electorally supported president can appeal to all four levels of constituents, since achieving a comfortable victory in the Electoral College rests on the participation of less active, less attached voters. The electorally challenged presidency finds the bulk of his supporters in the personal and primary categories. The issue and national groupings either voted for someone else or did not vote at all and thus are weakly connected to the president. Correspondingly, the electorally challenged president continually needs to rebuild his coalition issue by issue, as Seligman and Covington suggest.[14] For the electorally supported president, fewer groups and individuals are issue specific outside the core. Consequently, the electorally challenged president spends the bulk of his time working to make issue supporters into core supporters, by traveling to see them and articulating how their concerns are his concerns.

Shifting Presidential Leadership Strategies

Within the complicated media environment, which presents its own challenges,[15] presidents are either electorally supported or electorally challenged by their victory. A national audience is not the audience of a president elected by only

51 percent of the nation. Unlike crises and war, the domestic legislative agenda of a sitting president is not naturally unifying. Presidents cannot design legislative leadership strategies dependent on moving or motivating people who were not moved or motivated to vote for them originally. Presidents can, theoretically, expand their electoral coalitions—but only after having accomplished something that prompts reevaluation. Non-participants and non-supporters have no reason to come out for the president's preferred agenda, particularly in the first year, when they did not like the agenda enough to vote for him in the first place.

More significant, however, is the role that partisanship plays in the strategic reaction to the environmental constraints faced by the president. Whether electorally challenged or electorally supported, presidents in the new media age seek out specific groups to garner support for their agenda, and they continually remind audiences of what they have done and continually define the issues facing the nation. The strategy produces effective results: Local travel and rhetoric garner positive local news coverage and successfully influence key congressional voting on the president's major agenda items. The president, however, is less effectual in influencing national or state public opinion polls through local rhetoric.

The effectiveness of local rhetoric stems from linking leadership to participation. National views of the presidency tend to link leadership to citizenship and the ideological spectrum. In contrast, I link representation with participation. B. Dan Wood tests the different understandings of presidential representation by designing theoretical models that distinguish between the median voter and the median partisan voter.[16] Focusing on what Wood terms "issue-based liberalism," he argues that presidents ignore mass preferences in favor of strategies designed to persuade "those near the political center to move toward . . . [the president's] own positions."[17] In comparison to other leadership theories,[18] Wood contends that "presidents also appear unresponsive to incentives from changing public approval and elections."[19] Therefore, two vastly different methodological approaches indicate a rejection of national, or centrist, behavior. The preference for partisan behavior arises from the electoral environment from which presidents emerge.

The scholarship on presidential leadership divides strategies reliably into two camps: bargaining versus campaigning, or, put another way, inside the Beltway versus outside the Beltway. The bargaining view of presidential leadership dates to Richard Neustadt's first evaluation of FDR's success in 1960.[20] Although scholars have long considered presidential rhetorical leadership as a powerful tool of the presidency, notably Elmer E. Cornwell in 1965 and Jeffrey Tulis in 1987, not until Samuel Kernell in 1986 did presidential rhetorical leadership come into conflict with bargaining leadership.[21] As George Edwards notes twenty years after Kernell, "the permanent campaign is antithetical to governing."[22] Kernell argues that going public eliminates opportunities to bargain because presidents cement their positions publicly. Edwards extends the theory, arguing that the limited attention span of the public forces the reduction of choices to "stark black-and-white terms."[23] Fundamentally, the delineation of issue positions eliminates opportunities to build coalitions and eliminates the willingness to compromise—essential components of Neustadt's bargaining leadership.

The basis of these public leadership strategies rests on the assumption of a national audience and the corresponding behavior targeted toward that audience: Presidents reduce their language to the lowest common denominator and draw immovable lines in the sand. Scholarly arguments classifying presidential rhetorical leadership as "campaigning to govern" rather than "going public" focus on similar behaviors: speaking to the nation, rhetoric influencing public opinion, and delineating winning and losing opportunities. From a practical perspective, going public, campaigning to govern, and plebiscitary presidency[24] are all theories that analyze the use of rhetoric and campaign tools to explain the modern president's efforts to achieve his agenda by relying on the public rather than bargaining with Congress. As I described earlier, presidents speak frequently, but they do not use the key rhetorical language in their local rhetoric that would delineate fixed positions, ask their audience to contact members of Congress, or disparage Congress. These elements, which are the pillars of a strategy to force compliance by providing pressure from the public, barely exist at the local level.

Interestingly, the all-or-nothing approach to leadership, which subsumes the differentiation between individualized versus institutional pluralism, or bargaining versus public relations, rests on success. As noted in Chapter 2, a host of scholarship accepts the behavior of going public but simultaneously highlights the limitations of going public as a model of influence.[25] Focusing on the use of one particular campaign tool—public opinion polls—I argued in *Polling to Govern* that campaign techniques are present in the White House but that a campaign approach does not dominate leadership strategies.[26] The White House's use of the tools and techniques of a modern campaign while governing does not make advocating for policy the equivalent of running a campaign, regardless of conventional wisdom.[27] Consequently, there are two challenges to the credibility of individualized pluralism as the dominant presidential leadership strategy. First, Congress is not responsive to presidential approval ratings. A popular president is more likely to achieve the breadth of his goals in Congress.[28] However, on specific issues—particularly on the president's difficult agenda items—presidential desires fade behind party, group, and constituent pressures. Second, presidents are not doing what individualized pluralism requires. Given the infrequency of the presence of the core components of a going-public strategy while employing campaign tools suggests a schizophrenic approach as presidents try to employ outside-the-Beltway tactics without eliminating the ability to work inside the Beltway. The only way this leadership strategy is not quixotic is if the president travels around the nation to speak to people who are already part of the system.

Leading in a Wireless World

The findings in *The Presidential Road Show* are not rejections of public leadership in favor of bargaining. The exercise of presidential leadership at the local level is instead a strategic recasting of the going-public model to work within the constraints of the media environment and to redirect outreach to those who are responsive to it. The twenty-first-century version of the public leadership strategy is significantly more active, since it seeks out the president's audience while acknowledging his inability to reach a national audience. Because presidents will continue to need an extra-constitutional weapon as they battle Congress for their agenda, they will continue to adapt their public leadership strategies.

Although President Obama embraced the local strategy of his predecessors to marshal his partisan supporters in his legislative battles and to avoid the national press corps, the Obama White House extended its public strategy further. In his extraordinarily effective campaign in 2008, candidate Obama sophisticatedly employed technology, particularly social media, which gave him a tremendous advantage in getting his message to supporters and potential supporters. As president, Obama brought these methods of reaching his audience to the White House. Not only did the Obama White House use social media to find his constituents where they got their information, but it was also able to avoid a contentious national press while doing so.

In contrast to most views of presidential rhetoric, I contend that the bulk of presidential speech, which occurs at the local level specifically, targets those in the president's immediate presence. The leadership strategy accepts the benefit of local media providing the president with a wider effect but does not require it. The online presence of the Obama White House, interestingly, took the targeting feature a step further, as it bypassed all press in favor of a direct interaction with web users. A concerted, daily presence on the Internet is entirely new and potentially rewrites the rules of engagement between the president, the press, and the public. The shift occurring within White House communications is not the desire to reach the masses without a filter; it is the capacity to do so, as the presidential presence on the web preempts the media's ability to control access to information. The media cannot critique, fact check, or comment on all the online areas where presidential outreach occurs—especially where that outreach is direct (via direct e-mail) and/or targeted (to sympathetic audiences).

The Obama administration demonstrates the fluid nature of presidential efforts to employ the public in legislative battles. In 1980, Ronald Reagan relied on a national megaphone directed through the three major networks as he asked for the public's help in his battles with Congress. By 2000, even with a national megaphone the president could not always be heard over the cacophony of voices. Nearly abandoning entirely national rhetorical efforts, presidents designed local leadership efforts targeting participants in the political system for assistance with Congress. Throughout Obama's first term, his administration employed a continuum of public strategies, from national speeches to local speeches to YouTube conferences designed to assist the president in his legislative battles.

Presidential tactics change and evolve, but the need for help from the public remains the same. The future, then, for presidential leadership through rhetoric remains interestingly in flux due to the changing nature of the political environment. Partisanship will continue to wax and wane in terms of level of vitriol and adherence to messages that cannot be compromised. However, given the enduring nature of the Electoral College and the unlikelihood of an amendment to change it, half of my contextual argument will remain unchanged well into the future. However, as I note in Chapter 7, the popular vote may prove to be the preferred measure of constituency pressure if electoral outcomes remain closely contested.

Figure 8.2 demonstrates how an evolution in the way information is disseminated could affect presidential rhetorical leadership. I use the term "media organization" to highlight the proliferation of media outlets in the post-broadcast age. Whereas the big three television networks and a few major newspapers dominated twentieth-century political agenda setting, in the twenty-first century media age, there are multiple ways to get information. The changes to the media environment first came in the competition between hard and soft news. Citizens could get political information from television news programs or television entertainment programs. They could find political information in all sorts of new media, particularly on the Internet. During the 1990s and 2000s, the Internet grew exponentially, and Internet-only content providers began to equal the presence of traditional news sources' online options. *Politico* and the *Huffington Post* became legitimate outlets, no longer stamped with a scarlet

"I" for illegitimate, like the *Drudge Report* in late 1998 and 1999. However, the Internet is not yet the dominant information provider. If that change takes place, as when television supplanted both radio and newspapers, then presidential strategy will change accordingly.

In Figure 8.2, I delineate the different fragmented effects that would be produced by an Internet-dominated media. The hallmark of the Internet in comparison to other forms of media is the ability to instantaneously access information. In 2008, candidate Obama shattered the seeming inevitability of Hillary Clinton's nomination by reaching people online. Potential Obama voters gathered information directly from the candidate and donated money directly to the candidate, beyond the control of the traditional gatekeepers of the media or the party.

President Obama's first term revealed a glimpse of what an Internet-dominant political world might look like, with prepared video statements, a White House presence on large social networks and content providers, and a very interactive website. However, in the environment in which President Obama governed, the Internet was a meaningful source of information but not quite dominant.

Figure 8.2 Systemic Influences on Presidential Leadership as the Media Evolves

Electoral College victory	*Media organization*		
	Narrow	*Fragmented—old media dominate*	*Fragmented—new media dominate*
Large (>65% of total Electoral College vote)	Target a single audience Employ national rhetoric Less likely to travel	Target a single audience Employ national rhetoric Likely to travel	Target a single audience Employ national rhetoric Disseminate rhetoric via largest web content providers Less likely to travel
Narrow (<65% of total Electoral College vote)	Target multiple audiences Employ coalition base rhetoric Less likely to travel	Target multiple audiences Employ coalition base rhetoric Likely to travel	Target multiple audiences Employ coalition base rhetoric Disseminate rhetoric via content providers that match coalition Less likely to travel

If the Internet comes to dominate, presidential strategy will likely adjust to take advantage of the shift. For the electorally supported president, the Internet would offer the chance to return to the days of a smaller presidential road show. These presidents could travel less because they could reach their majority audience through major Internet content providers and social networks. The new top box in Figure 8.2—large Electoral College victory and dominated by new media—is similar to the top left box (large Electoral College victory and narrow media), except the method of disseminating information has changed. It is the other new box—narrow Electoral College victory and dominated by new media—that relies on a new application of the behavior identified in *The Presidential Road Show*, although the intent would remain the same.

In this new box, as in the bottom middle box, the president is electorally challenged. Consequently, the president must determine how to reach his supporters in the new media marketplace. The electorally challenged president in the post-broadcast age needed to travel to reach his supporters. The electorally challenged president of the future may need to travel, but over Wi-Fi, to find his constituents. This president will not be able to rely on large, nationally oriented content providers but instead will endeavor to have a web presence in places more specialized and targeted. Aided perhaps by the high-powered targeting that online data miners are currently able to do, administrations might be able to target political messages to citizens as banners while they surf the web or engage in other activities online.

The online tactics and online presence of the candidates in campaign 2012 reflect the growing importance of an Internet presence for candidates and presidents alike.[29] However, as Figures 1.1 and 8.2 demonstrate, the strength of a president's electoral victory matters as much as the media environment in which he governs when it comes to determining the type of rhetorical engagement a president may pursue. The president of the future will face a different media environment than his predecessors, but the constraints stemming from that environment, alongside those from the electoral constituency, will continue to focus the range of rhetorical leadership presidents can employ.

Notes

Chapter 1

1. President Barack Obama, "Remarks at a Town Hall Meeting and a Question-and-Answer Session in Los Angeles," March 19, 2009, *Public Papers of the Presidents of the United States*, Barack Obama, 2009, Book 1, 290–301.

2. For a discussion of the sources of the 2012 divisiveness, see Andrew E. Busch, "Political Movements, Presidential Nominations, and the Tea Party," in William G. Mayer and Jonathan Bernstein, eds., *The Making of the Presidential Candidates 2012* (Lanham, MD: Rowman and Littlefield, 2012), 59–92.

3. Larry M. Bartels, "Partisanship and Voting Behavior, 1952–1996," *American Journal of Political Science* 44 (2000): 35–50, p. 36; Richard Niemi and Harold Weisberg, *Controversies in American Voting Behavior* (San Francisco: W. H. Freeman, 1976).

4. Martin Wattenberg, *The Rise of Candidate-Centered Politics: Presidential Elections of the 1980s* (Cambridge, MA: Harvard University Press, 1991).

5. Steven Brams and Morton Davis, "The 3/2's Rule in Presidential Campaigning," *American Political Science Review* 68 (1974): 113–134, p. 115.

6. Ibid., p. 134.

7. Ibid., p. 128.

8. Larry Bartels, "Resource Allocation in a Presidential Campaign," *Journal of Politics* 47 (1985): 928–936.

9. Claude Colantoni, Terrence Levesque, and Peter Ordeshook, "Campaign Resource Allocation Under the Electoral College," *American Political Science Review* 69 (1975): 141–154.

10. Steven J. Rosenstone and John M. Hansen, *Mobilization, Participation, and Democracy in America* (New York: Macmillan Press, 1993).

11. Peter W. Wielhouwer and Brad Lockerbie, "Party Contacting and Political Participation, 1952–90," *American Journal of Political Science* 38 (1994): 211–219.

12. James Gimpel, Karen Kaufmann, and Shanna Pearson-Merkowitz, "Battleground States versus Blackout States: The Behavioral Implications of Modern Presidential Campaigns," *Journal of Politics* 69 (2007): 786–797.

13. David Hill and Seth McKee, "The Electoral College, Mobilization and Turnout in the 2000 Presidential Election," *American Politics Research* 33 (2005): 700–725.

14. Ibid.

15. Diane J. Heith, *Polling to Govern: Public Opinion and Presidential Leadership* (Stanford, CA: Stanford University Press, 2004).

16. See the *New York Times* interactive electoral map: "The Electoral Map: Building a Path to Victory," http://elections.nytimes.com/2012/electoral-map.

17. Darrell West, *The Rise and Fall of the Media Establishment* (Boston: St. Martin's Press, 2001); Matthew Baum and Samuel Kernell, "Has Cable Ended the Golden Age of Television?" *American Political Science Review* 93 (1999): 99–114.

18. W. Lance Bennett, "News as Reality TV: Election Coverage and the Democratization of Truth," *Critical Studies in Media Communication* 22, no. 2 (2005): 171–177; Doris Graber, *Mass Media and American Politics*, 8th ed. (Washington, DC: CQ Press, 2009).

19. Martha Kumar, *Managing the President's Message: The White House Communications Operation* (Baltimore, MD: Johns Hopkins University Press, 2007).

20. Jeffrey E. Cohen, *The Presidency in the Era of 24-Hour News* (Princeton, NJ: Princeton University Press, 2008), p. 176.

21. Ibid.

22. Thomas Patterson, *Doing Well and Doing Good: How Soft News and Critical Journalism Are Shrinking the News Audience and Weakening Democracy* (Cambridge, MA: John F. Kennedy School of Government, Harvard University, 2000).

23. Ibid.

24. Matthew Baum, "Soft News and Political Knowledge: Evidence of Absence or Absence of Evidence?" *Political Communication* 20 (2003): 173–190; Marcus Prior, "Any Good News in Soft News? The Impact of Soft News Preference on Political Knowledge," *Political Communication* 20 (2003): 149–171.

25. Matthew Baum, "Sex, Lies, and War: How Soft News Brings Foreign Policy to the Inattentive Public," *American Political Science Review* 96 (2002): 91–109, p. 92.

26. Patterson, 2000.

27. Baum, 2002, emphasis in original.

28. Patterson, 2000.

29. Baum, 2003; Matthew Baum, "Talking the Vote: What Happens When Presidential Politics Hits the Talk Show Circuit?" *American Journal of Political Science* 49 (2005): 213–234.

30. Patterson, 2000, p. 2.

31. John Zaller, "A New Standard of News Quality: Burglar Alarms for the Monitorial Citizen," *Political Communication* 20 (2003): 109–130, p. 110.

32. Bennett, 2005.

33. Cynthia Carter, Gill Branston, and Stuart Allan, "Setting New(s) Agendas: An Introduction," in Cynthia Carter, Gill Branston, and Stuart Allan, eds., *News, Gender, Power* (New York: Routledge, 1998), 1–12, p. 7.

34. Ibid., pp. 6–7.

35. Ibid.

36. John Nichols and Robert McChesney, *Tragedy and Farce: How the American Media Sell Wars, Spin Elections and Destroy Democracy* (New York: New Press, 2005), p. 130.

37. Liesbet van Zoonen, *Entertaining the Citizen: When Politics and Popular Culture Converge* (Lanham, MD: Rowman and Littlefield, 2005), p. 34.

38. Cohen, 2008.

Chapter 2

1. Colleen Sheehan, "Madison v Hamilton: The Battle over Republicanism and the Role of Public Opinion," *American Political Science Review* 98 (2004): 405–424, p. 405.

2. Ibid., p. 423.

3. Ibid.

4. Jeffrey Tulis, *The Rhetorical Presidency* (Princeton, NJ: Princeton University Press, 1987); Melvin Laracey, *Presidents and the People: The Partisan Story of Going Public* (College Station: Texas A&M University Press, 2002).

5. Tulis, 1987.

6. Laracey, 2002.

7. Ibid., p. 12.

8. Richard Rubin, *Press, Party and the Presidency* (New York: W.W. Norton, 1981).

9. Tulis, 1987; Laracey, 2002.

10. Richard E. Neustadt, *Presidential Power: The Politics of Leadership* (New York: Wiley, 1960).

11. Ibid.; Elmer E. Cornwell Jr., *Presidential Leadership of Public Opinion* (Bloomington: Indiana University Press, 1965).

12. Samuel Kernell, *Going Public: New Strategies of Presidential Leadership*, 4th ed. (Washington, DC: CQ Press, 2007).

13. Sidney Blumenthal, *The Permanent Campaign: Inside the World of Elite Political Operatives* (New York: Beacon Press, 1980).

14. Kernell, 2007.

15. George Edwards, *On Deaf Ears: The Limits of the Bully Pulpit* (New Haven, CT: Yale University Press, 2003).

16. Lori Cox Han, *Governing from Center Stage: White House Communication Strategies During the Television Age of Politics* (Creskill, NJ: Hampton Press, 2001).

17. Edwards, 2003.

18. Matthew Eshbaugh-Soha, *The President's Speeches: Beyond "Going Public"* (Boulder, CO: Lynne Rienner Publishers, 2006).

19. Brandice Canes-Wrone, *Who Leads Whom? Presidents, Policy and the Public* (Chicago: University of Chicago Press, 2006).

20. Brandon Rottinghaus, *The Provisional Pulpit: Modern Presidential Leadership of Public Opinion* (College Station: Texas A&M University Press, 2010), p. 195.

21. See Jeffrey E. Cohen, *Presidential Responsiveness and Public-Policy Making* (Ann Arbor: University of Michigan Press, 1997); and Donna Hoffman and Alison Howard, *Addressing the State of the Union: The Evolution and Impact of the President's Big Speech* (Boulder, CO: Lynne Rienner Publishers, 2006).

22. *DICTION 5.0: The Text Analysis Program: The Users Manual* (Austin: Digitext, 2000), p. 6.

23. Ibid., p. 44.

24. Ibid., p. 43.

25. Ibid., pp. 42 and 46.

26. Ibid., p. 47.

27. Jeffrey E. Cohen, "Presidential Rhetoric and the Public Agenda," *American Journal of Political Science* 39 (1995): 87–107; Cohen, 1997; Paul Light, *The President's Agenda: Domestic Policy Choice from Kennedy to Reagan* (Baltimore, MD: Johns Hopkins University Press, 1999).

28. Ronald Hinckley, *People, Polls and Policymakers: American Public Opinion and National Security* (New York: Lexington Books, 1992); Tulis, 1987.

29. Cohen, 1995.

30. Kernell, 2007.

31. George Edwards, *The Public Presidency: The Pursuit of Popular Support* (New York: St. Martin's Press, 1983).

32. Neustadt, 1960; George Edwards, *Governing by Campaigning: The Politics of the Bush Presidency* (Boston: Longman, 2008), p. 157.

33. Rottinghaus, 2010.

34. Edwards, 2008, p. 163.

35. Han, 2001.

36. James Jasinski, *Sourcebook on Rhetoric: Key Concepts in Contemporary Rhetorical Studies* (New York: Sage, 2001).

37. Aaron Wildavsky, "The Two Presidencies," in Aaron Wildavsky, ed., *Perspectives on the Presidency* (Boston: Little, Brown, 1975), 136–147.

38. Paul Brace and Barbara Hinckley, *Follow the Leader: Opinion Polls and Modern Presidents* (New York: Basic Books, 1992).

39. Bruce Miroff, "The Presidential Spectacle," in Michael Nelson, ed., *The Presidency and the Political System*, 7th ed. (Washington, DC: CQ Press, 2006), 255–282.

40 *DICTION*, 2000, p. 47.

Chapter 3

1. Lori Cox Han, *Governing from Center Stage: White House Communication Strategies During the Television Age of Politics* (Creskill, NJ: Hampton Press, 2001).

2. Samuel Kernell, *Going Public: New Strategies of Presidential Leadership*, 4th ed. (Washington, DC: CQ Press, 2007); Jeffrey E. Cohen, *The Presidency in the Era of 24-Hour News* (Princeton, NJ: Princeton University Press, 2008); Jeffrey E. Cohen, *Going Local: Presidential Leadership in the Post-Broadcast Age* (New York: Cambridge University Press, 2010); George Edwards, *On Deaf Ears: The Limits of the Bully Pulpit* (New Haven, CT: Yale University Press, 2003); Matthew Baum and Samuel Kernell, "Has Cable Ended the Golden Age of Television?" *American Political Science Review* 93 (1999): 99–114.

3. Chapter 6 will explore how the disparity between the Electoral College result and the popular vote influences leadership opportunities.

4. Kernell, 2007.

5. Robert A. Dahl, "Myth of the Presidential Mandate," *Political Science Quarterly* 105, no. 3 (1990), 355–372; Patricia Conley, *Presidential Mandates: How Elections Shape the National Agenda* (Chicago: University of Chicago Press, 2001).

6. Michael Burton, "The Contemporary Presidency: The 'Flying White House': A Travel Establishment within the Presidential Branch," *Presidential Studies Quarterly* 36, no. 2 (2006): 297–308.

7. David Mayhew, *Congress: The Electoral Connection* (New Haven, CT: Yale University Press, 1974).

8. The numbers of visits cited here are based on the speech criteria outlined in Chapter 2.

9. I use 2000 census data in order to split the difference between the administrations.

10. Corey Cook, "The Contemporary Presidency: The Permanence of the 'Permanent Campaign': George W. Bush's Public Presidency," *Presidential Studies Quarterly* 32 (2002): 753–764; Patrick Sellers and Laura Denton, "Presidential Visits and Midterm Senate Elections," *Presidential Studies Quarterly* 36 (2006): 410–432; Brendan Doherty, "Elections: The Politics of the Permanent Campaign: Presidential Travel and the Electoral College, 1977–2004," *Presidential Studies Quarterly* 37 (2007): 749–773.

11. Burton, 2006.

12. This material is now readily available online thanks to the heroic efforts of Gerhard Peters and John Woolley at the American Presidency Project (http://www.presidency.ucsb.edu).

13. Kernell, 2007, p. 159.

14. Richard E. Neustadt, *Presidential Power and the Modern Presidents: The Politics of Leadership from Roosevelt to Reagan* (New York: Free Press, 1990).

15. Kernell, 2007.

16. Ibid., p. 2.

17. Ibid., p. 41.

18. Lawrence R. Jacobs, Eric D. Lawrence, Robert Y. Shapiro, and Steven S. Smith, "Congressional Leadership of Public Opinion," *Political Science Quarterly* 113, no. 1 (1998): 21–41.

19. Kernell, 2007.

20. Ibid., p. 41.

21. Ibid.

22. Paul Light, *The President's Agenda: Domestic Policy Choice from Kennedy to Reagan* (Baltimore, MD: Johns Hopkins University Press, 1999).

23. Darrell West, Diane Heith, and Chris Goodwin, "Harry and Louise Go to Washington: Political Advertising and Health Care Reform," *The Journal of Health Politics, Policy and Law* 21 (1996): 35–68.

24. Ibid.

25. The president also gave an address to Congress two days later in which he laid out the administration's goals. In this speech, he mentioned all the agenda items discussed here: health care, the stimulus, AmeriCorps, and welfare reform.

26. William Lammers and Michael Genovese, *The Presidency and Domestic Policy: Comparing Leadership Styles, FDR to Clinton* (Washington, DC: CQ Press, 2000).

27. Kernell, 2007.

28. Jeremy Rosner, "Reading the Public: How Members of Congress Develop Their Impressions of Public Opinion on National Security," PhD dissertation, University of Maryland, 2007.

29. Ibid., p. 84.

30. Steven Kull, I. M. Destler, Celinda Lake, and Frederick Steeper, *Misreading the Public: The Myth of a New Isolationism* (Washington, DC: Brookings Institution Press, 1999); Catherine Paden and Benjamin Page, "Congress Invokes Public Opinion on Welfare Reform," *American Politics Research* 31, no. 6 (2002): 670–679; Fay Lomax Cook, Jason Barabas, and Benjamin I. Page, "Invoking Public Opinion: Policy Elites and Social Security," *Public Opinion Quarterly* 66 (2002): 235–264.

31. Rosner, 2007, p. 100.

32. Barbara Sinclair, *Party Wars: Polarization and the Politics of National Policy Making* (Norman: University of Oklahoma Press, 2006); Barbara Sinclair, *Unorthodox*

Lawmaking: New Legislative Processes in the U.S. Congress, 3rd ed. (Washington, DC: CQ Press, 2007).

33. Lori Cox Han, *A Presidency Upstaged: The Public Leadership of George H. W. Bush* (College Station: Texas A&M University Press, 2011).

Chapter 4

1. Sidney Blumenthal, *The Permanent Campaign: Inside the World of Elite Political Operatives* (New York: Beacon Press, 1980).

2. Samuel Kernell, *Going Public: New Strategies of Presidential Leadership*, 4th ed. (Washington, DC: CQ Press, 2007); George Edwards, *On Deaf Ears: The Limits of the Bully Pulpit* (New Haven, CT: Yale University Press, 2003); Brandon Rottinghaus, *The Provisional Pulpit: Modern Presidential Leadership of Public Opinion* (College Station: Texas A&M University Press, 2010).

Chapter 5

1. Bruce Miroff, "The Presidential Spectacle," in Michael Nelson, ed., *The Presidency and the Political System*, 7th ed. (Washington, DC: CQ Press, 2006), 255–282.

2. Richard Rubin, *Press, Party and Presidency* (New York: W.W. Norton, 1981).

3. Diane Heith, "The Virtual Party Campaign: Connecting with Constituents in a MultiMedia Age," in Meena Bose, ed., *From Votes to Victory: Winning and Governing the White House in the 21st Century* (College Station: Texas A&M University Press, 2011).

4. Ibid.

5. Diana Owen, "The Campaign and the Media," in Janet Box-Steffensmeier and Stephen Schier, eds., *The American Elections of 2008* (Lanham, MD: Rowman & Littlefield, 2009), 9–32.

6. Diane Heith, "President Obama, Public Opinion and the Media," in Colin Campbell, Bert A. Rockman, and Andrew Rudalevige, eds., *The Barack Obama Presidency: Appraisals and Prospects* (Washington, DC: CQ Press, 2011).

7. Ibid.

8. Barack Obama, "2004 Democratic National Convention Keynote Address," Boston, July 27, 2004, American Rhetoric Online Speech Bank, http://www.americanrhetoric.com/speeches/convention2004/barackobama2004dnc.htm.

9. Jeffrey M. Jones, "Obama Approval Averages 45% in September: Blacks, Democrats, Liberals Show Greatest Support for Obama," Gallup Politics, October 4, 2010, http://www.gallup.com/poll/143354/Obama-Approval-Averages-September.aspx.

10. Sheryl Gay Stolberg, "To Connect, Obama Heads into Backyard," *New York Times*, September 22, 2010, http://www.nytimes.com/2010/09/23/us/politics/23obama.html.

11. Ibid.

12. *DICTION 5.0: The Text Analysis Program: The Users Manual* (Austin: Digitext, 2000), pp. 6, 47.

13. Matt Bai, "The Way We Live Now: Don't Look Back," *New York Times*, January 8, 2009, http://www.nytimes.com/2009/02/01/magazine/01wwln-lede-t.html.

Chapter 6

1. Tip O'Neill Jr., *Man of the House* (New York: Random House, 1987).

2. Michael Grossman and Martha Kumar, *Portraying the President: The White House and the News Media* (Baltimore, MD: Johns Hopkins University Press, 1981).

3. Doris Graber, *Mass Media and American Politics*, 8th ed. (Washington, DC: CQ Press, 2009); W. Lance Bennett, *News: The Politics of Illusion*, 8th ed. (New York: Longman, 2009).

4. Jeffrey E. Cohen, *Going Local: Presidential Leadership in the Post-Broadcast Age* (New York: Cambridge University Press, 2010); Graber, 2009; Matthew Baum, "How Soft News Brings Policy Issues to the Inattentive Public," in Doris Graber, ed., *Media Power in Politics*, 6th ed. (Washington, DC: CQ Press, 2010), 113–128; Marcus Prior, "Audience Fragmentation and Political Inequality in the Post-Broadcast Media Environment," in Doris Graber, ed., *Media Power in Politics*, 6th ed. (Washington, DC: CQ Press, 2010), 153–164; Richard Davis, "A Symbiotic Relationship: Bloggers and Journalists," in Doris Graber, ed., *Media Power in Politics*, 6th ed. (Washington, DC: CQ Press, 2010), 244–261.

5. Jeffrey E. Cohen, *The Presidency in the Era of 24-Hour News* (Princeton, NJ: Princeton University Press, 2008); Cohen, 2010.

6. Richard Ellis, *Presidential Travel: The Journey from George Washington to George W. Bush* (Lawrence: University Press of Kansas, 2008).

7. Cohen, 2008.

8. Cohen, 2010.

9. Garry Young and William B. Perkins, "Presidential Rhetoric, the Public Agenda, and the End of Presidential Television's 'Golden Age,' " *Journal of Politics* 67 (2005): 1190–1205; Cohen, 2010; Matthew Baum and Samuel Kernell, "Has Cable Ended the Golden Age of Television?" *American Political Science Review* 93 (1999): 99–114.

10. "WH vs. NBC: NBC News' Response," Mediabistro TVNewser, May 19, 2008, http://www.mediabistro.com/tvnewser/wh-vs-nbc-nbc-news-response_b19373, accessed September 25, 2012.

11. Ibid.

12. Benjamin Page, Robert Shapiro, and Glenn Dempsey, "What Moves Public Opinion," in Doris A. Graber, ed., *Media Power in Politics*, 6th ed. (Washington, DC: CQ Press), 85–100; Franklin Gilliam Jr. and Shanto Iyengar, "New Coverage Effects on Public Opinion About Crime," in Doris Graber, ed., *Media Power in Politics*, 6th ed. (Washington, DC: CQ Press, 2010), 107–133.

13. Thomas Patterson, *Out of Order* (New York: Vintage, 1994).

14. Cohen, 2010, p. 55.

15. Ibid., p. 89.

16. Ibid., p. 121.

17. Ibid.

18. Ibid.

19. Ibid.

20. Matthew Eshbaugh-Soha and Jeffrey Peake, "The Presidency and Local Media: Local Newspaper Coverage of George W. Bush," *Presidential Studies Quarterly* 38 (2008): 609–630; Andrew Barrett and Jeffrey Peake, "When the President Comes to Town: Examining Local Newspaper Coverage of Domestic Presidential Travel," *American Politics Research* 35 (2007): 3–31.

21. Cohen, 2010.

22. George Edwards, *On Deaf Ears: The Limits of the Bully Pulpit* (New Haven, CT: Yale University Press, 2003); Matthew Eshbaugh-Soha, *The President's Speeches: Beyond "Going Public"* (Boulder, CO: Lynne Rienner Publishers, 2006); Brandice Canes-Wrone, *Who Leads Whom? Presidents, Policy and the Public* (Chicago: University of Chicago Press, 2006); Brandon Rottinghaus, *The Provisional Pulpit: Modern Presidential Leadership of Public Opinion* (College Station: Texas A&M University Press, 2010).

23. Paul Brace and Barbara Hinckley, *Follow the Leader: Opinion Polls and Modern Presidents* (New York: Basic Books, 1992); Charles Ostrom and Dennis Simon, "The Man in the Teflon Suit? The Environmental Connection, Political Drama, and Popular Support in the Reagan Presidency," *Public Opinion Quarterly* 53 (1989): 353–387.

24. Bush's job approval rating soared after 9/11 due to the predictable rally-around-the-flag effect. Two wars perpetuated the high ratings. After his reelection in 2004, both variables declined precipitously.

25. Edwards, 2003.

26. Rottinghaus, 2010.

27. Diane J. Heith, *Polling to Govern: Public Opinion and Presidential Leadership* (Stanford, CA: Stanford University Press, 2004).

28. Brandon Rottinghaus, "Strategic Leaders: Identifying Successful Momentary Presidential Leadership of Public Opinion," *Political Communication* 26, no. 3 (2009): 296–316; Rottinghaus, 2010.

29. Rottinghaus, 2009, p. 299.

30. Ibid., p. 303.

31. Ibid., p. 307.

32. Rottinghaus, 2010, p. 307

33. Rottinghaus 2009, p. 308.

34. Cohen, 2010.

35. Cohen and Powell argue that being able to explain an overwhelming amount of the variation in state-level approval allows for the use of the normed baseline. Jeffrey Cohen and Richard Powell, "Building Public Support from the Grassroots Up: The Impact of Presidential Travel on State-Level Approval," *Presidential Studies Quarterly* 35, no. 1 (2005): 11–27.

36. Cohen and Powell, 2005, p. 19.

37. Ibid.

38. Ibid., p. 22.

39. Ibid., p. 23.

40. Ibid., p. 19.

41. Jon Bond and Richard Fleisher, *The President in the Legislative Arena* (Chicago: University of Chicago Press, 1990); George Edwards, *At the Margins: Presidential Leadership of Congress* (New Haven, CT: Yale University Press, 1989); Charles Jones, *Passages to the Presidency: From Campaigning to Governing* (Washington, DC: Brookings Institution Press, 1998).

42. Andrew Barrett, "Gone Public: The Impact of Going Public on Presidential Legislative Success," *American Politics Research* 32, no. 3 (2004): 338–370.

43. Richard Powell and Dean Schloyer, "Public Presidential Appeals and Congressional Floor Votes: Reassessing the Constitutional Threat," *Congress and the Presidency* 30 (2003): 123–138.

44. Ibid., p. 130.

45. Ibid.

46. I use the first vote in the chamber, not the vote after conference.

Chapter 7

1. Stephen Skowronek, *Presidential Leadership in Political Time: Reprise and Reappraisal* (Lawrence: Kansas University Press, 2008), p. xi.

2. Google search using the term "Electoral College" with the terms "unfair," "outdated," and "undemocratic," February 23, 2012.

3. Lori Cox Han and Diane J. Heith, *Presidents and the American Presidency* (New York: Oxford University Press, 2012), ch. 3, p. 110.

4. Ibid. See also Thomas Cronin and Michael Genovese, *The Paradoxes of the American Presidency* (New York: Oxford University Press, 1998). For a full discussion on the Electoral College, see George Edwards, *Why the Electoral College Is Bad for America*,

2nd ed. (New Haven, CT: Yale University Press, 2011); and Gary Bugh, ed., *Electoral College Reform: Challenges and Possibilities* (Burlington, VT: Ashgate Publishing, 2010).

5. Ted Koppel, "Olbermann, O'Reilly and the Death of Real News," *Washington Post*, November 14, 2010. http://www.washingtonpost.com/wp-dyn/content/article/2010/11/12/AR2010111202857.html.

6. Jeffrey E. Cohen, *The Presidency in the Era of 24-Hour News* (Princeton, NJ: Princeton University Press, 2008); Jeffrey E. Cohen, *Going Local: Presidential Leadership in the Post-Broadcast Age* (New York: Cambridge University Press, 2010).

7. Lori Cox Han, *Governing from Center Stage: White House Communication Strategies During the Television Age of Politics* (Creskill, NJ: Hampton Press, 2001), p. 181.

8. Ibid.

9. Ibid.

10. Bill Clinton, *My Life* (New York: Knopf, 2004), p. 605.

11. Ibid.

12. George Edwards, *On Deaf Ears: The Limits of the Bully Pulpit* (New Haven, CT: Yale University Press, 2003).

13. Benjamin I. Page and Robert Y. Shapiro, *The Rational Public* (Chicago: University of Chicago Press, 1992).

14. Diane J. Heith, *Polling to Govern: Public Opinion and Presidential Leadership* (Stanford, CA: Stanford University Press, 2004).

15. Ibid.

16. "Presidential Approval Tracker," *USA Today*, http://www.usatoday.com/news/washington/presidential-approval-tracker.htm.

17. See John Mueller, "Presidential Popularity from Truman to Johnson," *American Political Science Review* 64, no. 1 (1970): 18–34; and John Mueller, *War, Presidents and Public Opinion* (Baltimore, MD: Lanham, 1973).

18. Mueller, 1973, p. 215.

19. Richard E. Neustadt, *Presidential Power and the Modern Presidents: The Politics of Leadership from Roosevelt to Reagan* (New York: Free Press, 1990).

20. See Brandice Canes-Wrone, *Who Leads Whom? Presidents, Policy, and the Public* (Chicago: University of Chicago Press, 2006).

21. "Martha Raddatz Interviews Vice President Dick Cheney," *ABC World News with Diane Sawyer*, March 19, 2008, Muscat, Oman, http://abcnews.go.com/WN/Vote2008/story?id=4481568&page=5#.T051zHOEa14.

22. Lawrence R. Jacobs, Eric Lawrence, Robert Y. Shapiro, and Steven S. Smith, "Congressional Leadership of Public Opinion," *Political Science Quarterly* 113, no. 1 (1998): 21–41.

23. Edward S. Greenberg and Benjamin Page, *The Struggle for Democracy*, 4th ed. (New York: Longman, 1999), p. 364.

24. Norman Meller, "Representational Role Types: A Research Note," *American Political Science Review* 61, no. 2 (1967): 474–477.

Chapter 8

1. Lester Seligman and Cary Covington, *The Coalitional Presidency* (New York: Dorsey Press, 1989).

2. Richard E. Neustadt, *Presidential Power and the Modern Presidents: The Politics of Leadership from Roosevelt to Reagan* (New York: Free Press, 1990).

3. Melvin Laracey, *Presidents and the People: The Partisan Story of Going Public* (College Station: Texas A&M University Press, 2002).

4. This is also why national opinion polls are so useless for realistic prediction during the presidential election, regardless of the effectiveness of the modeling. After all, public opinion pollsters and political science modelers predicted that Al Gore would win.

5. Diane J. Heith, *Polling to Govern: Public Opinion and Presidential Leadership* (Stanford, CA: Stanford University Press, 2004).

6. Samuel Popkin, *The Reasoning Voter* (Chicago: University of Chicago Press, 1991).

7. Seligman and Covington, 1989, p. 12.

8. Ibid., p. 1; Heith, 2004.

9. Heith, 2004.

10. Ibid.

11. Ibid.

12. David Mayhew, *Congress: The Electoral Connection* (New Haven, CT: Yale University Press, 1974).

13. Richard Fenno, "U.S. House Members in Their Constituencies: An Exploration," *American Political Science Review* 71, no. 3 (1977): 883–917, p. 887.

14. Seligman and Covington, 1989.

15. See Jeffrey E. Cohen, *The Presidency in the Era of 24-Hour News* (Princeton, NJ: Princeton University Press, 2008).

16. B. Dan Wood, *The Myth of Presidential Representation* (New York: Cambridge University Press, 2009).

17. Ibid., p. 118.

18. Lawrence R. Jacobs and Robert Y. Shapiro, *Politicians Don't Pander: Political Manipulation and the Loss of Democratic Responsiveness* (Chicago: University of Chicago Press, 2000).

19. Wood, 2009, p. 118.

20. Richard E. Neustadt, *Presidential Power: The Politics of Leadership* (New York: Wiley, 1960).

21. Elmer E. Cornwell Jr., *Presidential Leadership of Public Opinion* (Bloomington: Indiana University Press, 1965); Jeffrey Tulis, *The Rhetorical Presidency* (Princeton, NJ: Princeton University Press, 1987); Samuel Kernell, *Going Public: New Strategies of Presidential Leadership*, 4th ed. (Washington, DC: CQ Press, 2007).

22. George Edwards, *Governing by Campaigning: The Politics of the Bush Presidency* (Boston: Longman, 2008), p. 319.

23. Ibid.

24. Theodore J. Lowi, *The Personal President: Power Invested, Promise Unfulfilled* (Ithaca, NY: Cornell University Press, 1985).

25. Cohen, 2008; Jeffrey E. Cohen, *Going Local: Presidential Leadership in the Post-Broadcast Age* (New York: Cambridge University Press), 2010; George Edwards, *On Deaf Ears: The Limits of the Bully Pulpit* (New Haven, CT: Yale University Press, 2003); Matthew Eshbaugh-Soha, *The President's Speeches: Beyond "Going Public"* (Boulder, CO: Lynne Rienner Publishers, 2006); Brandon Rottinghaus, *The Provisional Pulpit: Modern Presidential Leadership of Public Opinion* (College Station: Texas A&M University Press, 2010).

26. Heith, 2004.

27. Ibid.

28. Andrew Barrett, "Gone Public: The Impact of Going Public on Presidential Legislative Success," *American Politics Research* 32, no. 3 (2004): 338–370.

29. See Richard Semiatin, "Introduction—Campaigns on the Cutting Edge," in Richard Semiatin, ed., *Campaigns on the Cutting Edge*, 2nd ed. (Washington, DC: CQ Press, 2013), 3–10; and Michael Turk, "Social and New Media," in Richard Semiatin, ed., *Campaigns on the Cutting Edge*, 2nd ed. (Washington, DC: CQ Press, 2013), 48–64.

Bibliography

Bai, Matt. "The Way We Live Now: Don't Look Back." *New York Times*. January 8, 2009. http://www.nytimes.com/2009/02/01/magazine/01wwln-lede-t.html.

Barrett, Andrew. "Gone Public: The Impact of Going Public on Presidential Legislative Success." *American Politics Research* 32, no. 3 (2004): 338–370.

Barrett, Andrew, and Jeffrey Peake. "When the President Comes to Town: Examining Local Newspaper Coverage of Domestic Presidential Travel." *American Politics Research* 35 (2007): 3–31.

Bartels, Larry. "Resource Allocation in a Presidential Campaign." *Journal of Politics* 47 (1985): 928–936.

———. "Partisanship and Voting Behavior, 1952–1996." *American Journal of Political Science* 44 (2000): 35–50.

Baum, Matthew. "Sex, Lies, and War: How Soft News Brings Foreign Policy to the Inattentive Public." *American Political Science Review* 96 (2002): 91–109.

———. "Soft News and Political Knowledge: Evidence of Absence or Absence of Evidence?" *Political Communication* 20 (2003): 173–190.

———. "Talking the Vote: What Happens When Presidential Politics Hits the Talk Show Circuit?" *American Journal of Political Science* 49 (2005): 213–234.

———. "How Soft News Brings Policy Issues to the Inattentive Public." In Doris Graber, ed., *Media Power in Politics*, 6th ed. Washington, DC: CQ Press, 2010, 113–128.

Baum, Matthew, and Samuel Kernell. "Has Cable Ended the Golden Age of Television?" *American Political Science Review* 93 (1999): 99–114.

Bennett, W. Lance. "News as Reality TV: Election Coverage and the Democratization of Truth." *Critical Studies in Media Communication* 22, no. 2 (2005): 171–177.

———. *News: The Politics of Illusion*, 8th ed. New York: Longman, 2009.

Blumenthal, Sidney. *The Permanent Campaign: Inside the World of Elite Political Operatives*. New York: Beacon Press, 1980.

Bond, Jon, and Richard Fleisher. *The President in the Legislative Arena*. Chicago: University of Chicago Press, 1990.

Brace, Paul, and Barbara Hinckley. *Follow the Leader: Opinion Polls and Modern Presidents*. New York: Basic Books, 1992.

Brams, Steven, and Morton Davis. "The 3/2's Rule in Presidential Campaigning." *American Political Science Review* 68 (1974): 113–134.

Brody, Richard. *Assessing the President: The Media, Elite Opinion and Public Support*. Stanford, CA: Stanford University Press, 1991.

Bugh, Gary, ed. *Electoral College Reform: Challenges and Possibilities*. Burlington, VT: Ashgate Publishing, 2010.

Burton, Michael. "The Contemporary Presidency: The 'Flying White House': A Travel Establishment within the Presidential Branch." *Presidential Studies Quarterly* 36, no. 2 (2006): 297–308.

Busch, Andrew E. "Political Movements, Presidential Nominations, and the Tea Party." In William G. Mayer and Jonathan Bernstein, eds., *The Making of the Presidential Candidates 2012*. Lanham, MD: Rowman and Littlefield, 2012, 59–92.

Canes-Wrone, Brandice. *Who Leads Whom? Presidents, Policy, and the Public*. Chicago: University of Chicago Press, 2006.

Carter, Cynthia, Gill Branston, and Stuart Allan. "Setting New(s) Agendas: An Introduction." In Cynthia Carter, Gill Branston, and Stuart Allan, eds., *News, Gender, Power*. New York: Routledge, 1998, 1–12.

Clinton, Bill. *My Life*. New York: Knopf, 2004.

Cohen, Jeffrey E. "Presidential Rhetoric and the Public Agenda." *American Journal of Political Science* 39 (1995): 87–107.

———. *Presidential Responsiveness and Public-Policy Making*. Ann Arbor: University of Michigan Press, 1997.

———. *The Presidency in the Era of 24-Hour News*. Princeton, NJ: Princeton University Press, 2008.

———. *Going Local: Presidential Leadership in the Post-Broadcast Age*. New York: Cambridge University Press, 2010.

Cohen, Jeffrey, and Richard Powell. "Building Public Support from the Grassroots Up: The Impact of Presidential Travel on State-Level Approval." *Presidential Studies Quarterly* 35, no. 1 (2005): 11–27.

Colantoni, Claude, Terrence Levesque, and Peter Ordeshook. "Campaign Resource Allocation Under the Electoral College." *American Political Science Review* 69 (1975): 141–154.

Conley, Patricia. *Presidential Mandates: How Elections Shape the National Agenda*. Chicago: University of Chicago Press, 2001.

Cook, Corey. "The Contemporary Presidency: The Permanence of the 'Permanent Campaign': George W. Bush's Public Presidency." *Presidential Studies Quarterly* 32 (2002): 753–764.

Cook, Fay Lomax, Jason Barabas, and Benjamin I. Page. "Invoking Public Opinion: Policy Elites and Social Security." *Public Opinion Quarterly* 66 (2002): 235–264.

Cornwell, Elmer E., Jr. *Presidential Leadership of Public Opinion.* Bloomington: Indiana University Press, 1965.

Cronin, Thomas, and Michael Genovese. *The Paradoxes of the American Presidency.* New York: Oxford University Press, 1998.

Dahl, Robert A. "Myth of the Presidential Mandate." *Political Science Quarterly* 105, no. 3 (1990): 355–372.

Davis, Richard. "A Symbiotic Relationship: Bloggers and Journalists." In Doris Graber, ed., *Media Power in Politics,* 6th ed. Washington, DC: CQ Press, 2010, 244–261.

DICTION 5.0: The Text Analysis Program: The Users Manual. Austin: Digitext, 2000.

Doherty, Brendan. "Elections: The Politics of the Permanent Campaign: Presidential Travel and the Electoral College, 1977–2004." *Presidential Studies Quarterly* 37 (2007): 749–773.

Edwards, George. *The Public Presidency: The Pursuit of Popular Support.* New York: St. Martin's Press, 1983.

———. *At the Margins: Presidential Leadership of Congress.* New Haven, CT: Yale University Press, 1989.

———. "Aligning Tests with Theory: Presidential Influence as a Source of Influence in Congress." *Congress and the Presidency* 24 (1997): 113–130.

———. *On Deaf Ears: The Limits of the Bully Pulpit.* New Haven, CT: Yale University Press, 2003.

———. *Governing by Campaigning: The Politics of the Bush Presidency.* Boston: Longman, 2008.

———. *Why the Electoral College Is Bad for America*, 2nd ed. New Haven, CT: Yale University Press, 2011.

Ellis, Richard. *Presidential Travel: The Journey from George Washington to George W. Bush.* Lawrence: University Press of Kansas, 2008.

Erickson, Keith. "Presidential Speeches: Political Illusionism and the Rhetoric of Travel." *Communication Monographs* 65 (1998): 141–153.

Eshbaugh-Soha, Matthew. *The President's Speeches: Beyond "Going Public."* Boulder, CO: Lynne Rienner Publishers, 2006.

Eshbaugh-Soha, Matthew, and Jeffrey Peake. "The Presidency and Local Media: Local Newspaper Coverage of George W. Bush." *Presidential Studies Quarterly* 38 (2008): 609–630.

Fenno, Richard. "U.S. House Members in Their Constituencies: An Exploration." *American Political Science Review* 71, no. 3 (1977): 883–917.

Fiorina, Morris. *Culture War? The Myth of a Polarized America.* New York: Longman, 2005.

Gilliam, Franklin, Jr., and Shanto Iyengar. "New Coverage Effects on Public Opinion About Crime." In Doris Graber, ed., *Media Power in Politics,* 6th ed. Washington, DC: CQ Press, 2010, 107–133.

Gimpel, James, Karen Kaufmann, and Shanna Pearson-Merkowitz. "Battleground States versus Blackout States: The Behavioral Implications of Modern Presidential Campaigns." *Journal of Politics* 69 (2007): 786–797.

Ginsberg, Benjamin, and Martin Shefter. *Politics by Other Means: Politicians, Prosecutors and the Press from Watergate to Whitewater.* New York: W.W. Norton, 1999.

Graber, Doris. *Mass Media and American Politics*, 8th ed. Washington, DC: CQ Press, 2009.

Greenberg, Edward S., and Benjamin Page. *The Struggle for Democracy*, 4th ed. New York: Longman, 1999.

Grossman, Michael, and Martha Kumar. *Portraying the President: The White House and the News Media.* Baltimore, MD: Johns Hopkins University Press, 1981.

Han, Lori Cox. *Governing from Center Stage: White House Communication Strategies During the Television Age of Politics.* Creskill, NJ: Hampton Press, 2001.

———. *A Presidency Upstaged: The Public Leadership of George H. W. Bush.* College Station: Texas A&M University Press, 2011.

Han, Lori Cox, and Diane J. Heith. *Presidents and the American Presidency.* New York: Oxford University Press, 2012.

Hart, Roderick P. *The Sound of Leadership: Presidential Communication in the Modern Age.* Chicago: University of Chicago Press, 1987.

Heclo, Hugh. "Introduction: The Presidential Illusion." In H. Heclo and L. Salamon, eds., *The Illusion of Presidential Government.* Boulder, CO: Westview Press, 1981, 1–8.

Heith, Diane J. *Polling to Govern: Public Opinion and Presidential Leadership.* Stanford, CA: Stanford University Press, 2004.

———. "President Obama, Public Opinion and the Media." In Colin Campbell, Bert A. Rockman, and Andrew Rudalevige, eds., *The Barack Obama Presidency: Appraisals and Prospects.* Washington, DC: CQ Press, 2011.

———. "The Virtual Party Campaign: Connecting with Constituents in a MultiMedia Age." In Meena Bose, ed., *From Votes to Victory: Winning and Governing the White House in the 21st Century.* College Station: Texas A&M University Press, 2011.

Hill, David, and Seth McKee. "The Electoral College, Mobilization and Turnout in the 2000 Presidential Election." *American Politics Research* 33 (2005): 700–725.

Hinckley, Ronald. *People, Polls and Policymakers: American Public Opinion and National Security.* New York: Lexington Books, 1992.

Hoffman, Donna, and Alison Howard. *Addressing the State of the Union: The Evolution and Impact of the President's Big Speech.* Boulder, CO: Lynne Rienner Publishers, 2006.

Jacobs, Lawrence R., Eric D. Lawrence, Robert Y. Shapiro, and Steven S. Smith. "Congressional Leadership of Public Opinion." *Political Science Quarterly* 113, no. 1 (1998): 21–41.

Jacobs, Lawrence R., and Robert Y. Shapiro. *Politicians Don't Pander: Political Manipulation and the Loss of Democratic Responsiveness.* Chicago: University of Chicago Press, 2000.

Jacobson, Gary. *A Divider, Not a Uniter: George Bush and the American People*. New York: Pearson Longman, 2008.

Jacobson, Gary, Samuel Kernell, and Jeffrey Lazarus. "Assessing the President's Role as Party Agent in Congressional Elections: The Case of Bill Clinton in 2000." *Legislative Studies Quarterly* 29 (2004): 159–184.

Jasinski, James. *Sourcebook on Rhetoric: Key Concepts in Contemporary Rhetorical Studies*. New York: Sage, 2001.

Jones, Charles. *Passages to the Presidency: From Campaigning to Governing*. Washington, DC: Brookings Institution Press, 1998.

Jones, Jeffrey M. "Obama Approval Averages 45% in September: Blacks, Democrats, Liberals Show Greatest Support for Obama." Gallup Politics, October 4, 2010. http://www.gallup.com/poll/143354/Obama-Approval-Averages-September.aspx.

Kernell, Samuel. *Going Public: New Strategies of Presidential Leadership*, 4th ed. Washington, DC: CQ Press, 2007.

Koppel, Ted. "Olbermann, O'Reilly and the Death of Real News." *Washington Post*. November 14, 2010. http://www.washingtonpost.com/wp-dyn/content/article/2010/11/12/AR2010111202857.html.

Kull, Steven, I. M. Destler, Celinda Lake, and Frederick Steeper. *Misreading the Public: The Myth of a New Isolationism*. Washington, DC: Brookings Institution Press, 1999.

Kumar, Martha. *Managing the President's Message: The White House Communications Operation*. Baltimore, MD: Johns Hopkins University Press, 2007.

Lammers, William, and Michael Genovese. *The Presidency and Domestic Policy: Comparing Leadership Styles, FDR to Clinton*. Washington, DC: CQ Press, 2000.

Laracey, Melvin. *Presidents and the People: The Partisan Story of Going Public*. College Station: Texas A&M University Press, 2002.

Light, Paul. *The President's Agenda: Domestic Policy Choice from Kennedy to Reagan*. Baltimore, MD: Johns Hopkins University Press, 1999.

Lowi, Theodore J. *The Personal President: Power Invested, Promise Unfulfilled*. Ithaca, NY: Cornell University Press, 1985.

Mayhew, David. *Congress: The Electoral Connection*. New Haven, CT: Yale University Press, 1974.

Meller, Norman. "Representational Role Types: A Research Note." *American Political Science Review* 61, no. 2 (1967): 474–477.

Miroff, Bruce. "The Presidential Spectacle." In Michael Nelson, ed., *The Presidency and the Political System*, 7th ed. Washington, DC: CQ Press, 2006, 255–282.

Mueller, John. "Presidential Popularity from Truman to Johnson." *American Political Science Review* 64, no. 1 (1970): 18–34.

———. *War, Presidents and Public Opinion*. Baltimore, MD: Lanham, 1973.

Neustadt, Richard E. *Presidential Power: The Politics of Leadership*. New York: Wiley, 1960.

———. *Presidential Power and the Modern Presidents: The Politics of Leadership from Roosevelt to Reagan.* New York: Free Press, 1990.

Nichols, John, and Robert McChesney. *Tragedy and Farce: How the American Media Sell Wars, Spin Elections and Destroy Democracy.* New York: New Press, 2005.

Niemi, Richard, and Harold Weisberg. *Controversies in American Voting Behavior.* San Francisco: W.H. Freeman, 1976.

O'Neill, Tip, Jr. *Man of the House.* New York: Random House, 1987.

Ostrom, Charles, and Dennis Simon. "The Man in the Teflon Suit? The Environmental Connection, Political Drama, and Popular Support in the Reagan Presidency." *Public Opinion Quarterly* 53 (1989): 353–387.

Owen, Diana. "The Campaign and the Media." In Janet Box-Steffensmeier and Stephen Schier, eds., *The American Elections of 2008.* Lanham, MD: Rowman & Littlefield, 2009, 9–32.

Paden, Catherine, and Benjamin Page. "Congress Invokes Public Opinion on Welfare Reform." *American Politics Research* 31, no. 6 (2002): 670–679.

Page, Benjamin I., and Robert Y. Shapiro. *The Rational Public.* Chicago: University of Chicago Press, 1992.

Page, Benjamin, Robert Shapiro, and Glenn Dempsey. "What Moves Public Opinion." In Doris A. Graber, ed., *Media Power in Politics,* 6th ed. Washington, DC: CQ Press, 85–100.

Patterson, Thomas. *Out of Order.* New York: Vintage, 1994.

———. *Doing Well and Doing Good: How Soft News and Critical Journalism Are Shrinking the News Audience and Weakening Democracy.* Cambridge, MA: John F. Kennedy School of Government, Harvard University, 2000.

Peterson, Mark. *Legislating Together: The White House and Capitol Hill from Eisenhower to Reagan.* Cambridge, MA: Harvard University Press, 1990.

Popkin, Samuel. *The Reasoning Voter.* Chicago: University of Chicago Press, 1991.

Powell, Richard, and Dean Schloyer. "Public Presidential Appeals and Congressional Floor Votes: Reassessing the Constitutional Threat." *Congress and the Presidency* 30 (2003): 123–138.

Prior, Marcus. "Any Good News in Soft News? The Impact of Soft News Preference on Political Knowledge." *Political Communication* 20 (2003): 149–171.

———. "Audience Fragmentation and Political Inequality in the Post-Broadcast Media Environment." In Doris Graber, ed., *Media Power in Politics,* 6th ed. Washington, DC: CQ Press, 2010, 153–164.

Rosenstone, Steven J., and John Hansen. *Mobilization, Participation, and Democracy in America.* New York: Macmillan Press, 1993.

Rosner, Jeremy. "Reading the Public: How Members of Congress Develop Their Impressions of Public Opinion on National Security." PhD dissertation, University of Maryland, 2007.

Rottinghaus, Brandon. "Strategic Leaders: Identifying Successful Momentary Presidential Leadership of Public Opinion." *Political Communication* 26, no. 3 (2009): 296–316.

———. *The Provisional Pulpit: Modern Presidential Leadership of Public Opinion.* College Station: Texas A&M University Press, 2010.

Rubin, Richard. *Press, Party and Presidency.* New York: W.W. Norton, 1981.

Rudalevige, Andrew. *Managing the President's Program: Presidential Leadership and Legislative Policy Formulation.* Princeton, NJ: Princeton University Press, 2002.

Seligman, Lester, and Cary Covington. *The Coalitional Presidency.* New York: Dorsey Press, 1989.

Sellers, Patrick, and Laura Denton. "Presidential Visits and Midterm Senate Elections." *Presidential Studies Quarterly* 36 (2006): 410–432.

Semiatin, Richard. "Introduction—Campaigns on the Cutting Edge." In Richard Semiatin, ed., *Campaigns on the Cutting Edge*, 2nd ed. Washington, DC: CQ Press, 2013, 3–10.

Sheehan, Colleen. "Madison v Hamilton: The Battle over Republicanism and the Role of Public Opinion." *American Political Science Review* 98 (2004): 405–424.

Sinclair, Barbara. *Party Wars: Polarization and the Politics of National Policy Making.* Norman: University of Oklahoma Press, 2006.

———. *Unorthodox Lawmaking: New Legislative Processes in the U.S. Congress*, 3rd ed. Washington, DC: CQ Press, 2007.

Skowronek, Stephen. *Presidential Leadership in Political Time: Reprise and Reappraisal.* Lawrence: Kansas University Press, 2008.

Stolberg, Sheryl Gay. "To Connect, Obama Heads into Backyard," *New York Times*, September 22, 2010. http://www.nytimes.com/2010/09/23/us/politics/23obama.html.

Tenpas, Kathryn, and James McCann. "Testing the Permanence of the Permanent Campaign: An Analysis of Presidential Polling Expenditures, 1977–2002." *Public Opinion Quarterly* 71 (2009): 349–366.

Tulis, Jeffrey. *The Rhetorical Presidency.* Princeton, NJ: Princeton University Press, 1987.

Turk, Michael. "Social and New Media." In Richard Semiatin, ed., *Campaigns on the Cutting Edge*, 2nd ed. Washington, DC: CQ Press, 2013, 48–64.

van Zoonen, Liesbet. *Entertaining the Citizen: When Politics and Popular Culture Converge.* Lanham, MD: Rowman and Littlefield, 2005.

Wattenberg, Martin. *The Rise of Candidate-Centered Politics: Presidential Elections of the 1980s.* Cambridge, MA: Harvard University Press, 1991.

West, Darrell. *The Rise and Fall of the Media Establishment.* Boston: St. Martin's Press, 2001.

West, Darrell, Diane Heith, and Chris Goodwin. "Harry and Louise Go to Washington: Political Advertising and Health Care Reform." *The Journal of Health Politics, Policy and Law* 21 (1996): 35–68.

Wielhouwer, Peter W., and Brad Lockerbie. "Party Contacting and Political Participation, 1952–90." *American Journal of Political Science* 38 (1994): 211–219.

Wildavsky, Aaron. "The Two Presidencies." In Aaron Wildavsky, ed., *Perspectives on the Presidency*. Boston: Little, Brown, 1975, 136–147.

Wilson, Woodrow. *Constitutional Government in the United States*. New York: Columbia University Press, 1908.

Wood, B. Dan. *The Myth of Presidential Representation*. New York: Cambridge University Press, 2009.

Young, Garry, and William B. Perkins. "Presidential Rhetoric, the Public Agenda, and the End of Presidential Television's 'Golden Age.' " *Journal of Politics* 67 (2005): 1190–1205.

Zaller, John. "A New Standard of News Quality: Burglar Alarms for the Monitorial Citizen." *Political Communication* 20 (2003): 109–130.

Index

Note: Page numbers followed by *f* or *t* refer to figures or tables, respectively.

M

N

O

About the Author

Diane J. Heith is associate professor and chair of government and politics at St. John's University. She is the author of several books on the presidency, public opinion, and the media, including *Presidents and the American Presidency* (2012), *Polling to Govern: Public Opinion and Presidential Leadership* (2004), and *In the Public Domain: Presidents and the Challenges of Public Leadership* (coedited with Lori Cox Han, 2005). Her work has appeared in *Public Opinion Quarterly*; *Presidential Studies Quarterly*; *Political Science Quarterly*; *Journal of Health Politics, Policy and Law*; *Journal of Women, Politics and Policy*; *White House Studies*; and *Congress and the Presidency*.